THE COMPLETE GUIDE TO MERGERS AND ACQUISITIONS

THE COMPLETE GUIDE TO MERGERS AND ACQUISITIONS

Process Tools to Support M&A Integration at Every Level

Timothy J. Galpin
Mark Herndon

JOSSEY-BASS
A Wiley Company
www.josseybass.com

Published by

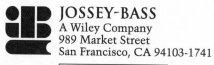

JOSSEY-BASS
A Wiley Company
989 Market Street
San Francisco, CA 94103-1741

www.josseybass.com

Jossey-Bass books and products are available through most bookstores. To contact Jossey-Bass directly, call (888) 378-2537, fax to (800) 605-2665, or visit our website at www.josseybass.com.

Substantial discounts on bulk quantities of Jossey-Bass books are available to corporations, professional associations, and other organizations. For details and discount information, contact the special sales department at Jossey-Bass.

We at Jossey-Bass strive to use the most environmentally sensitive paper stocks available to us. Our publications are printed on acid-free recycled stock whenever possible, and our paper always meets or exceeds minimum GPO and EPA requirements.

Library of Congress Cataloging-in-Publication Data

Galpin, Timothy J.
     The complete guide to mergers and acquisitions : process tools to support M&A integration at every level / Timothy J. Galpin, Mark Herndon.
          p.   cm. — (The Jossey-Bass business & management series)
     Includes bibliographical references and index.
     ISBN 0-7879-4786-5
     1. Consolidation and merger of corporations—Management.   I. Herndon, Mark.
     II. Title.   III. Series.
     HD2746.5.G35   1999
     658.1'6—dc21
                                                                    99-44484

FIRST EDITION
HB Printing   10 9 8 7 6 5

THE JOSSEY-BASS BUSINESS & MANAGEMENT SERIES

CONTENTS

PREFACE

The typical merger and acquisition (M&A) deal never realizes its intended financial and strategic impact. This failure is often due to the "people" side of the deal, and it occurs as a result of the change dynamics created by the merger. These dynamics heighten the resistance that people usually bring to the successful integration of two companies. Moreover, much of the needed talent—a key value driver for many deals—voluntarily leaves the organizations that are merging, and the departure of this resource also serves to derail the deal before its success can be achieved.

This Book's Purpose and Audience

The Complete Guide to Mergers and Acquisitions: Process Tools to Support M&A Integration at Every Level was written as a pragmatic "how-to" text designed to aid integration leaders (at the enterprise level and at the functional or divisional level) in realizing the advantages that can be created from a merger or acquisition. Its purpose is to provide executives and managers alike with tools, templates, and a proven process for efficiently and effectively combining two organizations.

Overview of the Contents

The twelve chapters in this volume highlight "best practices" as well as "lessons learned" with respect to the following areas and issues:

- Activities conducted and questions confronted throughout the process of the M&A deal
- Rates of success and failure for M&A deals and results that can be achieved through an approved approach
- Typical people-related dynamics created during an M&A deal
- Mistakes commonly made during integration
- Effective design and management of the integration process
- Specific actions for creating measurable positive results
- Implementation of a well-thought-out communication strategy
- Retaining and "rerecruiting" key talent
- Capturing deal synergies
- A clear process for staffing and selection
- Tracking progress

The book also includes numerous visual aids, tools, and templates, which should prove extremely valuable during the integration process, as well as three back-of-the-book resource sections that can serve as handbooks in themselves for facilitating effective, value-creating integration.

In all dynamic situations (and these occur in corporations every day) there is continuous progress where information, innovation, and understanding are concerned. As a result, any material in this book that touches on companies, their actions, their approaches to integration, and their accomplishments should be considered time-sensitive. Today's successful company may become tomorrow's poor example, and the laggard of today may become the leader of tomorrow. Therefore, the reader should view this material as illustrative of the specific points being made, and not as representative of timeless principles, which, especially today, do not exist.

Acknowledgments

We would like to acknowledge our clients and colleagues, who are too numerous to name here, but who have added much to our understanding of what a successful M&A integration entails. We would also and especially like to thank Jay Teinert: without his help, we would never have been able to complete this book.

August 1999   Timothy J. Galpin
Dallas, Texas   Mark Herndon

THE AUTHORS

TIMOTHY J. GALPIN serves as global practice leader for Merger and Acquisition Services with Watson Wyatt Worldwide. During the past several years, he has led projects incorporating the design, implementation, and evaluation of merger integration, human resources strategy, change management, culture change, productivity improvement, performance management, and project implementation that have resulted in improved performance for several national and multinational companies.

Galpin's clients include Sears, GE Capital, London Life Insurance, Equistar Petrochemicals, Lyondell Petrochemicals, ARCO, Quaker Oats, Armstrong Building Products, Prudential Insurance of Canada, MicroWarehouse, Inmac, Harrods (UK), Safeway (UK), Siemens, BlueCross BlueShield of Texas, Blue-Cross BlueShield of Illinois, and Amdahl.

Prior to joining Watson Wyatt, Galpin served as manager of organization development for Hughes Aircraft Company and as a consultant based in Europe and North America.

Galpin received his Ph.D. degree in organization development from the University of California at Los Angeles and his M.A. degree in management from Southern Illinois University, Carbondale.

An accomplished speaker, Galpin has been active in professional presentations on merger integration, human resources strategy, leadership development, organizational change, and business redesign. He has authored several articles appearing in *Mergers and Acquisitions, HR Magazine, Journal of Business Strategy, Training and Development,* and *Employment Relations Today* on the topics of merger integration, change management, corporate culture change, and organizational productivity. Galpin's two previous books are *Making Strategy Work: Building Sustainable Growth Capability* and *The Human Side of Change: A Practical Guide to Organization Redesign,* both published by Jossey-Bass.

MARK HERNDON serves as central region leader for Merger and Acquisition Services with Watson Wyatt Worldwide. As a consultant to major organizations, Herndon's work has focused on designing and implementing merger integration approaches that increase the speed and synergy capture of the deal.

Herndon's clients include American Express Financial Advisers, Amoco, Boeing, British Petroleum, Cessna Aircraft, Chevron, Dell Computer, Dow Chemical, Equistar Chemicals LP, Express Scripts/Value Rx, First Interstate Bank, General Electric, Hoechst-Celanese, J.C. Penney, Komatsu-Dresser, Magma Copper, Millennium Chemicals do Brasil, McNeil Consumer Products, Northern States Power, Quaker Oats, Shell Oil, The Toledo Hospital, TRW, and Willamette Industries.

Prior to joining Watson Wyatt, Herndon served as vice president of Performance Systems Corporation and was the director of a national leadership development program for a major division of the U.S. Department of Education.

Herndon earned an executive masters of business administration degree from the University of Texas at Dallas and is an honors graduate in economics and business administration from Oklahoma State University.

As a popular presenter at various trade and industry meetings, Herndon has addressed audiences in forty-four states and ten countries. His previous published works include *Peer Review — The Complete Guide, Watson Wyatt's Enterprise-Wide Merger Integration Manual,* and a variety of other articles, which appeared in *Management Review, Human Resource Executive, HR Magazine,* and numerous industry journals.

THE COMPLETE GUIDE TO MERGERS AND ACQUISITIONS

CHAPTER ONE

INTEGRATION: THE REAL DEAL

Beyond the statistics and optimistic press announcements are real organizations being disrupted, real executives being displaced, and real shareholders being disappointed.

A press release came to our attention recently that reflected the predeal optimism and strategic trumpeting to the financial community that are typical of such announcements: "ABC today announced an initial agreement to merge with XYZ. We view this as a true 'merger of equals' that creates superior access to resources and provides a strong global platform to accelerate growth. This deal will create significant value for shareholders and represents an outstanding opportunity for customers and employees alike." Announcements like this one have become so commonplace that M&A deals have become part of daily business, to the point where news reporters anticipate "merger Mondays" (a phrase that refers to the usual flurry of such activity at the beginning of the week). O'Donnell (1998) reports that 42 percent of respondents to a recent survey supported mergers as positive, whereas only 37 percent expressed the belief that mergers were bad; at any rate, the White House has promised to form a high-level group to review the current wave of mergers and determine whether competition will suffer. Meanwhile, industrywide consolidation has now grown so pervasive that it has spawned its own lingo, with such terms as *bolt-on, roll-up, tuck-under,* and *carve-out* describing various types of transactions. There is little doubt why this unique business phenomenon has become so entrenched in our society: the Securities Data Corporation's Web site reported 22,995 deals in 1998, for a combined deal value of $2.45 trillion—a record volume surpassing the previous records set in 1997 and 1996.

Yet in spite of this record volume, most M&A deals still fail to accomplish many of the strategic objectives so optimistically projected in the initial announcements. Consider the following statistics, gathered at random from several leading business publications:

- Just 23 percent of all acquisitions earn their cost of capital.
- When an M&A deal is announced, a company's stock price rises only 30 percent of the time.
- In acquired companies, 47 percent of executives leave within the first year, and 75 percent leave within the first three years.
- Synergies projected for M&A deals are not achieved in 70 percent of cases.
- In the first four to eight months that follow a deal, productivity may be reduced by up to 50 percent.
- CEOs and CFOs routinely cite "people" problems and cultural issues as the top factors in failed integrations.
- The average financial performance of newly merged companies is graded by their managers as a C-minus.

The results reflected in these statistics may be attributed to a number of factors— poor strategic fit, incomplete or haphazard due diligence (if there has been any at all), ineffective efforts at integration—but they all point to the same basic fact: it is much easier to "do" a deal than to implement one. The "real deal" is that integrating one business with another is inherently difficult, even for the most experienced acquirers, and the process must be managed exceedingly well if the effort is to succeed.

Indeed, beyond all the statistics and optimistic press announcements, real organizations are being disrupted, real executives are being displaced, and real shareholders are being disappointed—not for lack of effort, but largely for lack of effective planning and integration. Consider the well-publicized merger failures listed in Exhibit 1.1. As these failures show, the sobering truth is often far different from what is projected in an initial press release. Even more compelling than these actual cases, however, is the realization that relatively obvious key factors have been found by numerous researchers to be consistently associated with failed deals:

- A study of 190 CEOs, CFOs, and other top executives experienced in global acquisitions (Watson Wyatt Worldwide, 1998a) found that cultural incompatibility is consistently rated as the greatest barrier to successful integration but that research on cultural factors is the kind least likely to be done as an aspect of due diligence.

EXHIBIT 1.1. SEVEN TROUBLED MERGERS.

Companies Involved	Issues	Outcomes
1994 acquisition of WordPerfect Corporation by Novell, Inc.	Culture, including fundamentally different perspectives on customer service	Sold in 1996 for $1 billion less than it had paid two years earlier
1995 merger of Homedco Group and Abbey Healthcare to form Apria Healthcare Group	Intense competitive rivalry between the two organizations; distinct differences in decision-making process and authority levels	Year 1 financial results: Apria's stock price fell 50%; 4% revenue growth compared to double-digit premerger rate
1995 acquisition of Frame Technology Corporation by Adobe Systems, Inc.	Failure to understand the Frame business model, resulting in overly aggressive layoffs of telephone sales representatives	Frame sales fell by 50%; sales team had to be rebuilt
1996 hostile takeover of First Interstate Bank by Wells Fargo	Rapid combination of two major systems; Wells Fargo's blind faith in technology	Loss of approximately $300 million in retail and corporate accounts in 1996; fourth-quarter 1996 earnings fell to $1.12 per share, compared to $12.21 for the year
1997 merger of Aetna and U.S. Healthcare	Serious service degradation, including the mishandling of charges, reduction in coverage, doctors waiting for payment	Costs rose 14%, and new members increased only 10% in 1997; 37% of doctors turned down contract renewals as of 11/98; first-quarter 1998 earnings down 40%; third-quarter 1998 stock price dropped $9.50
1997 acquisition of Southern Pacific Railroad by Union Pacific Railroad	Logistical issues and staffing errors, leading to severe service problems and numerous safety incidents	Loss of $125 million in revenue; 1997 third-quarter earnings dropped 15%; key knowledge leaders have left the company
1998 proposed merger between Monsanto and American Home Products	Cultural and managerial differences regarding who would run what	Deal called off, Monsanto shares lost 24% on the announcement; AHP's shares fell by 10%

- A 1992 Coopers & Lybrand study (see Carleton, 1997) reported that in one hundred failed or troubled mergers, 85 percent of executives who were surveyed said that the major problem was differences in management style and practices.
- A 1996 British Institute of Management survey (see Carleton, 1997) also reported underestimation of the difficulties involved in merging two cultures to be a major factor in failure.
- In a 1997 Mercer Management Consulting study (see Lublin and O'Brien, 1997), poor postdeal integration was the major failure responsible for the fact that, in deals worth more than $500 million, only 43 percent of some three hundred merged companies outperformed their peers in total returns for shareholders.
- A study by the A. T. Kearney consulting firm (see Lublin and O'Brien, 1997) reviewed 155 M&A deals in multiple industries and determined most failures to be people-related.
- A study by Hewitt Associates that surveyed executives in 162 organizations, all of whom had been involved in at least one merger or acquisition, found that 69 percent of the respondents reported the top challenge to be integrating two organizational cultures.

As the data overwhelmingly suggest, organizations know the root causes of failed mergers, but they have not succeeded in doing much to manage the issues that are involved in successfully integrating an M&A deal. Even in companies where there has been painful personal experience of deals gone wrong, it is the rare executive who has led an organization to create anything more than a rudimentary plan for integration. Sadly, in spite of overwhelming evidence of the importance of effective postmerger integration, organizations and executives continue to fail.

Why Deals Are Done

Despite the risks and horror stories, mergers and acquisitions are here to stay. Driven by globalization, a long-term bull market, and economic or strategic barriers to organic growth, mergers and acquisitions have become the primary means by which many companies can quickly attempt to grow revenues. Largely because of these drivers, today's deals are fundamentally different from those that figured in previous waves of merger activity (see Exhibit 1.2).

In the 1980s, for example, a merger deal was primarily a financial transaction aimed at gaining control of an undervalued asset, which was then often

EXHIBIT 1.2. DEALS THEN AND NOW.

	1980s	Today
Reasons	Financial play	Operational leap
Risks	Overleverage	Integration
Targets	Diverse	Similar
Prizes	Hard assets	4 Cs: *customers, channels, competencies, content*
Mandate	Stabilize	Exploit instability
Market	Forgiving	Merciless

resold or left to stand alone as an independent entity. The target was often a dissimilar industry, or a business line distinctly separate from the acquirer's main business. Price premiums were less common, and the margin for error was often greater. The main risk involved taking enough cost out of the business to ensure sufficient cash flow for debt service. Today, the typical merger or acquisition is quite strategic and operational in nature. Executives are buying an installed customer base as well as new and better distribution channels and geographic markets. They are buying organization competencies and an infusion of talent that leverage and extend strategic opportunities, and they are gaining control over competitors' products and services. They are also consolidating business units or industries in a down cycle, to increase revenue and share price. The differences don't stop there, however. Given the all-out race for globalization, not to mention the constant short-term pressure for earnings growth, desirable targets are fewer in number, demand for them is much greater, and price premiums are far more common. There is less margin for error in actually achieving the economic projections of the deal. Costs must still be driven out of the business, but now without any sacrifice of the ability to capture revenue-generating synergies. Moreover, in contrast to the 1980s (an era when an acquisition normally could be integrated over a longer period, perhaps two or three years), today the businesses must be merged as quickly as possible—often within six to twelve months after the close. Managers and employees, instead of having to survive only one or two M&A transactions in their careers, must now be ready to do deals routinely, incorporating new businesses as a matter of course, one right after another, and often with multiple transactions occurring simultaneously. When the heightened expectations of Wall Street are factored in, it is clear that failure to integrate the businesses properly after the deal has closed can lead to disaster, as in Quaker Oats Company's acquisition of Snapple Beverage Corporation, one of the most ill-fated M&A deals in corporate history, in which Quaker Oats lost $1.4 billion in just twenty-seven months. Quaker's strength in supermarkets and mass distribution was a poor match with Snapple's convenience-store market. The new owners of Snapple replaced a popular ad campaign with new marketing programs that immediately flopped. In addition, Wall Street considered Snapple's purchase price to have been about $1 billion too high. All these factors and more resulted in a $1.6 million loss for every day that Quaker owned Snapple. It is no longer sufficient just to buy the right company at the right price. Today's deals start there, but they also demand effective execution of the right integration plan.

Integration: An Experience-Driven Skill Set

At a recent meeting in a major manufacturing company, a meeting called to prepare the integration plans for the fourth M&A deal in eighteen months, the CEO provided only one directive: "Give me an integration team that knows the drill." Indeed, managerial and organizational experience have long been referenced as factors that are key to a merger's success, and this concept has been further refined in a recent study by Singh and Zollo (see Pandya, 1998). Based on findings from more than five hundred bank mergers, the Singh and Zollo study is the largest to date on postacquisition management. The study concludes not only that past experience is the key to managing a successful merger but that this is true in two distinct areas. The first area, which the authors call "tacit knowledge," consists of subjective experience and exists largely in the minds of key executives. The second area, which they call "codified knowledge," consists of written procedures that a company articulates in the form of routines or norms that guide integration actions and decision making during the formation and implementation phases of the M&A deal. (Examples of codified knowledge might be procedures and guidelines for structuring the new entity and reconciling different practices with respect to compensation and benefits, or process models and instructions for staffing and selection.)

Every deal presents different challenges, of course, and requires customized adaptations of generic processes. Nevertheless, the existence of a structured approach to integration, and its skillful application by managers who "know the drill," have proved their ability to help organizations maximize the value of their M&A deals. When a structured integration process is well managed, significant results can be achieved. Executives and integration managers who responded to a recent survey (Watson Wyatt Worldwide, 1998a) cited several outcomes of structured integration (the respondents' comments are reproduced here):

- *Faster integration.* "To date we have captured an estimated $400,000 per day in synergy savings due to the speed of integration."
- *Lower costs.* "Task forces, subteams and employee groups affected by the change were able to get involved and identify significant cost-saving opportunities that were 'below the radar' for most executive dealmakers."
- *Achievement and surpassing of projected synergies.* "By the end of the kickoff session, all original synergies were understood and assigned to project teams responsible for planning and execution. Within the first week, task forces had identified five entirely new synergies estimated to be worth an additional $5 million. Financial analysts were particularly impressed by the synergy education and tracking process used to focus the organization's efforts on synergy capture."
- *Protection of productivity and maintenance of customer focus.* "The merger-integration scorecard process highlighted key operating, financial, customer, and organization issues that were most prone to disruption during integration and gave executives an early warning of where to focus attention in the successful day-to-day running of the business."
- *Smoother transition.* "The process works. It keeps the entire organization and the entire HR function focused and moving forward in a fast, efficient, and well-coordinated way."
- *Faster and more effective responses to workers' questions and concerns.* "One of the most positive things is that we have honestly addressed the 'me issues' and other concerns of the workforce. Our clear and open communications helped employees understand what was going on and see that we had a well-defined, objective process for planning the integration and resolving issues that affected them."

The Watson Wyatt Deal Flow Model

First, a disclaimer: there is no one best way to integrate two organizations. Second, an unfortunate reality: there usually is not any defined process method that can guide integration planning and decision making. One global acquirer that now averages ten or twelve deals per year summarizes the situation as follows:

Executives have historically focused exclusively on making the deal. Then they throw the whole process unceremoniously over to the business unit managers to integrate, all the while maintaining the same expectations for performance and participation in a myriad of other, equally high-priority corporate initiatives. As a result, every integration we do is different. For most, our process resembles Sherman's march on Atlanta: we win the territory but leave far too much in ruins. For others, no integration happens for the first year or so, and then managers try to slam-dunk some business-process decisions on the acquired business just because they bought the right to, and without any rational case. Others ignore the business process entirely and focus on "management seances" and "love-ins." As a result, we end up reinventing the wheel every time and hope for the best.

Most executives are subject-matter experts with regard to their specific functional responsibilities, but they have surprisingly little context knowledge of the entire "soup to nuts" process: the components of the transaction and their completion, the elements of due diligence, and the integration phase. Exhibit 1.3 shows the Watson Wyatt Deal Flow Model, a framework for conceptualizing the fundamental stages of the deal process. Exhibit 1.4 shows how this high-level M&A transaction model can be used to generate lists of stage-specific items for further detailed planning. Thus, for each of the five major stages in the model — *formulate, locate, investigate, negotiate, integrate* — the organization can create specific activities and products as needed to establish strategy, document policy, map processes, manage training, and so on. Issues and risks pertinent to each organization or major business unit can also be incorporated into the generic model, and knowledge captured from each new deal can be added to on-line and hard-copy libraries, to provide a living resource pool for subsequent dealmakers and integrators. The sections that follow describe and discuss the five stages of the model.

EXHIBIT 1.3. THE WATSON WYATT DEAL FLOW MODEL.

Watson Wyatt Deal Flow Model

Formulate	Locate	Investigate	Negotiate	Integrate
Strategy and Integration Process Development	Predeal (assessing, planning, forecasting value)		Deal (agreeing on value)	Postdeal (realizing value)

EXHIBIT 1.4. MAP OF M&A PROCESS AND ISSUES.

Watson Wyatt Deal Flow Model

	Formulate	Locate	Investigate	Negotiate	Integrate

Key Activities	• Set business strategy
	• Set growth strategy
	• Define acquisition criteria
	• Begin strategy implementation
		• Identify target markets and companies
		• Select target
		• Issue letter of intent
		• Develop M&A plan
		• Offer letter of confidentiality
			• Conduct due-diligence analysis
			  • *Financial*
			  • *People/cultural*
			  • *Legal*
			  • *Environmental*
			  • *Operational*
			  • *Intellectual capital*
			• Summarize findings
			• Set preliminary integration plans
			• Decide negotiation parameters
				• Set deal terms:
				  • *Legal*
				  • *Structural*
				  • *Financial*
				• Secure key talent and integration teams
				• Close deal
					• Finalize and execute integration plans:
					  • *Organization*
					  • *Process*
					  • *People*
					  • *Systems*

Issues/Risks	• Costs
	• Channels
	• Content
	• Competencies
	• Customers
	• Countries
	• Capital
	• Capacity
		• ROI/Value
		• Strategic fit
		• Cultural fit
		• Timing
		• Leadership fit
		• Potential synergies
		• Viability
			• Liabilities
			• Human capital retention
			• Human capital elimination
			• Viability of financial aspects
			• Integration issues
			• Synergies/economies of scale
			• ROI
				• Price
				• Performance
				• People
				• Protection
				• Governance
					• Speed
					• Disruption
					• Costs
					• Revenues
					• Results
					• Perception
					  • *Shareholders*
					  • *Public*
					  • *Customers*
					  • *Employees*

Stage 1: Formulate

In the first stage, the organization must set out its business objectives and growth strategy in a clear, rational, and data-oriented way. This should be more than the CEO's directive to "become a $1 billion company" in x number of years: instructions like these can do much to bias an organization to do a deal, any deal, just to stay off the boss's blacklist. Instead, specific criteria, which are based on the objectives that have been determined and on a strategy of growth through acquisition, should be established to describe what a viable target company would bring to the party. These criteria should be expressed in terms of goals like market share, geographic access, new products or technologies, and general amounts for financial synergy. In strategy development, it is often important to help the CEO's direct reports gain clarity about what the strategy means for him or her personally and develop specific action plans for implementing that strategy.

One aspect of strategy formulation that historically has been left out of the discussion is the determination of a specific method for the merger transaction and the subsequent integration. Many corporate M&A departments perceive their domain to be exclusively that of secretively finding target companies and signing the deals. In our experience, however, this dated approach does a tremendous disservice to the organization. The most effective M&A functions we have seen take a much more holistic approach, working with the CEO's office and with people in organization development, HR, and the business units to map the entire M&A process, define specific roles and responsibilities, and manage the knowledge-capturing process. The importance of accomplishing these tasks before the deal is started cannot be overemphasized: once the proverbial train is out of the station, it is too late to effectively create and refine these process tools and expectations.

This phase of planning carries with it all the typical strategy issues and risks as they apply to the specific M&A context. The organization should evaluate in advance what the ideal target company looks like in terms of various factors such as these:

- What type of cost structure does the ideal target have?
- What market channels would this target provide?
- What kinds of organizational competence and capabilities would provide maximum leverage and the greatest number of synergies?
- Are there strategic customer accounts or market segments to be gained?
- In what global regions or countries can we build additional capacity through this target?
- What is the optimum capital structure?
- What are the sources for new acquisitions?
- Will the ideal targets be businesses operated as independent holdings (in the portfolio approach), or does the organization intend to integrate the business partly or fully into its day-to-day operations?
- If joint-venture structures are to be used, what type of governance process and composition will ensure sufficient autonomy of the new enterprise while providing the parent companies the desired degree of involvement?

Stage 2: Locate

After the strategic template has been set and clarified among executive staff and M&A department members, the search for desirable target companies follows a much more focused and logical path. Initial financial and operational analysis leads to initial conversations between executive staffs. Initial conversations lead to high-level identification of potential synergies. With continuing interest from both parties, initial deal parameters, terms, and conditions are defined and ultimately submitted as a part of the letter of intent and the secrecy agreement.

Sophisticated acquirers have learned that it is necessary, at this early stage of involvement, to scope out many high-level recommendations and guiding parameters for the integration process and for the subsequent new organization (or, as we shall call the generic merged organization throughout this book, the Newco organization). Most letters of intent do an adequate job of describing the desired objectives and giving an overview of the proposed financial and operational aspects of the transaction. They include quite specific details on such items as the assets and business units involved, the equity positions of the parent companies, the assumption-of-debt requirements, intercompany supply agreements, employee liabilities, taxes, technology transfer, indemnification, public announcements, and other essential terms and conditions of the nonbinding understanding. However, equally clear agreement is just as necessary at this early stage regarding essential integration, cultural, and Newco organization issues such as the following:

- *In the case of a joint-venture arrangement, the governance structure of the partnership and specific issues for approval, input, or advisory notice from the parent companies.* In one case, for example, governance issues were left undefined until late in the process of negotiating a definitive agreement. There were major differences in each party's expectations about the number of people, and the specific individuals, who would serve on the partnership's governance committee. There was also such substantial disagreement over the parent company's role in setting Newco policy, budgets, senior-level staffing, and other major issues that the deal nearly fell apart. As a result, early statements indicating that the Newco organization would be a stand-alone entity were reversed by the majority parent company's mandate that the new company be managed as a wholly owned subsidiary. Perceptions in the Newco organization also shifted, from excitement about becoming a freestanding entity to bitterness and open hostility toward the majority parent company for turning the deal into an outright acquisition.
- *The overall process to be used for determining top-level organizational structure and staffing decisions.* For example, organization A was process-oriented. This company preferred a competency-based selection process, with involvement from external management psychologists and board members, to develop consensus on the most qualified candidate for each senior leadership role. By contrast, organization B used a command-and-control approach, with minimal documentation. Selection was typically based on whom the CEO knew and wanted

on his staff. The result of this difference was disagreement over the high-level structure and staffing process, which degenerated into a "swap meet" in which both organizations gained at least some representation, but not necessarily the best candidates for the requirements of the Newco organization. Within the first year of the Newco organization's operations, one vice president left abruptly over "cultural differences," and the CEO fired another for cause.

- *Agreement on the basic steps and provisions of the integration process to be used, including mutual participation, formation of key task forces, planning phases, and leadership roles.* Company A, for example, was an experienced acquirer with a defined process model for integrating new businesses. Company B, the new joint-venture partner, was conducting its first major expansion. Assumptions made by both parties resulted in two different sets of expectations, created during extensive internal communications, about the announcement of the deal and the integration plans. Neither organization was willing to reverse its position overtly, and the "hybrid" integration process that resulted was dysfunctional from the outset.

- *High-level reconciliation of major discrepancies regarding executive compensation, employee benefits, and incentive compensation plans.* For example, company A was a traditional European employer, compensating executives with a relatively modest base salary and extensive perquisites. Company B was a progressive fast-growth company that relied heavily on stock-based incentives for managers. There were some early attempts to define high-level guiding principles and action steps for researching and resolving compensation-based concerns, but resolution of these issues was postponed. As a result, company B abandoned a potentially favorable deal before either party was able to conduct an objective review of alternatives.

An important task of this phase is mutual identification of potential synergies. Historically, many organizations have undertaken this task with complete independence from the other party's involvement, but this norm is now changing under pressure from the increasing difficulty of finding and executing an economically viable deal. As a case in point, one organization was recently pursuing a joint-venture partner for a low-cost, commodity-oriented business segment. Price premiums for several potential targets were high because of current industry margins, but the industry itself was beginning a global down cycle. The majority partner, rather than risk the losses that could have resulted from an assessment of what it alone perceived to be the realistic synergies, facilitated a brainstorming and planning session with a team composed of its own key managers and those of a potential partner. With counsel from both sides in attendance (as protection against the disclosure of any specific information, which would have constituted an antitrust violation), the parties mutually identified and validated twenty-seven "first pass" synergies worth an estimated $80 million. Managers from the two companies, working together for the first time with their respective functional counterparts, creatively sought ways for the two companies to increase revenue and cut costs by combining their operations. High-level agreement was gained on key assumptions, exclusions, and terms of the deal that would be required in order for these synergies to be captured. The result of this exercise was enough consensus for the deal to be made and for both parties to commit themselves to moving forward collaboratively.

Stage 3: Investigate

The third phase of the model relies on thorough due diligence to explore every possible facet of the target company, in as much detail as practical prior to finalizing the definitive agreement. Therefore, due diligence must be exercised in the financial, operational, legal, environmental, cultural, and strategic arenas. Key findings should be summarized for executives' review, and any potential deal killers or "showstoppers" should be identified. Due-diligence findings are used to set negotiating parameters, determine bid prices, and provide the basis for initial integration recommendations.

A word of warning: given the fevered pace of merger activity, as well as increasing industry consolidation (so that organizations and executives know each other), there may be a temptation to hurry the fact-finding process, omit key parts of it, or gloss over it in the rush to do the deal. This temptation should be resisted. Much has already been written about the $14 billion merger in 1997 between HFS, Inc., and CUC International, Inc., to form Cendant Corporation. Roughly four months after closing the deal, Cendant disclosed that it had uncovered massive accounting irregularities at the former CUC. Widespread fraud was alleged as two managers filed affidavits indicating that senior CUC executives had ordered CUC managers to "invent" as much as 61 percent of CUC's 1997 net income. The day after the allegations broke, Cendant's stock price slid 46.5 percent and knocked $14 billion off Cendant's market capitalization. According to the *Wall Street Journal*, by August 1998 Cendant had lost another $20 billion in market value, Cendant's chairman had resigned, investors had filed at least seventy-one lawsuits, and nine of fourteen directors who had come from CUC had resigned (Nelson and Lublin, 1998). This may be a particularly grotesque example of failure to exercise due diligence, but wise acquirers will rightly want to redouble their own efforts in this regard. Consider that a company's financial data are typically the most carefully scrutinized of all the preacquisition information that is reviewed; therefore, if errors of the magnitude found in the case of Cendant can be made when the validity of this information is assumed, it is important to ask where else the organization may be at risk from unsubstantiated assumptions:

- *Market*. How large is the target's market? How fast are specific segments growing? Are there threats from substitute technologies or products? To what extent is the market influenced or controlled by governments?
- *Customers*. Who are the target's major customers? What are their purchase criteria: price? quality? reliability? Do buyers of product X also buy product Y, and do they buy both through similar channels? Are there unmet needs? Are changes in buying behavior to be expected?
- *Competitors*. Who are the target's major competitors? What is the degree of rivalry? What are the competitors' respective strengths and weaknesses vis-à-vis the target? What barriers to entry exist for new competitors? How will the competitors try to exploit the merger or integration issues to their own advantage?
- *Culture and human resources*. Which key people must be kept, which core areas of competence should be retained, and how possible is it to do either? Are there major cultural discrepancies with the target? If they could cause major defections or other losses of productivity, is the organization willing to resolve them? If so, at what cost? What are the historical biases or expectations that must be dealt with before credibility can be gained with, and confidence inspired in, the acquired company's workforce?

Missing the boat on any of these issues can be just as damaging as a discovery of fraudulent revenue-recognition practices. Only after this level of detailed evaluation has been conducted is an executive team adequately equipped to make intelligent decisions about the level of integration that will be required to support a specific deal.

In our work, we are frequently asked how to apply an overall method of integration to a particular type of deal (such as a joint venture or a small outright acquisition) or to a particular size and scale of transaction (such as the acquisition of a major global division of another company). The answer is almost always "it depends" because, unfortunately, few general principles are robust enough to be meaningful. Consider that for every fully integrated "merger of equals," we find another merged organization that is more effectively left as a separate holding company, and that for every "bolt-on acquisition" of an autonomous business division that is left to stand alone, we find another division that is more effectively integrated in full. Most experienced acquirers find that the determination of the desired level of integration depends less on the industry, the business cycle, the scale, or the type of transaction than on the specific business goals anticipated from the transaction, the specific context and complexity of the target, and the risks or obstacles to integration that must be successfully managed.

Exhibit 1.5 shows the approach that one acquirer uses in capturing the specific due-diligence issues for each new deal into a strategic decision-making process directed at the key desired outcomes and the desired level of integration. With this approach, the M&A team and the cross-functional deal teams work together to plot, in the far-left column, the primary integration-related issues or areas to be considered. The process includes separate pages or sections for organizationwide issues, specific functional and process-related issues, and major opportunities for synergy. For each integration-related issue, the teams must identify specific strategic or cost-related business goals made possible through the transaction. Initial dollar estimates are encouraged; typically at this stage, however, they are not yet completely validated. On the basis of the strategic goals, the teams consider three broad categories of potential integration (in the three central columns), and eventually they place each major issue into one of these three categories, to reflect the level of integration required for obtaining optimized results. Although many different kinds of categories and many definitions of integration could be used, this acquirer has discovered, over time, that these three tend to encompass most of the types of integration issues the company typically encounters:

- *Full integration.* All areas and processes companywide (or functionwide) are to be merged and consolidated. All management decisions for the acquired business (or function) will be integrated into the parent company's processes, with appropriate "best practice" knowledge transfer and revisions.
- *Moderate integration.* Certain key functions or processes (sales and marketing, for example, or manufacturing) will be merged and consolidated. Strategic planning and monitoring of the function will be centralized as an element of the parent company's processes, but day-to-day operations will remain autonomous.
- *Minimal integration.* Selected corporate and staff functions will be merged and consolidated, primarily to achieve staffing synergies and cost-efficiencies. All strategic and day-to-day operating decisions will remain autonomous and decentralized, with agreed-upon requirements for reporting to the parent company.

In the far-right column, deal teams capture the risks and obstacles likely to be encountered. If any "showstoppers" or deal killers are anticipated, alternative integration scenarios are evaluated, or strategic goals are revised and made more realistic.

EXHIBIT 1.5. STRATEGIC INTEGRATION-PLANNING ANALYSIS.

Integration Issue or Area	Desired Integration Objectives/Outcomes		Level of Integration Required to Accomplish Objectives	Risks and Obstacles to Achieving Integration Requirement
	Strategic	Costs		
Information systems (IS)	Use comprehensive enterprisewide systems capability to replace multiple legacy systems		Full: must consolidate both IS organizations and rationalize existing platforms/applications	■ Negative synergy due to capital investment in years 1–3 ■ Target company's partially completed module, which now may be irrelevant ■ Different IS philosophies and approaches as complication in planning
Leveraging combined product portfolio to all customer accounts	Estimate 10–15% increase in gross sales	Staffing synergies from redundant regional sales leadership	Moderate: centralize marketing leadership and product support, with field sales force integrated and reassigned	■ Timing: no full access to customer account, product, and price information until after deal close
Maximizing target company capability/ market share in Division X	Gain immediate leadership position in new segment		Minimal: consolidate nonstrategic staff functions	■ Must retain intact management team for division ■ Will likely require senior VP status for division lead, with direct report to CEO
Culture	Maintain primary characteristics of acquirer's culture while learning from target's strengths		Moderate: redefine core organizational processes in keeping with strategy	■ Sales organization not perceived to be as customer-responsive ■ Very strong commitment to open communications with employees
Manufacturing	Leverage best practices	Purchasing efficiencies	Moderate: leave plant-level leadership intact	
Staff functions	Add M&A team resources	Potential economies through shared services	Full: consolidate headcount to corporate and shared service locations	■ Current HR delivered through highly visible and involved field HR; no prior experience with other models

Stage 4: Negotiate

This stage includes process steps and requirements for successfully reaching a definitive agreement. Deal teams are briefed by due-diligence teams, and, together with senior executives, they formulate the final negotiating strategy for all terms and conditions of the deal. Considerations include price, performance, people, legal protection, and governance.

A particularly difficult aspect of many deals is the business of gaining agreement on the terms and conditions of transition services. Bridging arrangements are commonly provided by one organization to the other for various staff or functions, as a practical means of facilitating a more effective transition. For example, partner A buys payroll and benefit-administration services for the newly acquired employees during the first year, for an agreed-upon fee for service, whereas partner B agrees to continue operating the technical-support function of a sold asset for six months, until the new function has been fully integrated.

Conceptually, the task of bridging may be simple, but in practical terms it is immense. For example, one company reported getting "burned" on a recent deal because the deal team that created the services agreement had insufficient representation by subject-matter experts who used or provided the services being negotiated. The next time around, this company created cross-functional deal teams staffed with senior subject-matter experts who were able to stipulate the specific services that would be required and to analyze the various cost structures and fees that were being proposed. A high-level internal "peer review" was also established so that the deal teams could have a fresh look from other subject-matter experts, to validate the service requirements and associated costs. Finally, subject-matter experts (such as actuaries) were used to prepare negotiating routines, conduct practice sessions for the negotiators, and, in some cases, attend relevant sessions of the final negotiations.

Stage 5: Integrate

The fifth stage of the model, as already suggested, should be customized to each organization and adapted to each specific deal. This is the actual process of planning and implementing the Newco organization with its processes, its people, its technology, and its systems. In determining how to resolve the myriad issues that arise at this stage, the merging organizations must carefully consider such questions as how fast to integrate, how much disruption will be created, how disruption can be minimized, how people can be helped to continue focusing on customers, safety, and day-to-day operations, and how best to communicate with all the stakeholder groups (shareholders, employees, customers, and the general public).

The Watson Wyatt Deal Flow Model represents these five stages as linear. When the model is applied, however, these stages are almost always parallel but interlinked. Exhibit 1.6 shows how the five stages are interdependent and "concurrently engineered" to provide the right input and the right decision at the right time. As a case in point, consider GE Capital, a well-known and successful acquirer. During the last five years, the company has made more than one hundred acquisitions. These transactions have resulted in a substantial increase in its workforce, the rapid globalization of its businesses, and a doubling of its net income. To support this type of growth, GE Capital has conducted a coordinated and continuing campaign to develop competitive advantage through its organizational ability to integrate and manage acquisitions. Ashkenas, De Monaco, and Francis (1998, p. 168), writing about GE Capital, states, "Acquisition integration is not a discrete phase of a deal and does not begin when the documents are signed. Rather it is a process that begins with due diligence and runs through the ongoing management of the new enterprise."

EXHIBIT 1.6. THE WATSON WYATT DEAL FLOW MODEL IN PRACTICE.

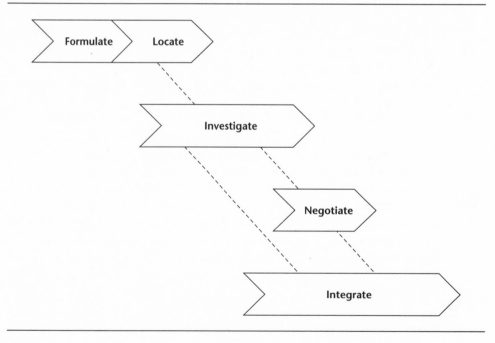

CHAPTER TWO

INTEGRATION BEGINS WITH DUE DILIGENCE

A large part of what makes a deal successful after you complete it is what you do before you complete it.

S. BARR, *CFO MAGAZINE,* JULY 1997

The CEO's comment was lobbed across the dinner table at his companion, like an artillery shell aimed for maximum effect: "If we'd known what your culture was really like, we never would have done the deal!" The remark exploded into intense debate, and it became clear that the two executives had never truly considered, until it was too late, the immense impact of issues that were far too important to leave to speculation.

In an era of widespread acknowledgment that mergers entail disproportionate risks and failures, the surprising factor is not that "culture" should become such a critical issue during integrations; rather, what is surprising is that organizational culture and other issues essential to integration have not yet become more central to executive-level deal making. Perhaps this oversight is finally being addressed as more and more organizations get burned for not conducting sufficiently broad due-diligence analyses aimed at catching and reconciling such issues. This chapter is intended to further this corrective development by providing an overview of three distinct sets of due-diligence analyses that an organization should conduct.

As Chapter One established, the most commonly referenced sources of merger failure are "people" issues and issues related to organizational culture. It stands to reason, then, that skillful acquirers should conduct due-diligence analyses of these issues with at least the same amount of effort that they give to due-diligence analyses in other, more traditional areas, such as the target company's financial data, operational assets, legal issues, marketing prospects, and other well-established conventions. Thus we assume in this chapter that, aside from a few notable exceptions mentioned in this book and elsewhere, acquirers will ensure that these traditional aspects of due diligence are rigorously addressed.

We focus instead on the areas that we perceive have the greatest shortcomings and the greatest potential impact on postmerger integration: initial risk factors, organizational culture, and human capital. These aspects of predeal assessment must be treated with as much discipline and structure as any other component of due diligence.

Many acquirers fail to attend to these less traditional components because they underestimate the potential significance of the findings. Others resist because "soft" due diligence is perceived as not directly related to executive-level concerns about making the deal. According to Reingold and Barrett (1998), the failure of still others to conduct even the rudimentary traditional due-diligence analyses is a direct result of the overwhelming frenzy of M&A activity. These authors also point out the greater propensity for sloppiness among executives who know each other and their respective organizations well and therefore rely on a higher level of trust than is prudent for deal making: "Companies are in the same markets; the executives know each other and how they behave reputationally. They believe that is their due diligence" (p. 72). Common experience suggests, however, that the information yielded by broader, more integration-oriented due-diligence inquiries is consistently at least as strategic and significant as findings of fraudulent revenue-recognition practices and other major misrepresentations. Consider the following deal breakers:

- A defense industry acquirer discovered a $300 million unfunded pension liability as a direct result of a comprehensive human capital due diligence.
- A chemical manufacturer determined that a $30 million investment would be required for the creation of a consistent information technology platform in the merged organization in order to accomplish what the majority partner saw as a mission-critical outcome.
- A retail merger unraveled after ten months when the top two executives of the Newco organization (one from each partner company) were unable to reconcile vastly different management styles and strategies. After numerous attempts at cultural integration, breakup was the only viable alternative that remained.
- Two financial services companies concluded that their organizations could never be integrated to any meaningful extent, given the dramatic cultural differences surrounding incentives, perks, and leadership expectations.

- A manufacturing firm failed to discover an all-employee profit-sharing plan in an acquired company that required a distribution to employees of 3 percent of net profits.
- Because two telecommunications firms' fundamental disagreement over approaches to executive compensation was not uncovered until it was too late, the Newco organization failed to retain essential leadership talent.
- Because of substantial omissions and errors regarding the estimated cost of consolidating a major division, a consumer products company failed to realize any net positive synergies during the first two years after the deal was made.
- A chemical manufacturer failed to consider the implications of foreign labor law for a plan to rationalize benefits and restructure the workforce, and the result was a net charge to the Newco organization equal to 25 percent of the total deal synergies.
- An industrial manufacturer failed to assess the extent to which an acquisition would increase its exposure to the risk of further union organizing, and two new unionization campaigns were conducted during the first year after the deal was signed.
- Because of contentious differences with its partner company's practices and styles in the areas of decision making, communication, employee involvement, and job design, a service company was unable to recruit essential managerial talent.

Redefining the Process of Due Diligence

To avoid these types of outcomes, sophisticated acquirers are redefining the process of due diligence, by using a structured approach to assess traditional and nontraditional components alike. This approach has several critical objectives:

- To identify risks and uncover potential liabilities before it is too late to do anything about them
- To quantify items affecting the sale price
- To ensure there are no "downstream surprises"
- To get data-based input into the negotiation process
- To facilitate a streamlined and effective launch of the integration-planning process

The enhanced due-diligence process, as shown in Exhibit 2.1, should begin during the earliest possible stages of locating the target company, and it should continue through negotiations and into integration planning.

EXHIBIT 2.1.   A NEW FOCUS OF DUE DILIGENCE.

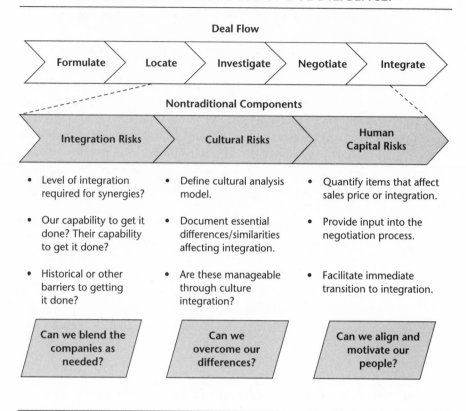

The first nontraditional component to be considered is that of basic integration risks: In order to achieve the deal synergies or capture the business opportunities that have been envisioned, can the companies actually be blended to the extent required? This question implies not only an initial determination of the overall degree of integration that will be required but also an objective determination of how able both organizations are to fulfill the strategy effectively.

The second nontraditional component requires a comprehensive cultural analysis, to identify the inevitable discrepancies and determine whether these issues will in fact be manageable during a well-planned cultural integration process. This question drives another, very important one about the extent to which both organizations are willing to adapt their cultural practices in order to achieve a reasonable resolution (that is, one that is not characterized by the phrase "Do it our way—or else").

The third nontraditional due-diligence component is a comprehensive assessment of the human-capital-related risks of the deal. Just as significant differences should be expected in the area of organizational culture, so also should acquirers expect significant differences in virtually every element of how the human resources function is positioned and in its key strategic objectives and roles, as well as in approaches to specific human-capital-related programs and processes. This due-diligence process must quickly catalogue the myriad risks and differences and then estimate how difficult and how expensive it will be to rationalize and align these practices so as to be effective in motivating the new workforce.

A fundamental redefinition also is needed in how the due-diligence process should be conducted. Executives often perceive due diligence to be a binary function—it is either done or not done, as a one-time affair—and yet practical experience suggests otherwise. Exhibit 2.2 shows that the due-diligence process is actually an iterative one, not unlike peeling an onion: it must be done and redone,

EXHIBIT 2.2. DUE DILIGENCE AS AN ITERATIVE PROCESS.

Phase	Responsible Parties	Purpose
Target verification	Executive staff, M&A department, strategic planning staff, or business development team	Capture sufficient public-domain information and industry-insider knowledge to analyze whether a specific target candidate is worth serious consideration
Synergy identification and validation	Executive staff, M&A department, strategic planning staff, or business development team; specific "deal teams" often launched at this phase	Provide sufficiently detailed brainstorming, planning, research, and validation of potential deal synergies, leading to completion of letter of intent between the parties
Detailed investigation	Deal teams and subject-matter experts	Conduct exhaustive review and analysis of core assets, processes, policies, programs, and functions, leading to reliable estimates of cost impact and identification of integration issues
Transition to integration planning	Deal teams, subject-matter experts, and integration task forces	Do knowledge transfer and comprehensive "as is" analysis of counterpart's business process, leading to specific best-practice design recommendations

at ever-deeper levels of detail and by more and more people, as the deal progresses from concept to letter of intent to definitive agreement and onward to full integration.

Due Diligence and Integration Risk Factors

Part of the fundamental redefinition of the due-diligence process is the realization that aspects of *both* organizations must be assessed before an objective determination can be made of whether to proceed with a deal. There are as many integration risks as there are deals and deal makers, but every organization should develop a template of its own key issues to be considered at the outset of each potential transaction. The following integration risk factors are among the most common:

- *Desired level of integration.* Should you fully absorb the company just because you have acquired outright control? What degree of autonomy will encourage key managers to stay? Does the corporate parent really intend to create a stand-alone entity, or will the acquired company eventually become a fully integrated subsidiary? What business processes and systems should be imported from the acquired company?
- *Availability of managerial and technical talent.* Get ready for the resource drain: M&As require the best of the best, but so does everything else you are doing. How will you manage the conflicting demands and priorities?
- *Cultural process mismatch.* If you are used to moving quickly and decisively and the acquired firm is not (or vice versa), every decision is a challenge.
- *Strategic context and financial performance.* Remember your basic Boston Consulting Group portfolio-analysis matrix? Guess what: cash cows, rising stars, dogs, and question marks may need to be integrated differently.
- *Predeal positioning.* Watch out for major "decisions" made by barter and "horse trading" before the opening gun sounds. These almost always cause grief later on.
- *Global complexity.* Do you think domestic deals are tough? Throw in multiple languages, multiple national cultures, very different regulatory environments, and lots of travel time.
- *Competition.* Look for intense rivalries to continue long after the combination has taken place. These situations create very difficult integration issues. To the employees of the acquired company, even a partnership or a joint venture may seem to be nothing more than conquest by a foe.
- *Relative dominance.* The first rule of mergers is that there is absolutely no such thing as a merger of equals; one of you is always the big kid on the block.

Therefore, it is better to find out now what the deal really means with respect to governance, control, culture, processes, and other guiding parameters.

- *M&A experience.* M&As can quickly overwhelm or wear down even the best and the brightest. It is an immense advantage if your team knows the drill and has been in the game before. Take specific stock of how many people from both organizations have the M&A skill set, and of who they are. To what extent has a proven method of successfully investigating and integrating acquisitions been developed by one or both organizations? How will differences in the two organizations' approaches be reconciled?

- *Ambiguities about power and authority.* One of the most irritating things for many employees and managers is that they won't know for a while who is really in control and how things really work. Watch out: extended ambiguity can torpedo productivity and cause talent to jump ship.

- *Concurrent pressures.* It's always something, and with M&As everything usually happens simultaneously: numerous deals in rapid succession, the board meeting, budgeting, a major systems installation, and, by the way, it's time to do performance reviews.

- *Hostility quotient.* Remember, the organization and its employees did not ask to be bought, so watch for potential backlash and ventilation. Moreover, partner companies that have extensive trade relations before a deal may need to contend with complex historical or interpersonal issues, such as contractual disputes from intercompany supply arrangements or a pattern of stealing talent from the new partner.

- *Organizational exhaustion.* Burnout can kill an integration process. If your troops are so far into one transaction that they just can't think about another deal, then they probably won't. Pacing is essential, as is getting new people into the integration discipline.

- *Incompatibility among top managers.* If the two teams or particular individuals on them despise each other, their feelings will inevitably influence both the deal and the perceptions of others involved in the due-diligence process, all the way through to integration. Look for this dissonance to trickle down to the Newco organization's leadership team as individuals from both sides naturally tend to carry previous perceptions and behavior forward.

- *Invalid assumptions about the business plan and processes.* Are the desired technologies and the best practices actually transportable? Are the two organizations' core capabilities or market opportunities being combined effectively, and in a way that could not be achieved without the transaction? Are the assumptions about sales channels and buyers' behavior valid?

- *Corporate arrogance.* It is sheer folly to mandate changes in business processes just because you have bought the right to do so. If either party perceives that there is nothing to be learned from the other, look out. Set the tone early with respect to the importance of learning and transferring knowledge, and maintain this tone throughout each stage of the deal.

Due Diligence and Organizational Culture

Consider the case of AT&T's acquisition of NCR in the early 1990s. According to Cary and Ogden (1998), AT&T was too late in discovering its significant cultural differences with NCR. Unionized employees objected to working in the same building as NCR's nonunion staff. NCR's conservative, centralized management culture was turned inside out by AT&T's insistence on calling supervisors "coaches" and removing executives' doors. Executive turnover among the NCR staff was so severe that by 1997 only four of the top thirty NCR managers remained. When AT&T finally sold NCR, the failure of the deal had cost AT&T more than $3 billion, and NCR lost approximately half its market value.

Now contrast that scenario with Southwest Airlines' acquisition of Morris Air in 1993. According to Lublin and O'Brien (1997), "Southwest spent two months exploring its cultural compatibility before finalizing the deal. Known for its can-do attitude and friendly esprit de corps, Southwest was committed to finding a partner with a similar orientation. As a result, the integration was completed successfully in only 11 months, rather than three years as was originally estimated."

Organization theorists Warner Burke and George Litwin were the ones who coined the most often quoted definition of organizational culture: "the way we do things around here." Organizational culture is like the air we breathe: many organizations and many executives are not actively aware of culture or its impact on their behavior until they are deprived of it or asked to change it. Carleton (1997) reminds us that organizational culture influences the way people treat and react to each other: "It shapes the way people feel about the company and the work they do; the way they interpret and perceive actions taken by others; the expectations they have regarding changes in their work or in the business; and how they view those changes" (p. 68).

And yet there is far more convincing and strategic evidence to indicate a direct financial and legal impact of organizational culture. For example, a 1989 ruling by the Delaware Supreme Court (*Paramount Communications, Inc. v. Time, Inc.,* 571 A.2d 1140, 1153. Del. 1989) established that organizational culture is a viable consideration in merger decisions. In this case, Paramount and two Time shareholder groups had brought suit against Time's directors for turning down Paramount's bid for the company in favor of the merger that created Time-Warner. The court found that it was proper for Time's directors to attempt to preserve the "Time culture" by merging with Warner, even though Paramount's bid would have meant more short-term profit for Time shareholders. Moreover, as Collins and Porras (1994) conclude in highlighting the results of a six-year study on "visionary" companies, those companies that have made an enduring commitment to values-based management have achieved an average stock market return fifteen times that of the general market. Further, Kotter and Heskett (1992) report astounding differences between the long-term financial results of companies that managed their cultures well and those that did not: revenue increases of 682 percent by contrast with 166 percent, stock price increases of 901 percent by contrast with 74 percent, and net income increases of 756 percent by contrast with 1 percent. Clearly, in the decision of which partner to merge with and how best to integrate disparate cultures and management processes, the potential risks and opportunities amount to more than just "fluff stuff."

A Six-Step Cultural Due-Diligence Approach

One experienced acquirer, intent on not becoming a negative "merger statistic," commissioned a full-fledged cultural due-diligence audit to be conducted as a part of a comprehensive predeal due-diligence process. A process model (see Exhibit 2.3) was created and approved by both partner companies. To prevent misunderstandings and streamline the process, thorough instructions and work steps were mutually agreed to, as listed here:

1. Initial planning.

> Determine objectives. Identify areas and issues to be audited. Discuss level of access available in the target company and who in the acquiring company will have access. Review initial organizational due-diligence checklist. Discuss data-collection needs and alternatives. Identify due-diligence team or representatives from among executives or deal-team members in the know. Confirm logistics, schedules, and responsibilities.

EXHIBIT 2.3. PROCESS MODEL FOR CULTURAL DUE-DILIGENCE ANALYSIS.

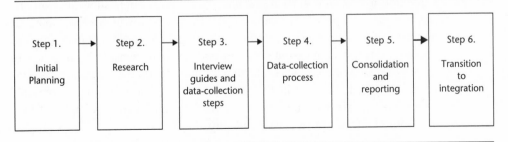

2. Conduct literature research.

> Review external data (annual report, press clippings, industry journals, recruiting information). Review available internal documentation (organizational charts, employee communications, policy manuals, employee census information, climate-survey data, data from deal teams. Review on-line information sources (Hoover's, company Web site).

3. Finalize interview guides and data collection steps.

> Capture key issues from preliminary research on structured-interview guide. Determine data-collection method (interviews, focus groups, surveys) on the basis of available access. Assign data-collection steps and contacts to due-diligence team members.

4. Data collection process.

> Interview key executives. Suggest minimum sample size of five executives, maximum of ten. Interview client company's deal-team members for verification of key issues. Conduct on-site observation, to the extent possible. Consider interviews with a few deal-team members from the target company.

5. Consolidation and reporting.

> Prepare and present a summary report to integration manager and officers. Incorporate key findings and issues into integration-process charters, assignments, and plans.

6. Transition process to integration.

> Present key findings to task force leaders at a kickoff meeting. Consider a survey of task force leaders to validate findings. In the discovery phase, ask the task force to conduct a detailed "as is" analysis.

Research and Interviews

In addition to research in such secondary sources as publications and on-line data, two forms of primary research were conducted: a written survey that was administered to a broad cross-section of managers from both companies, and structured interviews of executives from both organizations. It is important to remember that the process of conducting a cultural audit is similar to the process of conducting a behavioral interview in as much as the true value is typically captured through stories, anecdotes, expressions, and actual examples of how each cultural attribute is displayed and why.

In this case, after the data were collected and analyzed, the results were reported to key members of the executive staff. The written survey and the structured interview are described in more detail in the sections that follow.

Written Survey. To facilitate direct comparisons in scoring, the survey instrument (see Exhibit 2.4) was designed to capture reactions from respondents in both

EXHIBIT 2.4. SAMPLE FROM INITIAL CULTURE ASSESSMENT SURVEY.

Initial Culture Assessment

For each question, please base the first response on *your* current company's typical culture. Base your second response on your perception of the *partner* company's typical culture.

My current company affiliation is: Company A

Cultural Dimensions:

1. Organization-wide Information Transfer
To what extent is information readily disseminated throughout the organization? (Considerations: Financial performance? Operating performance? What is routinely communicated or held back? Employee perceptions of open information sharing and access to news?)

Company A: 1   2   3   4   5   6   7   8   9   10
              [Lesser Extent]   [Greater Extent]

Company B: 1   2   3   4   5   6   7   8   9   10
              [Lesser Extent]   [Greater Extent]

Comments and Observations:

_____

_____

2. Feedback and Interpersonal Communication
Is communication between individuals or departments more formal or informal in nature? (Considerations: Do essential communications regarding instructions, planning, and feedback take place primarily verbally or in writing? Through regularly scheduled meetings or informal conversations? Do employees and managers routinely access superiors through the "open door," voice mail, e-mail, or other avenues?)

Company A: 1   2   3   4   5   6   7   8   9   10
              [Lesser Extent]   [Greater Extent]

Company B: 1   2   3   4   5   6   7   8   9   10
              [Lesser Extent]   [Greater Extent]

partner organizations. Another, similar survey was also periodically readministered during the integration phase, to highlight slippage or pressure points that needed executive-level attention.

Structured Interview. It was necessary to ensure a consistent focus, across all the interviews with executives, on the cultural dimensions that the integration core team had determined to be most critical for this particular transaction. Therefore, a guide for these structured interviews was created (see Exhibit 2.5).

EXHIBIT 2.5. GUIDE FOR STRUCTURED INTERVIEWS OF EXECUTIVES.

Component / Questions	Notes / Comments
1. Strategic Direction What is the company/unit primary value proposition? What are the key business drivers behind the strategy? What key differentiators does the market recognize? How does the company express its mission, vision, values to the public? to employees? What are the key elements of the business plan? Other?	
2. Key Results Measures and Definitions What is measured and why? How are key measurement categories (customer service, production volumes, employee satisfaction) defined? How are these results communicated to external stakeholders? to employees? How are results and measures managed (by function or unit, by central source)? How are these metrics linked to rewards and incentives? To what degree is the organization focused on meeting the needs of the customer?	

The cultural dimensions most relevant to an audit will be different for each company and each new transaction, of course, but the core team ultimately settled on interviewing the executives with respect to twelve different dimensions:

1. Strategic direction

   What is the company's or unit's primary value proposition? What are the key business drivers behind the strategy? What key differentiators does the market recognize? How does the company express its mission, vision, and values to the public? to employees? What are the key elements of the business plan?

2. Key measures and definitions of results

   What is measured, and why? How are key measurement categories (customer service, production volumes, employee satisfaction) defined? How are results communicated to external stakeholders? to employees? How are results and measures managed—by each function or unit? by central source? How are these measures linked to rewards and incentives? To what degree is the organization focused on meeting the needs of customers?

3. Structure and protocols

   How is the company organized—by functions? geographical locations? business units? a matrix? organizational charts? How do staff and line units relate to each other? get services or deliverables from each other? What degree of customer-service perspective exists within staff functions? How do people access units or resources other than their own— by making direct contact independently? via some appropriate hierarchy?

4. Planning and control systems

   What formal systems are in place, and to what extent are they followed? Is there more adherence to informal or to formal approaches? How are strategic planning and budgeting handled? How are managers and employees engaged in strategic planning, budgeting, and so forth? How are decisions made, and at what levels? What level of authority do managers have, and for what types of decisions? What about for routine issues and decisions, by contrast with major ones? What degree of consensus or autonomy is typically expected in the formulation of decisions? What style of decision making would most employees perceive the organization as having: collaborative, delegative, or highly controlled and hierarchical? To what extent are policies, rules, and procedures prescribed and formalized? What degree of flexibility exists in applying policies?

5. Employee engagement

> How widespread are teams or other methods of employee involvement? If teams are used, what kinds—for work? for special projects? for positive employee relations? Is work performed with a primary focus on individual responsibility and accountability or on group responsibility? What level of input, influence, autonomy, or control do individuals have with respect to key aspects of their work (process, quality, rate, tools, resources, and so on)? Are employees linked to the business plan through processes for goal setting or performance management? To what extent are employees involved in special committees, social events, or task forces?

6. Use and philosophy of information technology (IT)

> What types of technology platforms and architecture currently exist? Is there compatibility of hardware? Is there planned investment in IT? Which business systems are in use? in development? How is technology currently being used to leverage staff expertise and increase productivity? How is mobile computing handled? What level of e-mail capability exists? What skill level exists with current software applications? With which suites and programs? How is the IT shop structured and staffed? What is the current level of service and capability? What level of service and support does the organization need? What are the current issues or concerns in IT? What major legacy systems and applications exist? How is the company dealing with Y2K compliance?

7. Physical environment

> What is the "look and feel" of the offices and plants? What is the level of constraint or opulence in finish-out, furniture, decor? Is there a dress code? Are offices open or private? Is there controlled or open access? What is the impact of the environment (with respect to interaction, camaraderie, and so on) on how work gets done?

8. Historical issues and expectations

> What major events (the worst and the best) created and affected the current organization? What perceptions and obstacles will most employees bring forward? most managers? What social activities, special incentives or opportunities, icons or images, and norms may people have a stake in preserving?

9. Organizationwide information transfer

> How readily is information (about financial performance, operating performance, and so on) disseminated throughout the organization?

What is routinely communicated? held back? To what extent do employees and managers believe that they have access to important information? What types of organizationwide communication channels, programs, and media exist?

10. Information transfer between and among individuals

Is communication between and among individuals and departments typically more formal or informal? Are instructions, feedback, and communication given primarily in writing or in person? To ensure fast and effective transfer of information, what types of regularly scheduled meetings exist throughout the organization? Do employees routinely have access to superiors through an "open door" policy? Via another feedback process?

11. Leaders' and managers' behavior

Are managers selected and rewarded primarily for coaching and facilitative leadership? for traditional command-and-control approaches? What type of boss-subordinate relationship represents the norm? What areas of competence are most predictive of success? How are these areas of competence identified, communicated, and developed?

12. Human capital

How is the human resources (HR) department positioned in the organization—as a strategic business partner? an administrative unit? How able is HR to affect significant change in the organization? How are reward programs designed to motivate desired types of behavior and align them with business objectives? How are benefits provided? What level of internal customer service is provided to employees? What is the general orientation of the company to its employees? Does it demonstrate that they are a valued resource? How?

Rationale for a Cultural Due-Diligence Process

The primary value of cultural due diligence is that it raises sensitivity to and awareness of issues that should be proactively managed during integration. A comprehensive cultural audit has other advantages, too, and can promote the accomplishment of several important practical outcomes.

First, a thorough cultural audit can help the acquirer avoid senseless mistakes. For example, when Union Pacific Corporation acquired Southern Pacific Rail Corporation, top managers failed to consider the immense cultural, historical, and emotional impact that one of its early decisions would have on the acquired workforce—specifically, the decision about the nomenclature that would be used to identify engines and routes. For Union Pacific, there was only one logical, rational choice: to follow its own numeric system. For Southern Pacific, however, losing the historically and emotionally significant Memphis Blue Streak—the company's oldest and most famous line—was tantamount to being betrayed, and a betrayal is exactly what the decision was taken to be. As one Union Pacific manager lamented, "We never recovered from that move" (Machalaba, 1997, p. A1). An effort to gain deeper cultural understanding could have prevented this early misstep, both by revealing what it would mean to Southern Pacific to be able to maintain some cultural heritage and by providing opportunities to identify a reasonable alternative to the unilateral imposition of Union Pacific's nomenclature.

Second, a careful cultural audit can help mitigate the effects of takeaways when they are necessary. In one common scenario, a cost-efficient, high-performance acquirer has a reward culture that is based on variable incentives, whereas the acquired company, a more traditional competitor, has a reward culture that is based on position- or title-related power, perquisites, and hierarchy. When the acquired company's reward culture is brought into closer alignment with a performance orientation, the result may be unnecessarily high turnover among capable talent unless a carefully thought-out retention plan is implemented. When individually tailored roles are created and the total value of the new approach is carefully communicated, it is possible to achieve a much higher retention rate and a higher level of performance.

Third, an effective cultural audit can stimulate much faster resolution of key disagreements that, left unchecked, could easily degenerate into organizational mudslinging contests. In one recent case, for example, the acquirer (company A) was a lean, low-cost operator, whereas the acquired organization (company B) was a well-to-do division of a major corporate entity. Company A's pervasive commitment to low costs was reflected in a directive from senior management that there should be no color overhead transparencies and "no fancy data projectors"; company B, by contrast, was run from a lavish corporate campus replete with a pond, a fountain, and a fully staffed corporate library. When executives from both companies were made aware of the cultural gap with respect to costs, and because they could point to several specific instances in which this gap was already creating substantial friction, they were able to reach consensus on how to handle key cost-related aspects of integration and consolidation, and they managed to produce clear, organizationwide instructions for cost containment during the transition.

Due Diligence and Human Capital

Steve Vernon is a colleague of ours whose expertise in due diligence has been used by dozens of major global employers. As a senior consulting actuary, Steve is often called on to assist with some of the thorniest problems related to human capital (for example, helping acquirers evaluate and negotiate target companies' pension plans, defined contribution plans, executive contracts, and retiree medical plans, to name just a few such problems). After one particularly challenging meeting with a client, Steve coached the M&A project team on the most important guidelines for due diligence with respect to human capital. "There are three rules for effective due diligence in this area," he explained. "(1) Pay attention to details. (2) Pay attention to details. (3) Pay attention to details." Good advice, since within the human resources functions are myriad details, any one of which could expose the company to millions of dollars in liabilities.

According to Roger Atkins, a senior international human resources consultant, any of these details is a potential deal killer: "We've routinely discovered unfunded pension liabilities of $30 million, $50 million, $80 million, and even $100 million in some of our work around the world. The most successful acquirers define a process for identifying both the human resources and financial issues [while attending to] broader organizational factors, in a way that resonates with senior management" (Atkins, Carter, Nies, and Rochelle, 1998).

GE Capital is an excellent case in point. After acquiring more than one hundred firms in five years, GE Capital not only has achieved remarkable financial results but also has made the transition from experiencing merger-related integration as an ordeal to seeing it as a business process for defining what is to be done on a routine basis. In 1997, the revenues for GE totaled $91 billion; GE Capital's portion of that total was approximately $40 billion, with twenty-eight different business components currently in operation and largely created through acquisitions in which the HR team was heavily involved.

Arapoff (1998, p. 17) cites Larry De Monaco, vice president of global human resources for GE Capital:

> Human capital due diligence helps to form a basis for the entire integration plan, and it helps to develop an assessment of the senior leadership of the company you're looking to acquire. It gets to the very core in understanding the cultural fit of one organization with another.
>
> I've been working here since 1987, and I've been involved in due diligence since the beginning. Getting HR involved early on in the M&A process—and

not getting intimidated by the scope of what you're doing—is the name of the game. If you can do that, it will minimize the time that you're actually involved in due diligence.

From De Monaco's standpoint, there are two facets of the HR function in due diligence, one defensive and the other offensive. Defensively, the goal is to glean information from the target company regarding its track record with union-ized plans, grievances, class-action suits, and other potential problems. Offen-sively, the goal is to bring all human-capital-related assets to the forefront and identify ways of maximizing their value.

"Due diligence should not only assess the financial aspects of the deal but also identify the human-capital elements of the target or partner organization and provide valuable data on them for the integration process," says De Monaco. From a global perspective, due diligence has even greater significance. Regard-less of the type of businesses involved in the deal, international mergers bring ad-ditional sets of investigative needs to the table. "The goals of due diligence are the same in New York or Paris or anywhere else from an HR standpoint," suggests De Monaco. "But you must do more homework on a much more complex set of regulatory requirements and country culture expectations, in addition to the stan-dard components—for example, the demographics of the merging company's workforce, leadership team, and company culture" (cited in Arapoff, 1998, p. 17).

Coordinating HR into the Due-Diligence Process

For most organizations, getting HR involved in the integration process is difficult enough. Many HR departments are never consulted at all until well after the due-diligence phase is completed—too late for them to issue effective warnings about key human-capital-related risks and liabilities.

Watson Wyatt Worldwide (1998a) surveyed 190 companies and found that, of those doing M&A transactions in the United States, 41 percent first involved HR during investigation (that is, at the due-diligence phase). Among those doing M&A transactions in the Asia-Pacific region and Brazil, the level of HR's early in-volvement was much lower: 21 percent and 14 percent, respectively. Likewise, among U.S.-based companies that did involve HR, fully 27 percent of M&A transactions did not bring HR in until the integration stage, whereas 44 percent of deals in the Asia-Pacific region and 50 percent of those in Brazil brought HR to the party late. (See Exhibit 2.6.) Further analysis of this survey reveals a par-ticularly noteworthy finding: in this sample, 46 percent of U.S.-based respondents saw productivity improve after the deal. When those respondents' organizations

EXHIBIT 2.6. STAGE AT WHICH HUMAN RESOURCES BECOMES INVOLVED IN THE DEAL PROCESS.

	United States	Asia-Pacific Region	Brazil
Initial planning	16%	19%	11%
Investigative stage	41%	21%	14%
Negotiation stage	16%	16%	25%
Integration	27%	44%	50%

Source: Watson Wyatt Worldwide (1998a).

are compared with organizations that did not experience improved postdeal productivity, a number of factors appear to be positively correlated with improved postdeal productivity. These include early involvement of HR, due diligence with respect to organizational culture, and due diligence with respect to HR policy. For several years, the importance of "people" issues and of issues related to organizational culture has been consistently cited in the management literature, but it is now increasingly clear that HR plays a much more instrumental role than previously thought in delivering business results during M&A transactions. It seems that the difficulty in gaining sufficiently early HR involvement is often due more to historical bias than to any inability on HR's part to make a legitimate contribution.

In many organizations, this pattern of leaving HR out until it is too late is unlikely to change much until HR can demonstrate that it understands M&A transactions and what the business needs at various stages of the deal process. For example, one of our clients, the vice president of human resources for a major global manufacturer, recently made the following request: "We do ten or twelve acquisitions per year, and HR has yet to be involved before the deal is announced. Help me find a way to position HR as a legitimate player in the predeal due-diligence process." Exhibit 2.7 illustrates a process similar to the one proposed in response to this client's request. In this case, there was no clearly defined M&A transaction process. For years, the details of deal making had been a closely guarded secret. As a result, even the M&A department itself was unsure about when to involve the various stakeholders, and on what issues these stakeholders should be consulted. After a series of interviews with executives, and after research into the documentation of previous deals, a clear process map was drawn up and validated by all the parties to deal making and M&A transactions. Steps were then proposed for human-capital-related due diligence and were modeled against the

EXHIBIT 2.7. COORDINATING HR INTO THE DUE DILIGENCE PROCESS.

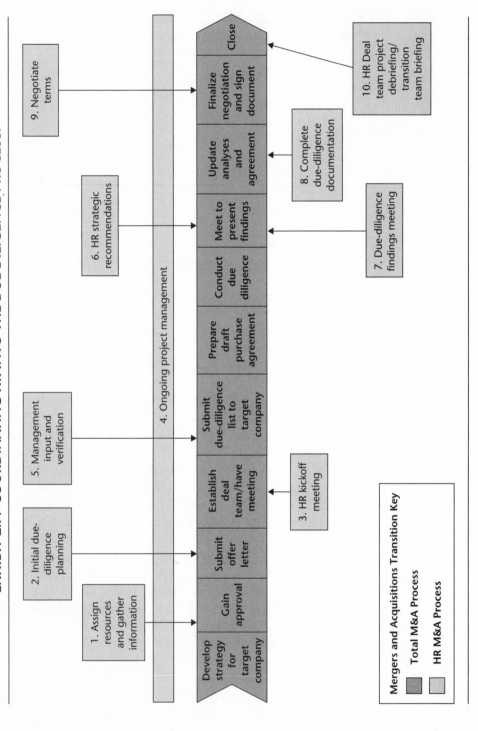

overall transaction phase. Specific roles and responsibilities were drafted along with comprehensive checklists and parameters for such specific areas as aligning different compensation philosophies and different retirement plans. Finally, document templates were developed for everything from defining the due-diligence team to using outside consultants or legal counsel to reporting key findings to senior managers.

Culture and HR Due Diligence for Partner Company Selection

In today's frenzied M&A market, there are often many potential buyers for every company and many potential joint-venture candidates for every business expansion. An increasingly important critical success factor is the ability to discern which of the several partner candidates represents the most strategic play and the best organizational fit. This was the challenge recently faced by a major global computer manufacturer. Intent on quickly forming the first captive-leasing and financial services joint venture among its industry peers, the company commissioned a comprehensive human-capital and cultural best-practices analysis of three finalist candidates.

Beginning with a thorough orientation to the uniqueness of the acquirer's culture and business model, the project team quickly created a human-capital and cultural best-practices model that succinctly summarized the strategic objectives in each of eight essential human-capital categories; a similar model is shown in Exhibit 2.8. After general philosophical directives had been clarified for each of these eight categories, a comprehensive list of issues was created for each area. The issues were classified into one of two lists: those essential to the selection of the candidate and the establishment of basic short-term operations, and those important in carrying out such longer-term goals as supporting the deal synergies and achieving full integration. A representative sample of human-capital-related issues is shown in Exhibit 2.9. As the final step in preparation, subject-matter experts were assigned to conduct research in the secondary literature, study each candidate's joint-venture bid, and interview the candidates' executives to determine the best human-capital and cultural match. Particular emphasis was laid on the business objectives of the financial services venture and on the two organizations' complementary strengths. After all of the data had been gathered, each of the three finalist candidates was profiled against the acquirer's human-capital best-practices model and was compared with the other two finalists; Exhibit 2.10 shows a sample of the document template that was used in constructing these profiles. A briefing was then conducted with key members of the deal team, and a recommendation was made, from a human-capital and cultural standpoint,

EXHIBIT 2.8. BEST-PRACTICES BASELINE MODEL.

Critical "People" Practices	Objectives
Culture development	Create an organization that has a clear vision and that values client satisfaction, quality, and the importance of involving employees.
Leadership	Ensure the provision of leaders who carry the vision and values to meet the needs of the organization and its customers.
Staffing and selection	Recruit and select people who have the skills and behaviors to meet the workforce's needs.
Rewards and recognition	Align individual and team rewards with the organization's performance relative to the business plan.
Benefits	Provide pension, health, and other programs that offer choice and that support the workforce demographics.
Training and continuous learning	Help people acquire and develop skills and knowledge critical to the organization's competitive success.
Performance management	Align individual and team goals with company goals, provide employees with continuous feedback and coaching, assess performance and results, and manage the consequences of poor performance.
Employee communications	Share information with employees to promote two-way communication across the organization.

regarding the team's assessment of the most strategic, most complementary joint-venture partner. The organization considered to provide the best human-capital and cultural fit was in fact later selected as the joint-venture partner. Data that had been discovered during the due-diligence process led directly into human-capital-related integration planning. Within two weeks from the time the selected candidate was identified, the high-level HR strategy, structure, and program-design direction had been set. Within two months, the detailed HR program designs had been carried out. Within four months, the new financial services joint venture was in operation.

EXHIBIT 2.9. SAMPLE HUMAN-CAPITAL-RELATED ISSUES.

"People" Practice Area	Up-and-Running Issues	Longer-Term Issues
Rewards and recognition	• Who is the competitive labor market for talent? Does this vary by job level? • How is base pay positioned against the marketplace, and how should it be? • What does the base pay structure look like? • How is incentive compensation positioned against the marketplace, and how should it be? • What is the appropriate mix of direct compensation? • What are the available alternatives for long-term incentives? • What are the critical performance measures that affect rewards? • How will executives be compensated?	• How will employees receive increases in base pay? • What reward and recognition plans are appropriate to reinforce the business strategies and culture? • How will reward plans be communicated to ensure they are effective? • What are the success criteria for reward plans, and how will they be measured?

EXHIBIT 2.10. SAMPLE OF DOCUMENT TEMPLATE FOR BEST-PRACTICES PROFILE.

Candidate Organization	Key Findings
ABC Company	Finding 1: Finding 2: Finding 3: Finding 4: Finding 5:
LMNO Company	Finding 1: Finding 2: Finding 3: Finding 4: Finding 5:
XYZ Company	Finding 1: Finding 2: Finding 3: Finding 4: Finding 5:

CHAPTER THREE

WELCOME TO THE BIG LEAGUES OF CHANGE MANAGEMENT

E ven though the predominant mergers and acquisitions of today are carefully designed to ensure a tight strategic fit between two companies, the task of integrating the companies remains difficult and may be getting even harder than in the past. One way of meeting the challenge is to treat the integration process as nothing less than a far-reaching change-management initiative for both companies.

Change management—largely regarded as a discipline that realigns operating companies so that they can deal with economic, technological, and other forces shaking up their marketplaces—is significantly related to the M&A process. For one thing, a timely M&A is among the important developmental responses to market-based change. For another, few initiatives or responses change the configurations or the environment of a company more visibly and dramatically than an acquisition does; indeed, the changes introduced in this way come far more quickly and are more significant than those to which most organizations are accustomed. Therefore, the concepts and tools of change management should be used by both parties to the M&A deal. Even if the buyer is a multibillion-dollar enterprise that is bringing in a smaller concern—say, in the area of $100 million in annual sales—chances are that the acquirer also is experiencing significant change because of the transaction.

Whether a company's strategy is to grow its existing markets, introduce new products, gain access to new customers, or expand its distribution systems, an

M&A provides the means of executing this strategy quickly and effectively. Therefore, the deals of the 1990s tend to stress such characteristics as compatibility, fit, and complementarity of core areas of competence. But even these favorable traits are not enough to guarantee smooth integration, and to assume that they are is to take a great risk, one that may be exacerbated by the fact that focused acquisitions increase pressure on management to deliver on strategic promises within a shorter time.

In short, integration presents a change-management challenge unlike any other. What is surprising, however, is that many executives who are responsible for making mergers and acquisitions work fail to see the link between M&As and the change-management discipline.

Organizational Dynamics Created by Mergers and Acquisitions

Exhibit 3.1 lists twelve critical areas entailing organizational dynamics that only occasionally come into play during other kinds of change efforts (such as a reorganization or a downsizing) but that all show up in a merger or an acquisition. We have found that these change dynamics are often overlooked during the due-diligence process and are further ignored as integration gets under way. These dynamics are inevitable, however, and they tend to hit merging companies with full force once the deal has closed.

Poor handling of the change dynamics during postmerger integration is a principal reason why many mergers and acquisitions fail. In fact, during the recent acquisition of a chemical company by another chemical producer, these dynamics were displayed in both organizations, a situation that came as a total

EXHIBIT 3.1. CHANGE-MANAGEMENT DYNAMICS BROUGHT ABOUT BY A MERGER OR AN ACQUISITION.

Aggressive financial targets	Growth-related challenges
Short timelines	Restructuring
Intense public scrutiny	Reengineering
Culture clashes	Questions about where to downsize
Politics and positioning	Problems with retention of personnel
Communication-related issues	Issues related to employees' motivation

surprise to senior managers. The surprise was not that these issues needed to be addressed in the acquired company but that they also needed to be addressed in the acquiring company. For example, many managers and employees in the acquiring company began to feel threatened by the seemingly more efficient processes and high level of talent in the acquired company, where they also saw a younger, more dynamic workforce. These change dynamics actually created the need for more communication, and for more attention to politics and positioning in the acquired company, than top managers ever would have realized had these dynamics not begun to appear. Top managers should have been better prepared for these reactions in the acquiring company's workforce, and they should have initiated action to address these reactions through (at the minimum) earlier, more frequent communication with the acquiring company's managers and employees. Fortunately, however, the message that integration and change management are connected is starting to get through. For example, during a recent consulting assignment, we conducted a one-hour briefing for the top twenty managers of two merging companies, a briefing that centered on the very dynamics just cited. One of the two CEOs commented, "We thought we knew what we were getting into, but this merger has it all. We are now in the big leagues of change management."

Concepts of Change Management

Because a merger creates immense change-management issues, actions aimed at integration should help mitigate the risks and stack the odds in favor of making the deal work. In the sections that follow, we discuss seven change-management concepts that embody the lessons we have learned while assisting companies with merger integration:

1. Addressing "me" issues quickly
2. Applying defined, clear leadership
3. Providing extensive communication
4. Ensuring a focus on customers
5. Making tough decisions
6. Creating focused initiatives
7. Managing resistance at every level

These concepts have proved to be facilitators of successful organizational change initiatives, and they should also be applied to merger integration.

Addressing "Me" Issues Quickly

Major change not only requires daring moves, it requires that they be made rapidly. In the earliest stages of a merger or an acquisition, once people are in the know about what is happening, they begin trying to grapple on a number of fronts with the newly introduced uncertainty. Nevertheless, the first topic to become a matter of great concern among people at all levels of the organization, from executives down to front-line employees, is personal uncertainty: the "me" issues. Before people become curious about combined market share or start thinking about the integration of databases, they consider the personal impacts. Will I lose my job? Will my pay be affected? To whom will I report? Will I have to move? These questions underscore the real issues in the minds of managers and employees. Moreover, in the case of an acquisition or merger, personal concerns proliferate not just among the personnel of the target company but also among those of the acquiring company. In conducting numerous integration efforts over the past several years, we have seen that managers and employees keep asking these questions until they get answers, and the time that the workforce spends worrying about these questions is time that is not being spent on the business.

Productivity, morale, and performance almost always decline at all organizational levels during a time of change, and these declines can be especially vexing during merger integration. What Exhibit 3.2 makes clear, however, is that patterns of decline (decreased customer service, for example, or lower levels of operational and financial productivity) for senior managers, middle managers, and employees are staggered over time as the merger or acquisition unfolds.

This pattern comes about because senior managers are typically the first to be informed of a merger or an acquisition. Next, middle managers are told, and, finally, the employees are filled in. The staggered learning that results has some tangible implications. Specifically, senior managers stop communicating about what is going on: they themselves are informed and know where they stand on the "me" issues, and so they relax, believing that the worst is now behind them, and often begin looking ahead to the next deal. As a result, they give lower priority to managing the current integration; their attitude is often "Why doesn't the workforce just get back to work?" They forget that middle managers and employees are just learning about the deal and are only now receiving information that the executives were given some time ago. The bottom line is that senior managers must manage the integration on the basis of where the majority of the organization is, not on the basis of where they themselves are.

Merger integration is like pulling off a bandage: it can be slow and painful, or it can be fast and painful. Slow movement through the integration process

EXHIBIT 3.2. STAGGERED PATTERN OF DECLINING PRODUCTIVITY, MORALE, OR PERFORMANCE.

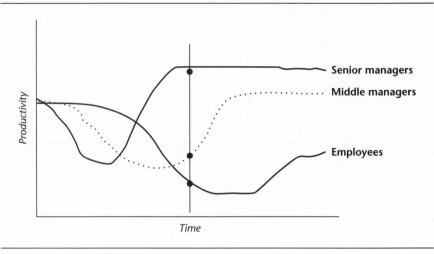

prolongs the period of unrest and uncertainty, and people in both firms have more time to dwell on their personal issues, which are a distraction from maintaining peak productivity and performance. Moving quickly—but not recklessly—through the integration process clears up uncertainty and leaves less time for a decline in productivity to develop; both the depth and the duration of the drop are mitigated. Fast-track integration—that is, integration conducted at prudent (but not reckless) speed—also ensures that the expected gains will be realized as soon as possible. Synergies of cost and growth in a merger or an acquisition can be significant and should be accelerated: shaving even one month off the integration timetable can generate millions of dollars for the combined organization.

Here is an easy-to-grasp example. Say that a company acquires a thousand-person asset from another company. Each of the thousand managers and employees of the acquired asset talks about the acquisition for just one hour per day instead of doing his or her job. ("Who do you think will get which jobs?" "What processes will we use?" "What changes will they make?" "What about our pay and benefits?") At five days per week, five thousand hours of productivity are lost each week. At an average of four weeks per month, twenty thousand hours of productivity are lost each month. In our experience, the traditional integration period in most companies has been approximately eighteen to twenty-four months. Therefore, at least three hundred sixty thousand hours of productivity can be lost during an acquisition of just a thousand-person operation. Moreover, you can be sure that managers and employees are not talking about the deal for just one hour per day, and that the conversations do not occur only before or after work or at lunch. People will be distracted by the integration for major portions of the work-day, *every* day, until their "me" issues are resolved and the integration is complete. Therefore, completing the integration in twelve months rather than eighteen can mean a savings of twenty thousand hours of productivity per month, or one hundred twenty thousand total hours of productivity. At an average per-employee rate of $25 per hour in pay and benefits, the total savings would be $3 million.

Applying Defined, Clear Leadership

In any change effort, leadership is important in providing clear direction for the move into an uncertain future. Unfortunately, however, leadership is difficult to obtain in major change efforts, especially in mergers and acquisitions: two new groups of people are coming together, and many obvious "champions" naturally opt for playing politics instead of providing leadership to the organization. This tendency only makes it more difficult for people to get resolution of the "me" issues that generate so much uncertainty and low morale. When people see top managers merely jockeying for political position in the new company, putting little or no focus on the business, its customers, or its employees, the seeds of a failed integration are sown. Ensuring that someone is in charge of the integration and defining clear lines of authority can mitigate the politics and create a "back to business" attitude.

Like the implementation of a new system, the move to a new facility, or any other change, a merger integration is a very large and complex project. Unless a specific person is accountable for the project's success, the effort will be stymied by delays, false starts, and overwhelming confusion. To be successful, the person in charge needs several key characteristics: skills in project management and project coordination, both clout with and respect from (the two do not always go hand in hand) the acquiring organization, and solid strategic decision-making ability. Like a camera's lens, the "merger manager" should be able to zoom in quickly on the details and just as comfortably zoom out to view the broader picture. Both views are essential to efficient and effective problem solving, decision making, and direction setting.

Providing Extensive Communication

Communication, a huge part of any major change effort, is critically important in a merger or an acquisition. An M&A transaction is a setting of great uncertainty, frequent rumors, and constant decisions that change the scene. Clear and constant communication throughout the integration process can provide decisive answers and dispel rumors.

Beyond seeking answers to their immediate personal questions, people want to know about the operational, marketing, systems, and financial aspects of the newly formed organization because these matters will also have a direct impact on their personal situations. When they do not hear recurrent messages from top managers about the direction of the company, about why the merger is happening, about who is involved, about how the integration will unfold, and about the time frame that has been erected for meeting goals, they perceive leadership, direction, and control to be lacking. Clear, consistent, and frequent communication (at least weekly, and perhaps more often), even when it only takes the form of cursory updates on progress, will go a long way toward recapturing the commitment of middle managers and employees during the integration. The most frightening message of all is silence: something that must be avoided at all costs.

According to May and Kettelhut (1996, p. 9), "Open communication and collaboration are essential [to effective change]. Open communications clarify expectations and reduce ambiguity." Haslett (1995) also emphasizes communication as a key first step in any change effort. Jack Welch of GE offers a real-life example of employing communication to lower resistance. In his interview with Sherman (1993, p. 84), he comments as follows: "How do you bring people into the change process? Start with reality. Get all the facts out. Give people the rationale for change, laying it out in the clearest, most dramatic terms. When everybody gets the same facts, they'll generally come to the same conclusion. Only after everyone agrees on the reality and resistance is lowered can you begin to get buy-in to the needed changes." Longo (1996, p. 69), too, emphasizes that companies generally do a poor job of communicating change to their people: "The second biggest problem [beyond a lack of involvement] is communication. Getting people to buy into [change] isn't easy because people put little stock in what management is selling. Senior managers dilute, filter, and distort information."

Unfortunately, experience shows that organizations need to do a better job of communicating, not only initially but also throughout their integration efforts. For example, consider what happened when a systems-integration consulting firm was acquired by a large manufacturer of computers. As the integration process unfolded, the director of communications from the consulting firm sent out information about the acquisition process only when there was "something important" to tell people. This practice meant that communications about the deal were separated by an average time of one month or even longer, but the director of communications repeatedly insisted that managers and employees in his firm were receiving enough information, and that they did not want to be bothered by too many communications. About three months into the acquisition process, top management of the computer manufacturer held a gathering for key managers from the acquired consulting company, to welcome them to the new and larger organization. As this gathering began, a question-and-answer session was conducted by a panel made up of top management. The first question put to the panel by a manager in the audience was "How can I tell my people what needs to be done to integrate the companies, when I have heard nothing about what is going on?"—a comment immediately echoed by three other managers. These managers went on to say that there had been good communication until the deal closed, almost three months before this meeting, but that they had heard nothing since then. After this meeting, communication became much more frequent.

Ensuring a Focus on Customers

Any kind of major organizational change requires that a company become introspective, and this requirement is especially important during a merger integration. And, once the deal has been announced, the focus of both organizations and the people in them turns inward.

Shortly after a merger, many organizations experience lower sales, as well as increased complaints about customer service—problems that they cannot afford. The spotlight is already on the deal, with analysts, top and middle managers, employees of both organizations, and customers anxious to know the outcome. When sales and service suffer, people in these groups tend to blame the merger, and they immediately question the viability of the combination. Moreover, customers may begin to flee to competitors, in the belief that service has been abandoned or impaired in the merger of the two organizations.

If the merging organizations lose sight of the market, then sales and service—the points of contact with the customer—become the most vulnerable areas. Therefore, managers must ensure that the organizations' critical outreach to customers, one of the most valuable franchises a company can own, is protected. They should pay particular attention to maintaining the standards of sales and service that their customers expect, and to installing any mechanisms that are needed to sustain good relationships with customers. As necessary, care of customers should include special initiatives like short-term sales incentives, merger training and information for customer service personnel at help desks and call centers, and special advertising aimed at communicating to customers that there is a continued commitment to service. Actions to boost sales and service must be overtly planned and quickly executed.

Making Tough Decisions

A change of any consequence requires tough decisions to be made, and the integration environment makes these decisions even tougher because of the more intense time pressure. Often, however, managers who do not want to offend the newly acquired organization (or alarm their own people) may unwisely delay these tough decisions.

In a merger or an acquisition, it is almost impossible to be perceived by everyone as totally fair. The difficult issues that must be dealt with during integration include organizational structure, reporting channels, spans of control, roles and responsibilities, identification of positions, and selection of people. Seldom are there easy, clear-cut answers in these areas, but top managers must make decisions quickly, implement them, and abide by them; otherwise, both companies get the message that top management is unorganized and indecisive, and that the merger lacks leadership. Delaying a decision in the hope that the perfect solution eventually will surface is itself a poor decision.

Creating Focused Initiatives

When a deal closes, each functional area (finance, systems, human resources, operations, marketing, and so on) launches its own integration actions and proceeds with the very best of intentions. Unfortunately, however, go-it-alone managers and employees in specific areas unintentionally create harm that is manifested in several ways:

- The actions of the specific areas are uncoordinated and leave the impression that the total integration plan is disjointed.
- Because the efforts are uncoordinated, they often overlap.
- Divergent activities allow too many details to fall through the cracks, never to be retrieved.
- The aims, timing, and outcomes of uncoordinated actions often wind up in conflict with one another.

In any change initiative, tolerance of divergent activities can seriously hinder success. Therefore, all the elements of the combined organization must be fully coordinated, even while they may be taking separate actions, and the merger integration should be managed as a fully coordinated project with a visible project-management structure.

Managing Resistance at Every Level

People resist change, and the degree of change involved in integrating two organizations is massive. The extent of the change often fosters resistance that may seem insurmountable and can destroy even the best-planned merger.

This perception is sustained throughout the writings on strategic organizational change. For example, Clemons, Thatcher, and Row (1995) conducted a study, across various industries, of why major change efforts have failed in large companies. They found that the failures were unrelated to the technical aspects of organizations; in general, companies have the skill (or can hire it) to implement the technical aspects of change efforts. Rather, the authors contend, a major reason for failure is what they call "political risk," which they describe as the risk that changes will not be completed because of organizational resistance, or because of the progressive fading of commitment to the change effort. They contend that when resistance is substantial, organizations falter at both the development and the implementation of a change project. Peck (1995), who also studied major change projects, identifies "organizational resistance" as the top barrier to success and reports that 92 percent of his respondents identified it as the main problem they had encountered. This finding is supported by Longo (1996), who notes, in writing about the difficulty of change efforts, that the "number one source of difficulty with implementation of [change] is the disregard for, or misunderstanding of, the resistance to change" (p. 69). Moreover, in a *Financial Times* article about creating "high performance workplaces" ("Mastering Management," 1996), resistance to change is reported to be a major obstacle to success: "Institutional obstacles, resistance to change, un-supportive cultures, and incoherent strategies . . . explain why high performance workplaces have not diffused more widely" (p. 3). Finally, the first two "frequently asked questions" on the World Wide Web site of one group of consultants (Organized Change, 1996) are "How do I obtain commitment to our plans from my organization?" and "How do I minimize resistance from middle management in implementing this change?"

Why is there so much misunderstanding, among managers at all levels, about people's resistance to mergers and acquisitions? One answer is that it can be attributed to the education and training that most managers receive. Although the situation is shifting, many MBA programs and management training courses focus primarily on the "hard" (technical, operational, financial) aspects of business, dealing only in a very cursory way with organizational change. As a result, management training does a poor job of addressing how to manage through the resistance that is encountered during a change effort (such as a merger or an acquisition). Another answer is that managers' practical experience during the planning of a merger or an acquisition, with its focus on the "hard" aspects of the deal, merely serves to reinforce their training and education while undermining their ability to gain a sound understanding of why and how people in both organizations may resist the deal after it has closed.

It is important to recognize that resistance is not necessarily an indication that something is going wrong with the integration. Rather, it may simply be a sign of people's understanding that something big is happening. Managers who grasp this point may be more able to view employees' resistance as a normal reaction to integration—that is, as a reaction that does not necessarily require an equally forceful reaction from managers. Instead, during a major change, the wise manager will focus his or her efforts on those individuals or groups whose resistance is not so evident—for example, the people who are undecided about the changes taking place. These people are typically the largest group in the organization. They are management's "swing vote"—and, most important, they are ultimately the ones who will or will not implement the desired changes effectively.

In any case, if two companies are to be integrated successfully, then resistance to change must not be allowed to remain a mystery to those companies' managers. Exhibit 3.3 shows a three-level "resistance pyramid" that illustrates the reasons for people's resistance to change during the integration effort that follows a merger. The three levels represent a progressive hierarchy of the reasons why change is resisted. The base level ("Not knowing") represents people's lack of knowledge and information about the integration effort. The middle level ("Not able") represents people's lack of ability to perform the tasks made necessary by the merger. The top level ("Not willing") represents people's personal reluctance to make the effort to change. Each level of the resistance pyramid suggests a tangible action for managing resistance (see Exhibit 3.4). At the base level, what is required is communication, to keep people informed about the integration effort. At the middle level, what is required is training. At the top level, what is required is performance management, given that communication and training only begin to lower people's resistance.

We have already seen the importance of providing extensive communication, both before a merger and during the integration effort. Beyond providing information and knowledge, it is necessary, in lowering resistance to integration, to provide training—that is, to equip people with the new skills that they will need in order to use another company's procedures, systems, and the like. May and Kettelhut (1996, p. 8), discussing training as a tool for managing resistance to change, concur: "Individuals need to feel competent and to continually develop their competence. Change generally involves new knowledge, skills or abilities, and this often places people in positions where they initially lack that which they

EXHIBIT 3.3. THE RESISTANCE PYRAMID.

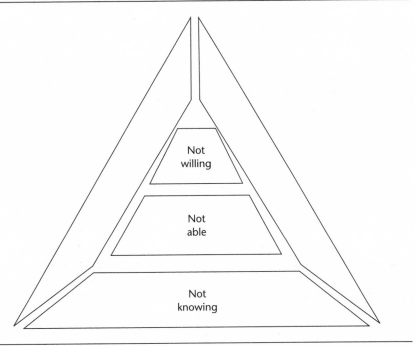

Source: Adapted from Galpin (1996).

need to feel competent." Although many executives view training and development as luxuries and an added expense, they are a necessity during merger integration because two companies, no matter how similar, will have different systems, procedures, rules, policies, and so forth.

As Exhibit 3.4 shows, willingness can be induced through a solid process for performance management, one that includes goals, measures, feedback, and rewards (including recognition). Therefore, as a first step, new goals and measures for the integration effort must be developed. These goals should be clearly understood by managers and employees alike, and the measures should be directly linked to the desired goals. As a second step, incentives in the form of rewards must be developed because people will work toward a goal—in this case, successful integration—that they are given an incentive to achieve. Incentives can take many forms: cash, stock, trips, time off, promotions, and other considerations. As for recognition, it can be provided in the form of publicity, letters and visits from

EXHIBIT 3.4. MEETING RESISTANCE WITH ACTION.

PERFORMANCE
MANAGEMENT
(Goals, measures,
feedback, rewards)

Not
willing

TRAINING

Not
able

COMMUNICATION

Not
knowing

executives, thank-yous and pats on the back from top management, awards lunches and dinners, plaques, and trophies, to name just a few possibilities.

All the indications point to heavy M&A activity for the foreseeable future. The structuring, financing, and closing of a deal are only preliminary steps; the real work comes after the deal is signed, when integration becomes a daunting and unique change-management challenge. The complexities that would accompany any other kind of change effort are all due, in this case, to the merger of two companies, and the resulting organizational dynamics are intensified because they have to be addressed not just in one organization but in two. The stakes are too high to take the attitude that you pay your money and take your chances. A well-managed integration effort can increase the chances of success in an era of deal making that is compelled by the need to respond to constant upheavals in product and service markets. Welcome to the big leagues of change management.

CHAPTER FOUR

THE MERGER INTEGRATION
WORK STREAMS MODEL

Merger integration is without a doubt the ultimate change-management challenge.
Unless the organization is equipped with a well-defined, replicable, flexible process,
it is doomed to repeat its mistakes in every future deal.

After a long string of twelve- to fifteen-hour days, at the depths of a merger
integration process, the executive leading the project confided in us: "This
is quite possibly the most complex 'simple' process I've ever seen." That is a sen-
timent that resonates for any manager or executive who has been through the
same drill. The steps and the process mechanics are not unique or challenging
in and of themselves, but the environment of change—the pace, the pressure,
the stress and uncertainty, the widespread fears and skepticism—combine with
the sheer volume of difficult decisions to create a Herculean task that can quickly
overwhelm even the most capable manager and the most sophisticated organization. As if the excitement of the formation and planning phase were not difficult
enough, companies are then left with the seemingly never-ending (and rather
boring) work of the execution phase. Either phase, if poorly led and managed,
can sink an otherwise successful endeavor.

As a result, merger integration is without a doubt the ultimate change-
management challenge. Unless the organization is equipped with a well-defined,
replicable, flexible process, it is doomed to repeat its mistakes—or make new
ones—in every future deal. Most organizations do a reasonably good job of identifying the generally accepted principles and the critical success factors for major
change initiatives. Platitudes such as those in the following list are useful in setting the tone for integration, but in reality they often represent nothing more than
hopes, dreams, and aspirations; consider how frequently we have all made these

statements to employee groups, and yet how inconsistently these principles have been applied in the heat of battle:

- "Senior management must actively support and be involved in the change process."
- "We will provide open, honest communication."
- "We will involve those affected by the changes."
- "We will provide a seamless transition for our customers."

These platitudes do reflect important beliefs, but organizations are still quite uninformed about the key principles that are more likely to drive the success of a merger integration in a consistent way. Fortunately, various studies have already validated certain core elements that have been empirically demonstrated to produce just such successful results; for example, consider these elements listed by Hodge (1998), who reports on a study of 270 mergers and acquisitions:

- *Effective planning and execution.* Companies that have effective policies for managing the postmerger period can improve their odds of success by as much as 50 percent. Experienced acquirers (those making six or more deals per year) succeed significantly more than deal makers do who have less experience. Further, companies that have strong integration plans, by contrast with those that have weak ones, have produced shareholder returns above industry average.
- *A compelling vision that is understood and embraced by managers, employees, and shareholders.* Each deal is part of a larger strategy. The vision of that larger strategy becomes a fundamental theme around which all postmerger priorities and action plans revolve.
- *Effective alignment.* A practical, methodical approach is used for the "heavy lifting" of determining how best to integrate and align two organizations' structures, processes, systems, and cultures. Adequate resources and time are dedicated to translating the vision, as necessary, and aligning all organizational and business-process elements around it. An action plan is created to guide the organizations beyond the initial transition and toward full integration. The organizations' cultures are integrated by design rather than by chance.
- *Fast and focused transition.* Successful organizations do not wait for the dust to settle. They prepare in advance, at the point when employees and customers are primed for change, to take advantage of the deal's momentum. The pace of any deal, of course, is determined by the degree of overall integration required and by the nature of the functional and process implications, but most deals proceed too slowly for their own good. On six qualitative measures of organizational performance, for example, Hodge found that a faster integration process yielded

better results than a slower one. Results that were improved through the faster pace showed up in speed to market, technological progress, employees' commitment, the company's focus on its customers, the clarity of the company's direction, and turnover among employees.

Though such elegant principles are easy to understand, they are hard to put into action. It is clear that what is needed is a comprehensive method that can be customized to each specific organization and purpose, one that is built to apply these and other principles, drive actual individual and organizational behavior, and lead both companies through the uncertainty.

The Merger Integration Work Streams Model

We believe, on the basis of our work with merger clients around the world, that there are at least nine different but strongly interdependent and continuing sets of responsibilities, or "work streams," that are mission-critical for the success of any merger integration:

1. Executive leadership roles and responsibilities
2. Integration planning and implementation
3. Communication
4. Structure and staffing
5. Rerecruiting
6. Cultural integration
7. Human-capital-related integration
8. Measurement and feedback
9. Project management

By packaging and coordinating the appropriate components of these work steams for each deal, an organization can equip itself to handle, in an effective way, the myriad tasks that must be performed. None of these work streams is our unique discovery, and every organization has made use of one or more in previous mergers. Nevertheless, the strength of this model is based on the coordinated, simultaneous deployment of work streams in combination, as part of an integrated method rather than as independent series of actions. The more "strands" of the "change cord" that an organization successfully and purposefully binds together, the stronger the process, and the better the end results.

Each work stream begins with strategic planning, represented in Exhibit 4.1 by the lead-in arrows. As a general rule, the earlier the overall direction of each

EXHIBIT 4.1. THE MERGER INTEGRATION WORK-STREAMS MODEL.

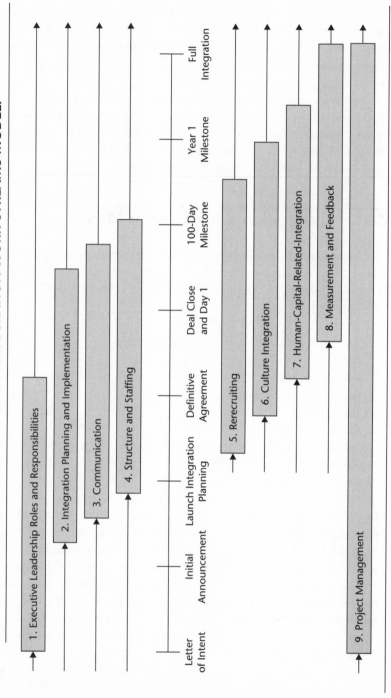

work stream can be agreed on, the better. Initial plans lead quickly to the establishment of a comprehensive project approach in each work stream. This critical mass of activity is represented in Exhibit 4.1 by the shaded box. Each work stream generally continues through the end of full integration, if at a reduced pace and level of intensity (represented in Exhibit 4.1 by the tailing arrows), as determined by the project's needs.

In addition to identifying the core work streams to include for successful integration, this model emphasizes other critical distinctions from less successful approaches:

- *Process-driven rather than event-driven.* Instead of considering integration a collection of disparate events to be managed, it should be approached as a coordinated series of change processes. For example, organizations generally do a good job of communicating critical events through initial announcement of the deal, day 1 celebrations, and the like. But those events are often followed by long periods of silence because the organization lacks both an ongoing strategic communication process and the senior-level resources needed to manage this crucial responsibility.
- *Concurrent rather than sequential.* Merger integration cannot be accomplished effectively through a purely linear or sequential approach. Logical, methodical steps can cause delay and ambiguity in many critical-path issues if management insists that a particular integration step be 100 percent complete before moving on to the next one. Such an approach is impractical because everything in merger integration tends to unfold in an evolutionary way. For example, one recent client was reluctant to undertake anything but staffing decisions until the staffing phase was complete. The reasoning was that no effective operational integration planning, and certainly no communication about these pending decisions, could be done until everything was finalized. Experience has shown the opposite to be true: early and deep involvement in operational or functional planning provides essential context and understanding in support of managers' abilities to make important selection decisions. Indeed, the great difficulty of merger integration is that everything must happen concurrently, and nothing ever seems to be completely resolved. Thus a concurrent-work-streams approach is the only practical way to coordinate the chaos and respond to the panoply of needs.
- *Sooner rather than later.* Although the transaction timeline in Exhibit 4.1 is admittedly simplified and purely representative, it makes clear just how much planning should have taken place by the time deal closure is achieved. Although every acquirer must scrupulously adhere to legal antitrust guidelines and other

regulatory requirements, many miss opportunities to do substantially more planning early in the transaction phase without incurring potential liabilities.

Later chapters offer more details about most of the work streams; for now, Exhibit 4.2 shows how the nine components work together to bring about the desired results.

It is surprising but true that one of the most often ignored integration work streams is the first one, executive leadership roles and responsibilities. This oversight may be due to the adage "Executives do deals, managers integrate them" or

EXHIBIT 4.2. KEY WORK-STREAM COMPONENTS.

Work Stream	Key Components	Impact
1. Executive leadership roles and responsibilities	Initial strategic planning; identify top-level leadership; change leadership; business and technical expertise	Ensures integration issues are considered during initial deal making. Ensures integration becomes part of overall transaction process.
2. Integration planning and implementation	Task force infrastructure; charters; subteam work process; transition and synergy-capture plans	Establishes and coordinates consistent process for all functions/business units to follow. Ensures thorough planning and fast implementation.
3. Communication	Overall communications strategy; ongoing processes and feedback channels; special meetings and events	Manages rumors. Ensures fast two-way flow of facts and perceptions. Engages the entire organization in the integration. Helps the organization embrace the change.
4. Structure and staffing	Create, approve, and support the processes for determining the organization structure and staffing decisions	Ensures the organization is "set" quickly. Ensures the "best player" wins the job. Minimized cronyism and favoritism.
5. Rerecruiting	A specific policy, process, tool to identify key talent and gain their commitment to stay with the Newco organization	Retains key talent. Increases short-term commitment. Refocuses attention on longer-term opportunities.

(continued)

EXHIBIT 4.2 (*continued*)

Work Stream	Key Components	Impact
6. Cultural integration	Structured approach to identify and clarify key management processes that establish how we will do things in the Newco organization	Deals proactively with major failure factors. Analytical approach to specific issues for changing/alignment. Early-warning process.
7. Human-capital-related integration	Targeted alignment/ rationalization of all people processes to more directly support the Newco organization's business objectives	Eliminates proliferation of practices that no longer support business needs. Quickly and powerfully reinforces desired Newco culture. Drives employee behavior toward key objectives.
8. Measurement and feedback	Merger integration score-card; synergy planning and tracking; integration-process feedback	Tracks and reports key operational, financial, customer, and organizational issues most subject to merger-related disruption and risk.
9. Project management	Consolidated project plan; contact rosters; information-distribution protocols; key action items for core team and executive attention	Links all efforts to specific milestones and accountabilities. Ensures continued focus on timely completion of tasks.

to some other, equally out-of-date notion. In any case, a failed merger is, more often than not, ultimately a failure of leadership. The following sections describe just a few of the areas in which executives can get more directly involved to create successful mergers.

Initial Strategic Planning

Integration must begin with a clear consensus on the strategic direction and objectives of the Newco, and a clear determination of the primary value-drivers of the combined entity. Agreement should be gained from both partner companies regarding the integration process and the timeline to be used. An important initial determination is how and when the transaction process (that is, the process of making and approving the deal) will flow into and overlap with the merger integration process. The partner companies' executive teams should concur on the initial announcement messages and their timing. Key governance issues and the desired level of integration for the Newco organization should also be discussed as early as possible because these decisions will have a significant impact on strategic planning for the integration. Finally, the partner companies need to select, from both companies, the project managers for the integration.

Top-Level Leadership Team

One of the most difficult and delicate tasks for senior leaders is to select the Newco organization's executive team. Countless deals have faltered or failed over disagreements in this area, or over a poor selection process. There are a number of explanations for the difficulties that may be encountered:

- The stakes are high, and the selection discussions take place in a politically charged climate.
- Because the selection process is usually undertaken very early in the transaction and integration phases, the parties may not have complete information about the candidates or their abilities.
- The best candidates may not be made available to the Newco organization (as often happens in the case of a joint venture or a divestiture arrangement).
- There is a historical bias toward creating a "balanced" executive team by selecting individuals from each partner company for some key roles.

The most successful integrators resist these pressures and insist early on that an objective selection process be followed throughout the organization, and that it start with the top of the house. (These issues are discussed in more detail in Chapter Eight.)

After the top-level leadership team has been selected, some expedient process should be conducted to help this team be effective. It is often assumed that the senior officers of the Newco organization can meet and immediately become a fully functional staff. In our experience, senior leaders tend to struggle with group effectiveness more than many newly formed groups of middle managers do. Because of the extreme time pressure, or perhaps because there is no perceived need to establish even basic ground rules for collaboration, these rules are often ignored until something goes awry. Once again, though, as experienced acquirers can attest, the faster a firm foundation is established, the faster the work will proceed. Make no mistake: a minor fissure that appears at this point between individual team members or team factions will soon widen into a gulf that, later on, may be unbridgeable. It is best to take precautions at the outset to ensure this group's clarity of vision, focus, strategy, and approach.

Change Leadership

It has been said so often that it is now more trite than true: any change effort will fail without senior management's support and commitment. Unfortunately, however, this statement is only partially true. Senior management's support and commitment are "table stakes"; they may keep you in the game, but they won't win you the prize. A merger integration today requires active change leadership. The alternative is failure. What makes the difference between change leadership and failed leadership? The following list was compiled on the basis of feedback from employees and from leaders of integration task forces:

- Communication with employees
- Regular attendance of executive staff at key events related to the integration team and to customers
- Regular integration updates (covering the status of the integration, key issues to be resolved, and areas requiring the executive staff's attention) at meetings of executive staff in both partner companies
- Provisions for accountability and recognition with respect to creating and adhering to the desired new culture
- The planning and holding of a business meeting (just before or after the deal closes) with the top several hundred managers of the Newco organization, to launch the business plan, create collegial networks, set expectations for the culture, and ensure that the essential early requirements for the transition are understood

Business Processes

Most of the literature emphasizes the role of change leadership in isolation from technical or functional expertise and guidance. One group of managers, for example, when asked recently what an effective change leader does, gave only responses like "acts as a coach," "engages in open communication," "is fair-minded," and "listens to the organization." These are all necessary and positive actions; with all due respect, however, change leadership must mean more than that in a merger. The most effective change leaders also apply their functional and technical expertise in a way that gives focus, clarity, and direction to the rest of the organization.

Senior leaders should be working actively with functional task forces during the planning stage, to translate the Newco organization's strategies and business plans into reality. They should be painting and repainting key business-process parameters and expectations, to ensure a seamless transition for customers. They should be reviewing and endorsing the task force's integration plans, and they should be working with functional leaders to implement those plans. And, of course, the members of the executive team must work together to resolve issues related to priority conflicts, capital-allocation budgets, resource availability, and the realignment of existing major initiatives.

Deploying the Model

Each of the work streams must be given a place in every deal. To create the focus and the outcomes specifically required by a particular deal, however, the process and the steps involved in implementing the work streams should be carefully tailored.

A major manufacturer recently presented a typical challenge:

- A joint-venture deal was designed to capture enhanced market share, broaden the product slate, and eliminate redundant costs.
- The majority partner had an open and entrepreneurial culture, whereas the other partner had a traditional command-and-control culture.
- A target was set of $125 million in annual synergies within two years.
- Extremely complicated issues of customer service and logistics were involved.
- Each of the organizations was at a different point in implementing SAP enterprise information systems.
- Customers' early reactions to the deal were mixed and in some cases were unfavorable.
- The achievement of the major revenue-enhancing synergies depended on the creation of a fully integrated sales force as quickly as possible.
- The deal was scheduled to close in approximately four months.
- Reaching a definitive agreement would require complex negotiations to identify and price a variety of transition service agreements.
- Regulatory approval of the deal was still in process (but not perceived to be at risk).

After initial discussions with executive teams from both partner companies, and after several planning meetings with the integration project manager and assistant manager, an integration project map was designed. The map gave a high-level overview of how and when specific aspects of the work streams would be deployed in responding to the unique complexities of this particular deal (see Exhibit 4.3).

EXHIBIT 4.3. CUSTOMIZED DEPLOYMENT OF THE WORK-STREAMS MODEL.

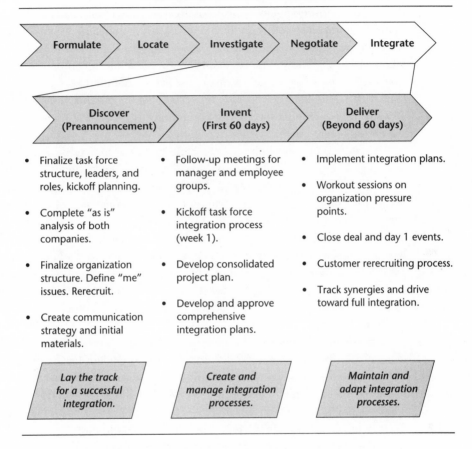

Discover (Preannouncement)	Invent (First 60 days)	Deliver (Beyond 60 days)
• Finalize task force structure, leaders, and roles, kickoff planning.	• Follow-up meetings for manager and employee groups.	• Implement integration plans.
• Complete "as is" analysis of both companies.	• Kickoff task force integration process (week 1).	• Workout sessions on organization pressure points.
• Finalize organization structure. Define "me" issues. Rerecruit.	• Develop consolidated project plan.	• Close deal and day 1 events.
• Create communication strategy and initial materials.	• Develop and approve comprehensive integration plans.	• Customer rerecruiting process.
		• Track synergies and drive toward full integration.

Lay the track for a successful integration.	Create and manage integration processes.	Maintain and adapt integration processes.

The Discovery Phase: Before the Announcement

Because both organizations were committed to a fast integration process, the first work stream became integration planning (work stream 2 in Exhibit 4.1). An assessment was made of both organizations' structures, business units, and key processes. Ultimately, an integration infrastructure was defined that created task forces or subteams for each major function and process. Coleadership of all task forces was used to ensure effective transfer of knowledge and capture of best practices. Participation in each task force and subteam was also designed to maximize interaction among subject-matter experts from both companies. An initial timeline for the integration project was established, and materials were produced in advance for use during the task force kickoff meeting.

Significant cultural differences began to emerge almost as soon as the conversations between the organizations began. A quick risk assessment was conducted to determine potential areas of greatest conflict and friction, and action items were implemented to buffer these risks. A twelve-dimension cultural "litmus test" was implemented via interviews with key deal makers and managers who were in the know. The results were compiled into a comparative list, and both organizations were made aware of the perceived differences, as well as of the similarities. This exercise was essential to helping the organizations establish acceptable protocols and processes for communication and decision making during the period before the deal closed.

A group of business unit managers and human resources professionals, recognizing the importance of establishing the final organizational structure and making staffing decisions as quickly as possible, partnered to define a mutually acceptable staffing process. The criteria included competency-based job specifications, a very brief job description, minimal documentation, and sufficient input from both organizations on the selection of all key roles. Documents and forms were developed, and an initial schedule was approved for cascading the selection process throughout the organization. This schedule was communicated throughout the organization during the initial announcement meetings and did much to set expectations and alleviate anxiety about "when the other shoe was going to drop."

An existing "talent war" in the local market, and in the chemicals industry generally, further compounded the risk of losing key talent because of the deal. Technical and managerial recruiters warned that, as soon as the deal was announced, many people in important job roles would receive multiple job offers, which would include significant increases over their current base compensation. To lock in key talent, a rerecruiting policy was written, and a specific list of financial and nonfinancial incentives was developed and approved for use at managers' discretion. Planning tools and facilitation guides were drafted, to ensure that key managers proactively assessed their risk and were prepared to respond with the right incentives delivered in the right way.

Finally, a comprehensive communication strategy was created that identified all key stakeholder groups and key messages that needed to be delivered. A variety of continuing communication processes and special events were defined and prepared, to ensure an effective announcement-day "blitz." An electronic newsletter and a confidential toll-free hotline were established and prepared for use as of the morning of the announcement. In addition, as further insurance that the deal would get off to the best possible start, all key executives scheduled to take part in live presentations to the public or to employee groups were briefed and drilled on their presentations and on effective communication techniques.

The Invention Phase: The First Sixty Days

Immediately after the initial public and internal announcements of the deal, those associated with the communication work stream launched the second phase of their efforts, with a series of more detailed face-to-face meetings throughout the organization. The top-line organization chart and key executive appointments were announced, along with a complete explanation of the integration infrastructure, and it was announced that task force leaders would immediately begin work on making the transition and capturing the expected synergies of the deal.

A formal kickoff meeting was conducted during the first week after the initial public announcement. Participants included the integration project manager and assistant manager, the coleaders of each task force, and legal counsel from both organizations. All the Newco organization's executive staff members were involved, to present key portions of the kickoff agenda or respond to questions about the business plan and the transition. The task forces were given eight weeks to orient all their members and subteams and to develop comprehensive integration plans for their respective areas. Each task force presented its plans to the other task force leaders, to ensure effective cross-functional coordination and complete understanding of essential day 1 instructions. After the executive staff endorsed all integration plans, the task forces prepared their respective organizations for day 1 operations and prepared to begin implementing these plans immediately after deal closure.

To establish a clear Newco identity and communicate the business strategy, values, and leadership expectations to the organization, a business meeting was held just before deal closure. The top two hundred managers from the Newco organization attended, and for many of them this was the first chance to meet their counterparts and the first opportunity to gain detailed information about business processes and capabilities across the organization.

The Delivery Phase: Beyond Sixty Days

On the day the deal closed, a variety of day 1 events were coordinated, to celebrate the formation of the company and recognize the work that had been accomplished during the initial planning for the transition. The full implementation of the integration plans was now launched, and a special customer "rerecruiting" process was put into action, to ensure that all customers knew what the deal meant for them and whom they could contact with questions.

All competitively sensitive information had been restricted until the deal closed, so the full transfer of key information was coordinated by the task forces, to eliminate any unnecessary delay. A unique and particularly successful aspect of this integration was the rapid launch of the newly consolidated sales and marketing function. On the day after the deal closed, the entire sales and marketing team came together for a comprehensive briefing on customers, products, pricing, and sales strategy. As a result, the Newco organization achieved its integrated sales force within twenty-four hours of formally completing the legal transaction.

While the task forces pursued the implementation of their integration plans and synergy projects, periodic measures were conducted, to assess progress and detect cultural or transition-related issues that were limiting results. As issues were identified, the core team and the respective task forces formed ad hoc problem-solving teams, to clarify issues and propose solutions.

At this point, an educational process was launched, to focus the entire organization on the deal synergies. A formal process for verification and tracking was implemented, to approve new synergy projects and consolidate results for reporting. A periodic synergy newsletter captured highlights of synergy projects in process and gave recognition to teams that had completed their synergy projects. The integration infrastructure was disbanded, and the long-term integration projects were transferred to the appropriate units, when a review of the consolidated project plan indicated completion and meeting of approximately 75 percent of all tasks and milestones.

CHAPTER FIVE

ORGANIZING AND INVOLVING INTEGRATION TASK FORCES

The best way . . . is to get people working together quickly to solve business problems and accomplish results that could not have been achieved before.

R. N. ASHKENAS, L. J. DE MONACO, AND S. C. FRANCIS,
HARVARD BUSINESS REVIEW, JAN.–FEB. 1998

Some time ago, we responded to an urgent request that perfectly illustrates the importance of establishing an integration infrastructure robust enough to withstand the chaos of divergent efforts. The merging organizations, before seeking outside assistance, had identified sixteen different functional groups or business-process teams for which integration was required. In an attempt to give each group some degree of autonomy, management literally let each group do its own thing. The results were both predictable and costly: sixteen different requests for proposals for consulting assistance, sixteen different approaches, sixteen different project plans and timelines, and sixteen different sets of problems. As this acquirer soon learned, the integration infrastructure must be flexible enough to meet the need of diverse functions yet consistent enough to minimize confusion and duplication of effort.

Establishing the Integration Infrastructure

Companies being combined must be coordinated through a single project team that has been given clear roles, responsibilities, and expectations. One such model is shown in Exhibit 5.1. As this model suggests, the Newco organization's executives have ultimate accountability for the success of the integration. They

EXHIBIT 5.1. COMMON PLANNING MODEL FOR THE INTEGRATION'S INFRASTRUCTURE.

Example:

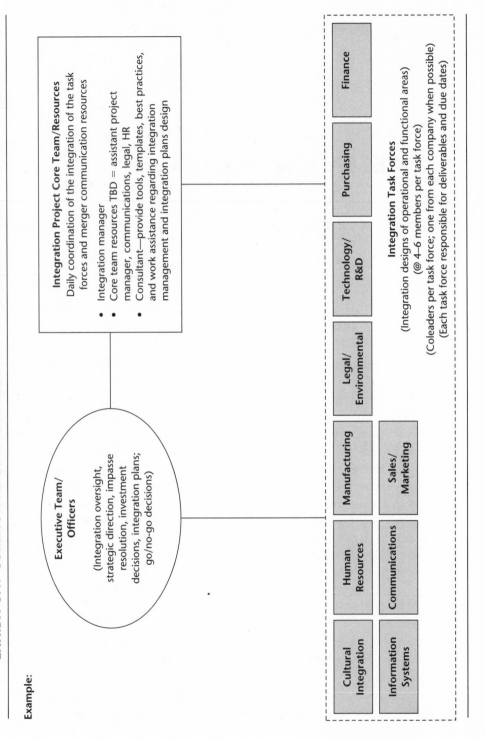

Executive Team/ Officers

(Integration oversight, strategic direction, impasse resolution, investment decisions; integration plans; go/no-go decisions)

Integration Project Core Team/Resources
Daily coordination of the integration of the task forces and merger communication resources

• Integration manager
• Core team resources TBD = assistant project manager, communications, legal, HR
• Consultant—provide tools, templates, best practices, and work assistance regarding integration management and integration plans design

| Cultural Integration | Human Resources | Manufacturing | Legal/ Environmental | Technology/ R&D | Purchasing | Finance |

| Information Systems | Communications | Sales/ Marketing |

Integration Task Forces
(Integration designs of operational and functional areas)
(@ 4–6 members per task force)
(Coleaders per task force; one from each company when possible)
(Each task force responsible for deliverables and due dates)

are actively positioned throughout the project to provide strategic direction, establish boundaries for the effort and for the individual task forces, resolve impasses, make go/no-go decisions on integration plans, and provide oversight to the core integration team. During the early stages of the deal, these responsibilities are shared between the executive staffs of both partner companies, so that coordination and communication become a critical link.

The integration project's core team assumes primary day-to-day responsibility for coordinating the task forces and the overall process. This is a full-time role: overseeing the establishment of the task forces, managing the selection of the task force leaders, arranging the kickoff session that begins the planning, ensuring effective coordination between and among the task forces, and managing the business of identifying issues, communicating them, and working them through. Additional full-time resources are necessary so that the core team can provide a nucleus for networking, problem solving, and communicating with the organization. Other resources for the core team may include an assistant project manager, a legal representative, a human resources representative, and a representative of the cultural integration and/or communication task forces.

Integration managers have been drawn from disciplines as diverse as engineering, accounting, human resources, and law. Far more important than an integration manager's technical background, however, is this individual's knowledge of the business and his or her ability to lead people and serve as a change agent. The size of the organization has something to do with the choice, but successful integration managers have been vice presidents, directors, managers, and, in some cases, internal consultants with a strong operations background. In particularly large or complex deals, a member of the executive staff may serve more effectively in this capacity.

As a general rule, if the project manager is selected from the acquiring company, then the assistant project manager should be selected from the acquired organization. The role of the assistant project manager is particularly important in that this person is in the single best position to capture feedback data from the acquired organization and channel it to the core team and the executive team for discussion and resolution.

Task forces make up the majority of the integration infrastructure and, together with their respective subteams, are primarily responsible for designing transition plans, capturing synergies, and implementing the action items required for successful business integration. The number, focus, and composition of the task forces will depend entirely on the business structure and the process requirements. More often than not, however, the task forces will tend to be organized around basic functional areas. Specific business processes (such as order entry and customer service) should have dedicated teams, and "superteams" of highly interdependent functions (for example, a product team that includes man-ufacturing, engineering, research, marketing, or other contributors to a global product line) should be used to ensure adequate cross-functional thinking. In addition, a variety of special-issue task forces should be considered to focus on client retention, culture, synergies, and specific operational projects.

Given the importance of the task forces and subteams, the selection of the right task force leaders becomes mission-critical. Task force leaders should be individuals who are senior enough to have the authority that gets things done but not so senior as to be out of touch with the details of the business process. Ex-hibit 5.2 outlines one client's position description for the role of task force leader. This document was circulated along with an explanatory letter to the executive staffs of both companies involved in the deal, and nominations were provided to the members of the core team. The core team conducted discussions with the su-periors of all the nominees, and with the nominees themselves, to ensure qualifi-cations, interest, availability, and fit. The core team then prepared and sent to both companies a slate of candidates for review.

The task forces, like the core team, should include balanced representation from both partner companies. This type of balance serves both a symbolic and a purely practical business necessity. In a recent merger integration, for example, the acquirer had a particularly nasty reputation in the industry as an old-line command-and-control organization, whereas the acquired organization was an entrepreneurial spin-off noted for its open, people-oriented management style. A particularly long regulatory review process caused much of the integration plan-ning to be delayed until just before the deal closed. The assistant project manager, a member of the acquired organization, later said, "The mere fact that so many of our key people were invited to play such a significant role in the first official in-tegration event clearly helped turn the tide of negative perceptions." More im-portant, however, is the reality that deal synergies often prove elusive and difficult to capture unless each organization has a thorough understanding and apprecia-tion of its counterpart's business processes, technology, and core capabilities. This level of awareness comes only when people are brought together to work on busi-ness issues.

Task forces should be encouraged to create subteams (also composed of peo-ple from both companies) to serve as primary subject-matter experts, planners, and implementers of major subcategories of issues. For example, a task force for sales and marketing might want to create subteams for various product lines or geographical areas; a task force in human resources should create subteams for compensation and rewards, retirement, health and welfare, workforce transition, leadership and learning, and so forth. When synergy projects have been identified,

EXHIBIT 5.2. POSITION DESCRIPTION FOR A TASK FORCE LEADER.

INTEGRATION PROCESS
Task Force Leader Position Description

Task Force Leader Objectives

The task force leader is a focal point for accomplishing all task force work, including development of transition/integration plans; coordinating issues, as needed, with other task forces; producing detailed integration recommendations for approval of the integration team and officer group; and overseeing the implementation of integration activities.

Task Force Leader Responsibilities

- Serve as a member of the integration project core team, and report task force progress and issues to the integration project core team
- Ensure completion of and adherence to the task force charter
- Coordinate overall activities of the task force
- Participation in a common communication process, and use tools for exchanging information among task force members and among other task forces
- Coordinate task force meetings, ensuring meetings take place as often as necessary, and ensuring participation from both owner companies throughout
- Arrange for appropriate meeting notes to be summarized into specific action items/responsibilities, and distribute to members
- Submit weekly, one-page e-mail progress reports to the integration manager in advance of the weekly integration project core team meetings
- Ensure appropriate links to other task forces for overlap and coordination issues

Selection Criteria

- Senior-manager level
- Technical expertise/credibility in area
- Strong leadership competence
- Conceptual and analytical abilities
- Comfort with ambiguity
- Sense of urgency/action orientation
- Strong people and relationship skills
- Facilitation/group-process skills

dedicated subteams should be formed to validate, plan, and execute these initiatives, with the same level of involvement and accountability expected of other subteams. Each team is also responsible for coordinating with other subteams and task forces on issues of mutual dependence. They are often called on to supply services to other task forces or subteams, as in the case of connectivity, staffing support, training, and so forth, between information systems and telecommunications.

Launching the Planning Process

Over the course of many deals, we have never ceased to be amazed at the level of positive energy that a merger integration can create. Some people merely equate involvement with continued employment, but we have developed the conviction that most people want to do what is best for the business and will go to extraordinary lengths to accomplish the desired results—if and when they are given a chance for involvement. To harness this enthusiasm and get everyone on the "same page," we recommend launching the planning process for the task forces as early in the transaction phase as it is practical to do so. For deals not at substantial risk of regulatory challenge, we have often defined the integration infrastructure and selected the task force leaders before the initial public announcement, convening the entire core team for the integration during the first week after the announcement.

As a general rule, there are two perfectly lawful reasons for one party to a merger to provide business information to the other party during merger negotiations: first, due-diligence analyses must be completed, and, second, the parties may need to begin planning (but not implementing) the integration of the two businesses. Integration planning during these pre-deal-closure phases does heighten the need for strict adherence to antitrust and exchange-restraint considerations, but this kind of planning is usually warranted by business necessity. Counsel should be obtained with respect to setting the appropriate time for integration planning to begin and to establishing deal-specific protocols that will govern the sharing of information and the coordination of activities. Ordinarily, it is possible to define reasonable and practical precautions that will enable the planning process to precede the actual closing of the deal. For example, in one recent deal that was undergoing intense regulatory scrutiny, counsel for both organizations permitted the integration task force kickoff to occur on schedule, approximately ninety days before the deal was expected to close. As a part of the kickoff orientation meeting, the task forces were trained on the following guidelines and document-handling procedures:

Sharing of Information

- Entering into a confidentiality agreement and scrupulously adhering to its terms
- Marking all documents to indicate that they were received in an appropriate manner and to facilitate their destruction or return
- Making sure that there is a legitimate business reason for requesting information from the other party, and ensuring that any such requests are closely related to the requesting party's evaluation of the deal or to planning for the postacquisition period
- Determining who will have access to information, and making sure that access is limited to those who are required to have the information
- Not sharing information about overlapping or potentially overlapping products (with respect to current or future nonpublic information on costs, prices, profitability, competitive strategies, marketing plans, plans for product development, or customers), and, if it is necessary to provide such information, aggregating whenever possible, and not requesting specific information without consulting counsel

Coordinating Activities

- Continuing to act as if both parties will be in the business for the foreseeable future
- Continuing to make bids, solicit customers, and so on, if these activities would be undertaken in the absence of the possibility of the pending transaction
- Consulting with counsel before making what ordinarily would be a normal business decision, but about which there is now some uncertainty because of the possibility of the pending transaction
- Not allowing the other party to the negotiations dictate business activities, and not giving the other party any role in decisions having to do with business activities that have competitive significance
- Being cautious about disclosing future plans to the other party

Kickoff Meeting for Task Force Leaders

A meeting (or a series of meetings) will be needed in order to provide a coordinated start to the planning process. The specific objectives of such a meeting include gaining clear understanding of the task forces's purpose, roles, responsibilities, deadlines, deliverables, and other issues. Exhibit 5.3 shows a sample kickoff meeting agenda.

EXHIBIT 5.3. SAMPLE KICKOFF MEETING AGENDA.

1. *WELCOME AND ORIENTATION*
   - Project goals and milestones
   - Project structure, roles, responsibilities

2. *STRATEGIC BUSINESS CASE*
   - Opportunities and challenges of the deal
   - Synergy review and discussion

3. *LEGAL BRIEFING*
   - Antitrust
   - Communication issues

4. *HUMAN RESOURCES BRIEFING*
   - Status update on pay, benefits, and staffing

5. *INTEGRATION PROCESS WORK STEPS AND DELIVERABLES*
   - Task force work-steps model
   - Deliverables and due dates
   - Task force status updates
   - Instructions for initial working session

6. *INITIAL TEAM LEADER PLANNING*
   - Complete draft charter:
       Verifying synergy assignments
       Identifying issues
       Determining subteam resources required
       Identifying data/inputs needed
       Establishing task force logistics (meeting locations, times)

7. *GROUP DEBRIEF SESSION*
   - Review progress and issues
   - Clarify next steps
   - Closing comments

Many organizations choose to begin with a welcome dinner, which provides an opportunity to meet and get acquainted with the members of the partner company's core team and its task force leaders. Other organizations have also had success with a premeeting, attended by only their own representatives to the integration task force and held a few days before the kickoff meeting. This practice allows much of the basic information transfer to take place with respect to roles, responsibilities, and process instructions, and it frees up valuable time that can be used during the kickoff meeting to focus on beginning the actual planning.

As a general rule, the first part of the kickoff meeting should be devoted to giving the task force leaders an overview of the deal, the business case for the deal, the expected synergies, and any givens or strategic parameters that have already been decided as a result of the negotiations. There should be very clear instructions about deliverables, mandatory or voluntary process steps, timelines, and documentation requirements. This meeting provides a very important early opportunity to identify and discuss potential cultural differences and to demonstrate that, regardless of any differences, both organizations and both cultures have far more similarities that can be leveraged.

Specification of Deliverables

At the initial kickoff meeting, a significant amount of time should be allowed for task force leader breakout sessions.

Charter. Similar to other project team initiatives, a chartering exercise is often a good way to begin the planning process, and, given the complexity of a merger integration, many of our clients have improved the effectiveness of their task forces' initial planning by providing detailed, customized charter templates to help their subteams get started quickly. Resource A shows an example of such a template; the format and the level of detail should be customized to the specific requirements, of course, but task force leaders have responded quite favorably to the structure and detailed guidance shown in this example.

The charter is the first of each task force's deliverables. As such, it serves several important purposes, which include planning, role clarification, resourcing, scheduling, establishment of accountability, and education of subteams. Because it is so significant, the charter should be completed in as much detail as possible and reviewed by the core team for thoroughness and accuracy. Typically, the charter would include the following components:

- *Overall objective statement.* An example of such a statement might be "to review the commercial processes (including operations planning, sales, marketing, and commercial development) in a way that will ensure that all processes make a successful transition to the Newco organization and that all the potential synergies are identified and captured."

- *Specific synergy targets.* This component verifies and lists all the currently known synergy possibilities that fall under each task force's responsibilities. A brief description of the project is given, along with the estimated dollar value of the target, the timeline for its accomplishment (six months, six to twelve months, twelve to twenty-four months, and so on), and a list of any other task forces that are linked with this synergy.
- *Data and documentation requirements.* This list gives specific requests for information that will be needed for sufficient understanding of the partner organization and its relevant business processes.
- *Initial identification of issues.* This component gives an initial "brainstorm" outline of all transition-related issues, tasks, responsibilities, policies, decisions, synergy clarifications, and other points that require thorough planning or the development of recommendations for the transition.
- *Links to other task forces.* This list or matrix is sorted on the basis of issues, functional owner or owners or supporting task force, and primary contact person.
- *Subteam resourcing requirements.* This component is an organizational chart or a list of the key individuals who should be involved in the various issues and responsibilities of the task forces.
- *Logistics and communications of the task forces.* This is a plan for how and when to launch each task force's respective subteams. It includes plans, as necessary, for facilitation or support and for the continuing communication between and among the subteams.

Integration Planning Model. Exhibit 5.4 shows a ten-step model given to task forces and subteams, to facilitate their work. This model, by providing a consistent process for each task force and subteam to follow, ensures a greater degree of thoroughness and consistency in the planning process.

"As is" analysis is particularly important to make sure teams are in fact searching for the "best of both" solutions for the Newco organization. A common and pervasive mistake acquirers make is to mandate changes to business process or policies just because they have bought the right to order those changes. To avoid this demoralizing and costly error, task forces on both sides should create structured information-exchange briefings, to help their counterparts walk through key elements of the process or technology being evaluated. Process maps, plan descriptions, side-by-side comparative matrices, and other tools will help task force members visualize essential differences and similarities that they should consider before they begin to identify the best solutions.

EXHIBIT 5.4. TASK FORCE PLANNING PROCESS.

STEP ONE	A: Current situation orientation O: Basic understanding of the current situation	WHERE ARE WE?
STEP TWO	A: Data collection O: Information, process maps (if applicable), and measures	
STEP THREE	A: Solution identification O: Integration designs	WHERE ARE WE GOING?
STEP FOUR	A: Develop integration plans O: Road map for installation	HOW DO WE GET THERE?
STEP FIVE	A: Gain approval O: Steering committee and/or merger team give the go-ahead	ARE WE IN AGREEMENT?
STEP SIX	A: Detailed installation preparation O: Announcements, training materials, logistics, scheduling	ARE WE READY?
STEP SEVEN	A: Installation activities O: Conduct training, make moves, do announcements	GO
STEP EIGHT	A: Measurement and monitoring, adjusting O: Progress reports, process adjustment	COURSE CORRECTIONS
STEP NINE	A: Handoff to local management O: Management ownership	FINISH
STEP TEN	A: Project completion O: Finish celebration	

Legend: *A = Action*   *O = Output*

Weekly Update Process

In addition to their major deliverables—the charter and the integration plan documents—the task forces are responsible for participating regularly in a process for achieving effective cross-functional communication and coordination. By way of a weekly update, each task force leader completes and e-mails a brief memo and participates in a weekly one-hour conference call with the core team members and all other task force leaders.

The e-mail memo should follow the same format each week, and it is suggested that it be limited to very brief bulleted items addressing the following points:

- Key actions taken during the preceding week
- Key successes or early wins
- Unresolved or anticipated issues, and next steps
- Other comments, questions, or information, as necessary

The weekly schedule for e-mail updates (see Exhibit 5.5) should be adhered to consistently.

The weekly conference call is a fast, convenient way for the integration task force leaders to communicate and coordinate directly with the entire integration infrastructure. Moreover, if the task force leaders congregate for the conference call at their organizational headquarters or at some other agreed-on site, this provides additional opportunities for increased interaction.

To ensure that the call delivers consistent value and stays on schedule, an agenda is prepared. In the course of the conference call, announcements and general updates are given by core team or executive staff members, and these are fol-

EXHIBIT 5.5. PROCESS FOR WEEKLY UPDATES.

By 5:00 P.M. Wednesday	Thursday A.M.	Friday 8:30–9:30 A.M.	By 1:00 P.M. Friday
TFLs complete and e-mail 1-page update (bulleted-point format)	Project core team reviews for issues, successes, and action items	Project core team and TFLs conduct weekly integration-update conference call	Project core team distributes summary meeting minutes to all key stakeholders

lowed by brief status reports from each major task force. (To prevent the call from getting bogged down, participants engage in detailed problem solving at another time and place.) After the call, members of the core team summarize the meeting in minutes that are provided in memo format and e-mailed to all task force leaders, executive staff members, subteam members, and other key stakeholders. This information pipeline becomes a key element of fast planning and integration, and it helps keep unproductive rumors to the minimum.

Integration Plan Documentation

The task forces should be given a template (see Exhibit 5.6) that outlines specific expectations for the integration plan and gives examples of the types of data and level of detail required. These expectations and the level of detail will depend, of course, on the transaction's scope, timing, complexity, objectives, and specific synergy targets that have been identified.

Historically, for example, many companies have focused their integration efforts on a one-hundred-day plan. By definition, the primary focus of this approach is a fast transition to the combined operation, with little attention to major projects for capturing synergies or integrating the two cultures. The implication is that these tasks will be left to the Newco organization's management or incorporated into some other initiative. This approach can work quite well for smaller deals, for transactions in which the integration requirements are minimal (as when a fully autonomous or completely free-standing entity is acquired), for deals in which there is minimal overlap in operations and administrative functions, and for deals in which few potential synergies are of critical importance.

Most deals will require a higher degree of consolidation or integration to achieve the economies of the transaction. These circumstances call for a more intensive approach to planning so that complex processes can be fully aligned and rationalized and larger-scale synergies can be captured.

As for the level of detail in planning, many organizations, as a practical matter, choose a comfortable midpoint on the continuum represented in Exhibit 5.6. Particularly if the integration planning process precedes the actual closing of the deal, some information that is sensitive from a competitive standpoint will not be available until after the legal formation of the Newco organization. As a result, it may be necessary in many transactions to divide the planning into two smaller, more focused phases.

This was the situation recently for a client whose transaction had been delayed by regulatory review. As the target date for closure of the deal drew closer, both companies' executive staffs wisely decided that if they were to achieve a seamless initial transition of the business, the planning had to begin immediately,

EXHIBIT 5.6. DETERMINE THE LEVEL OF DETAIL FOR TASK FORCE PLANS.

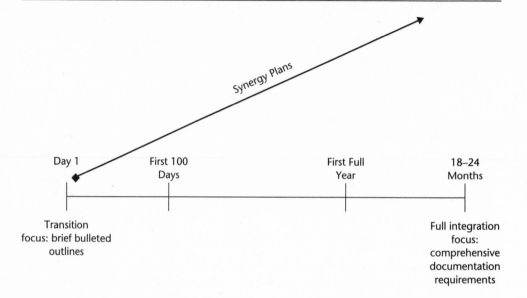

Day 1   First 100   First Full   18–24
                          Days   Year   Months

Transition   Full integration
focus: brief bulleted   focus:
      outlines   comprehensive
                                                                                  documentation
                                                                                   requirements

Example: Example:

• Essential transition action items   • Operating strategy/objectives
  necessary for basic functionality   • Work process/design and
• Minimal analysis and documentation   integration policies
                                                          • Organization structure/staffing
                                                            and role descriptions
                                                          • Full synergy project plans
                                                          • Capital investment and resource
                                                            requirements
                                                          • Information systems, facilities,
                                                            and logistics requirements
                                                          • Policies and practices
                                                          • Measures and baselines
                                                          • Current initiatives to delay or stop
                                                          • Work sheets and supporting data
                                                          • Integration of shared services

regardless of the status of the regulatory review. That way, they could minimize potential disruption more effectively and capture the synergies of the deal more quickly. To help the task force with planning on a short-term basis, the core team defined what it considered to be the categories and the level of detail representing the minimum business requirements for a successful initial transition; Resource B shows a template of the team's recommendations and sample output. The task forces were given approximately six to eight weeks to complete their initial recommendations and prepare for implementation.

- *Overall work flow and key operating rules.* Capture specific instructions and transition-process recommendations to ensure seamless operations. Focus should be on how work will actually get done. If certain roles or responsibilities will change substantially, these should be highlighted. Actual process redesign or alignment will come later, but a brief summary of process steps may be needed. Transition-specific organizational charts and headcount estimates should be provided. Names of contacts and contact information for key people in both companies should also be provided. Plans should be included for informing and training all key stakeholders responsible for implementing and carrying out transition-specific practices.
- *Synergies: "quick hits" and "low-hanging fruit."* Focus short-term actions on immediately achievable synergies, and start high-level planning for longer-term, high-impact projects. No implementation will be possible until the deal closes, so the intent is to plan, make transition-specific decisions, and be ready to implement the plans as soon as possible after day 1. Where exchange-restraint considerations limit the sharing of competitively sensitive material before closure of the deal, assign a project owner from one of the partner companies to begin, independently, as much planning as possible, or consider having an independent third party review both companies' processes and make initial short-term recommendations on time-sensitive transactions.
- *Initial systems and facilities requirements.* Focus on how best to minimize the disruptions caused by relocations and new assignments by providing fast connectivity when and where it is needed. Identify new people at each location, and specifically indicate what basic connectivity and software applications will be needed by whom, and where and when they will be needed. The need for adjacency or colocation should also be indicated.
- *Transition cost estimate.* Focus on giving the best financial estimate for planning, and on achieving the most cost-effective transition. Task forces and subteams should use a consistent spreadsheet format with predefined

cost categories, and they should note specific assumptions and basis information to support the calculations.

- *Transition timeline.* Focus on identifying and publishing information about key projects, tasks, milestones, and areas of accountability during the period that has been determined. A single software application and a consistent format should be used so that the data can be incorporated into a consolidated project plan.

- *Issues and recommendations for the executive staff's attention.* Focus on identifying, clarifying, and setting priorities for essential issues that are beyond the immediate control of the task forces, or that involve resource demands or have other business impacts that need to be sorted out at the level of the executive staff. These issues and priorities should be encapsulated in brief descriptions, with supporting data, as necessary. Although these issues and priorities are beyond the control of the task forces, their identification at this early stage, before the integration plans are submitted, helps to ensure that no potential obstacles will be overlooked.

Once the initial transition plans were drafted, approved, and in the process of being implemented, the task forces turned their attention to completing plans to achieve full integration and the more complex synergies. An additional six to eight weeks were provided for development and review of full recommendations in the following areas:

- *Strategy review and objectives.* On the basis of the strategy and business plan of the Newco organization, revisit your functional plans and objectives, and determine what adjustments or changes may be needed in direction, resourcing, budgeting, priorities, and other areas.

- *Synergy project plans.* Following the defined format, each synergy project should have a high-level plan to submit for review and approval. Requirements include a description of the respective synergy and its estimated value, a description of the plans and process for verifying and validating the possibility of achieving this synergy, identification of who has primary responsibility for achieving this synergy and what the supporting functions are, a description of the major project milestones or key steps that will be required, and a statement of other cost- or process-related data that will be required in planning and verification.

- *Business-process recommendations.* Process maps, role descriptions, and operating instructions should be provided. There should also be a description of the implications that the recommended business processes (as optimally aligned or rationalized) are likely to have for headcount and organizational structure.

- *Alignment of policies and practices.* Each task force should conduct a structured review and a gap analysis of all policies and practices in use at both partner companies. A recommendation should be made for each area with respect to policies that will be adopted, adapted, changed entirely, or blended with other policies in the interest of complete alignment and reinforcement of the desired operations and culture.
- *Revision and updating of systems and facilities requirements.* As necessary, note any changes since the initial transition report.
- *Revision and updating of transition cost estimate.* As necessary, note any changes since the initial transition report.
- *Comprehensive timeline for full integration and all synergy projects.* Expand the task force project plan to include middle-term and longer-term tasks and milestones.
- *Communication and education requirements.* Determine how functions, business units, teams, individuals, and the organization as a whole will be informed after plans are approved, and determine what training will be required.
- *Issues and recommendations for the executive staff's attention.* Provide an update regarding any remaining concerns, or clarify those already conveyed.

Managing the Integration Project

The Merger Integration Work-Streams Model (see Chapter Four) establishes project management as a separate and distinct function. In practice, however, project management is a central part of the integration planning process. Sophisticated acquirers know that successful merger integration owes much to basic "blocking and tackling": careful planning followed by effective implementation and follow-up (documentation, communication, listening, and responding to issues). Therefore, making project management a dedicated core function of the integration process will pay off in important ways. As a general rule, we recommend several tools and processes to help in project management.

High-Level Summary Timeline

Exhibit 5.7 shows one experienced acquirer's overall integration timeline. It was used in planning meetings, as well as in countless communication sessions, to give everyone in the organization an effective grasp of key steps and milestones. Note that both companies' executive staffs were briefed on the integration process, and both, well in advance of the initial public announcement, commissioned the project to go forward. This arrangement provided enough time for the

EXHIBIT 5.7. HIGH-LEVEL SUMMARY TIMELINE.

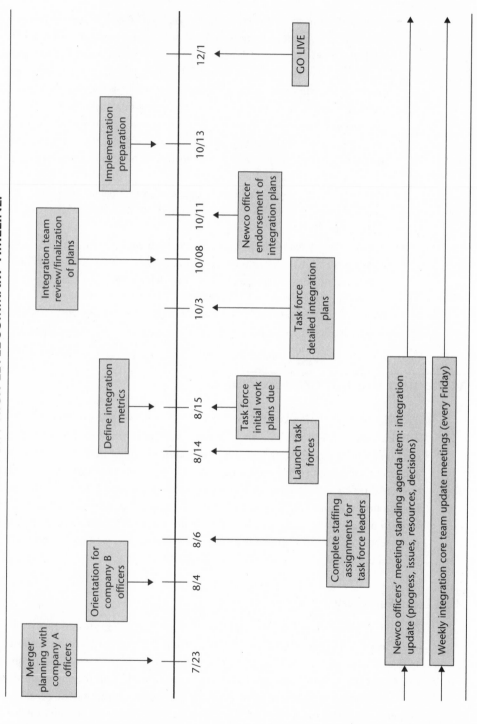

project managers to be selected, the structure of the task force to be designed, the task force leaders to be selected, and the kickoff planning session to be held immediately after the initial public announcement. This aggressive timeline should be revised as the project progresses and is best used as a regular element of communication meetings, to advise the organization of what progress has been made and of essential next steps. Another version of the summary timeline is depicted in Exhibit 5.8. In this application, the organization was well into the implementation phase of the detailed integration plans, so it chose to emphasize specific functional plans and pending projects.

Consolidated Project Plan

A fundamental tool in keeping the overall integration effort moving forward and on track is the consolidated project plan. As Exhibit 5.9 shows, this tool entails the consolidation of the individual task forces' plans into one comprehensive plan for integration. The particular components are owned and managed by the individual task forces, but the core team should own and manage the overall consolidated plan and its distribution. The core team's oversight can also help ensure that the tasks and milestones that are posted are at the appropriate summary level. This is an important role, given the number of specific projects: clients often document between one thousand and three thousand separate and distinct major issues, tasks, and milestones over the course of full integration.

Despite the size and complexity of the consolidated plan, the document serves many important purposes, especially in the following areas:

- *Relentless prioritization.* Projects and action items must continually be reviewed, ranked, and resourced to determine which items will directly drive deal value and are mandatory for accomplishing the core work.
- *Tracking and accountability.* The executive staff, the core team members, and the task forces should establish an ongoing periodic review of the consolidated project plan. This review should be aimed at assessing progress, slippage, and priorities. A recent client of ours, a CEO, perceived this integration document as the most important single tool for his executive staff to keep up with, and he regularly used it in all staff meetings.
- *Communication and involvement.* According to Ashkenas, De Monaco, and Francis (1998, p. 174), "one vital issue when integrating any acquisition ... is how to speed the process of getting dozens, hundreds, or thousands of people to work together in harmony." We believe that the consolidated project plan should play a central part in furthering communication and involvement. Clients have variously posted their consolidated project plans to the company intranet, created a dedicated shared drive on the company network, e-mailed

EXHIBIT 5.8. HIGH-LEVEL SUMMARY TIMELINE: FIRST 120 DAYS.

December	January	February	March
• Day 1! 12/1	• Dynamic fleet-management model completed	• Order entry fully operable	• Develop pipeline optimization plan
• Launch brochure and advertising campaign to customers	• Terminal capability study	• Advanced polymer process control strategy finalized	• Phase I best practices identified by technology centers
• Conversion of product specs to process	• Test-run process finalized	• Finalize 1998 R&D programs	• Maintenance purchase savings opportunities and action plan approved
• Product-line consolidation plan approved	• Completion of basic product training for sales and customer service (including legacy systems, processes, products, customers)	• Final SAP configuration complete	• Transition to long-term legacy system support process (post IT retention date)
• Critical control policies, including capital and expenditure approval process	• Materials-management design rolled out to plants	• New railroad freight contract negotiated	• Logistics, S&OP, credit functionality
• Define short-term crisis management organization and notification system	• Butane cracking online		• Quality management functionality at appropriate remote sites
• Begin legacy maintenance, ongoing	• Sales territory transitions		• Order fulfillment functionality
• Vision/values rollout	• Year end accounting for owners		
• Product certification process	• National agreements negotiated with suppliers		
• First official publication of synergy scorecard	• Completion of companywide facility-siting strategy		

EXHIBIT 5.9. SAMPLE CONSOLIDATED PROJECT PLAN.

ID	Task Name	Finish	% Complete	Resource Names	1999 (A M J J A S O N D J F)
1	**Purchased Safety Services**	**Fri 6/30/00**	**32%**		
2	Complete detailed analysis and prioritization of current purchased services	Fri 8/14/98	100%	R. Smith/ B. Jones	100%
3	Generate updated synergy target based on above	Tue 9/1/98	40%	R. Smith/ B. Jones	40%
4	Consolidate purchases identified in target, as contracts permit	Fri 6/30/00	25%	R. Smith/ B. Jones	
5	Provide functional support to achieve target (ongoing)	Fri 6/30/00	25%	R. Smith/ B. Jones	
6	**Corporate Safety Consolidation**	**Mon 2/1/99**	**41%**		
7	Develop organization plan and headcount recommendation	Tue 9/1/98	100%	P. Baker/ J. Thomas	100%
8	Review above with appropriate officers	Tue 9/15/98	100%	P. Baker/ J. Thomas	100%
9	Modify and finalize plan, as necessary	Thur 10/1/98	85%	P. Baker/ J. Thomas	85%
10	Develop consolidated safety-management philosophy and programs	Mon 2/1/98	10%	P. Baker/ J. Thomas	1
11	Implement	Wed 7/1/98	50%	P. Baker/ J. Thomas	50%
12	**Regional Safety Consolidation**	**Tue 9/1/98**	**50%**		50%
13	Confirm organization plan and headcount recommendation	Tue 9/1/98	20%	P. Baker	20%

copies of the plan to the entire organization, and provided full copies on request, all for the purpose of communicating openly about what was going on and engaging people's thinking throughout the company.

- *Reporting of progress and celebration of accomplishment.* Organizations and their leaders gain enormous credibility with employees, shareholders, and external stakeholders when they can say with certainty that the integration is 50 percent, 75 percent, or 95 percent complete, basing their statements on a consolidated project plan that consists of well over two thousand different tasks or milestones. In fact, without this type of objective standard, leaders will never be able to give a definitive answer to the questions "How is it going?" and "Where are we in the process?"

List of Oversight Vehicles

One of the most frustrating aspects of any integration is ambiguity about decision making and levels of review. The Newco organization's executive staff members may sometimes feel compelled to get deeply involved in details when they do not have a firm grasp on what is happening or confidence that a task is being properly managed. Some organizations have resolved this problem by listing, for members of governance committees and owners of parent companies, the variety of reports and processes through which the integration is being managed. This approach can be used to identify and clarify specific issues that a governance committee or new owners may want to decide directly, be involved in, or be advised of without direct involvement. Exhibit 5.10 shows one such list, developed in conjunction with the governance committee of a major joint venture. This tool was extremely helpful in establishing the issues and processes in which the governance committee had a legitimate interest in being involved. It also helped in gaining this group's confidence with respect to issues that had been determined to fall outside their direct purview. Particular attention was paid to ensuring that the governance committee and the executive team clearly understood each other's goals, roles, procedures, and relationships.

Miscellaneous Tools for the Core Team

The core team plays a very active role in leading the day-to-day integration efforts. Therefore, added importance is taken on by the business processes that this group uses in carrying out its responsibilities. To improve the effectiveness of their core teams, successful acquirers have used a number of techniques:

- *List of key action items (issues log).* This document is intended to capture tasks and areas of accountability for the core team itself. A number of items might be

EXHIBIT 5.10. LIST OF OVERSIGHT VEHICLES.

VEHICLE/(CONTACT)	VALUE ADDED	OWNER USE

1. **Consolidated project plan** (responsibility)
A. Detailed timeline by functional area
B. Executive rollup chart
	• Identifies functional critical path and milestones
	• Facilitates tracking of progress and task force emphasis
		• Review for
		  Completeness
		  Focus on appropriate elements
		  Owner decisions needed
		• Discuss gaps/inquiries with appropriate Newco officer

2. **Integration key action items list** (responsibility)
C. Major strategic themes
D. Key tactical items
	• Identifies major issues related to milestone achievement
	• Identifies major themes
		• Review to identify
		  Emerging decisions
		  Potential obstacles owners can address/remove on Newco's behalf
		• Discuss gaps/inquiries with appropriate Newco officer

3. **Synergy report card** (responsibility)	• Creates task force focus • Provides baseline for tracking	• Review for progress • Discuss gaps/inquiries with appropriate Newco officer

4. **Business plan** (responsibility)	• Enumeration of
	  Base economic assumptions
	  Industry analysis and scenarios
	  Business strategies/drivers
	  Tactical execution items
	• Identifies desired business results and means of measurement
		• Review for
		  Strategic direction
		  Completeness
		  Goals to be achieved
		  Owner decisions needed
		  "Pressure Test"
		• Discuss gaps/inquiries with appropriate Newco officer

5. **Newco officer meeting agendas and minutes** (responsibility)	• Provides insight into strategic focus areas of the Newco officers	• Identify emerging issues, major decisions, priorities • Inform Newco officers of missing owner requirements
6. **Closing status and responsibility checklist** (responsibility)	• Identifies critical-path milestones • Enables progress tracking	• Determine whether deal closing is on track • Identify potential obstacles • Inform Newco of missing owner requirements

7. **Weekly integration task force leader meeting notes** (responsibility)	• Communicates highlights for individual task forces
	  Actions
	  Successes
	  Issues
	  Assistance needed
		• Understand scope and objectives of activities
		• Assist where possible in removing obstacles or identifying additional owner needs

included—the continuing management of each of the eight major integration work streams, for example, or the planning and conducting of special meetings and events to address unique issues, or cross-functional concerns that have impacts on many of the task forces. This planning tool then assumes a central role in the core team's routine as the team members conduct status updates, follow through on action items, and set priorities for the issues that will be addressed.

- *Contact roster.* In any grand endeavor, somebody has to manage the bread-and-butter work. Given the number of people involved in merger integration, as well as the speed with which assignments may change, the core team is in the best position to keep and distribute a regularly updated directory of the project team's members.

- *Communication-distribution matrix.* During a merger integration, practical and logistical frustration can become overwhelming. When it comes to distributing information and documents throughout an organization, for example, what was once a clearly defined, easy process ("e-mail it to them") may now be very complex. Especially during the early days of integration planning, it is entirely likely that the two partner organizations will have very little direct e-mail connectivity (other than perhaps by way of the Internet) and very little software compatibility. Moreover, it is often necessary to translate materials into several languages and distribute them to multiple locations in different countries and even on different continents; indeed, it is often almost impossible merely to issue one report at a single time in a single format to the entire organization. A helpful exercise is to catalog all distribution channels and instructions in a planning matrix. Typically, this matrix would include information about who the audience (or a key individual) is and where the audience (or this individual) is to be found, in addition to information about preferred and secondary methods of distribution (e-mail, fax, courier), with notes about any peculiarities of these methods, as well as the name of a local contact person who (in the case of a plant or another large group) will take responsibility for distribution. The matrix should also include notes pertaining to each major group or level in the organization and specifying the types of communications to be routed to them and giving the names of people who are responsible for these routings.

CHAPTER SIX

TELL IT LIKE IT IS: HONEST COMMUNICATION

The company is being sold." "There will be massive cuts." "People will be let go." Unfortunately, those are familiar words to many employees. When you ask people where they first heard such statements, they often say, "In the lunchroom" or "At the coffee machine." In other words, they heard it through the grapevine.

To beat the grapevine, especially during an M&A transaction, top managers need to use communication effectively so that rumors do not become the main source of information. As Ashkenas, De Monaco, and Francis (1998) write, "Communicate, communicate, and then communicate some more. . . . Keeping the communication process going—and making it reach broadly and deeply throughout the organization—requires more than just sharing information bulletins" (p.13). One way to beat the grapevine is to adapt some traditional models of interpersonal communication for use in an organizational context.

The Johari Window

Remember the Johari Window? This communication model, developed in 1969 by Joseph Luft and Harry Ingham, helps people improve their interpersonal interactions by assessing the ways in which they give and receive information. The Johari Window (see Exhibit 6.1) is a grid divided into four regions representing

EXHIBIT 6.1. THE JOHARI WINDOW.

	Known	Unknown
	◄——— F e e d b a c k ———►	
Known	**1. Arena** Shared information	**2. Blind spot** Information known to others but not to oneself
Unknown	**3. Facade** Information that favors only oneself	**4. Unknown** Information unknown to others and to oneself

(Vertical axis label: E x p o s u r e)

Source: From *Group Processes: An Introduction to Group Dynamics, Third Edition* by Joseph Luft. Copyright © 1984 by Joseph Luft. Reprinted by permission of Mayfield Publishing Company.

areas of knowledge about oneself that are exchanged during communication. The grid's horizontal or *Feedback* axis represents the path along which one receives or fails to receive information about oneself. The vertical or *Exposure* axis represents the path along which one discloses or fails to disclose information about oneself. The basic concept behind the Johari Window is that open, two-way communication can enhance interpersonal interactions. In the broader context of an organization, the Johari Window can help improve organizational interactions and therefore effectiveness, again through open, two-way communication. Before we discuss its organizational applications, however, it is important to describe how the model represented by the Johari Window functions at the personal level.

The Personal Level

Region 1, *the Arena*, represents information known both to oneself and to others. When people share information and understand each other, their interpersonal relationships tend to be better. The larger the Arena—the more shared information there is—the more effective, productive, and mutually beneficial an interpersonal relationship is likely to be. Region 2, *the Blind Spot*, represents information that is known to others but not to oneself. The Blind Spot can cause damage in interpersonal relationships because it makes true understanding almost impossible. Region 3, *the Facade,* represents information known to oneself but not to others. The Facade thus hinders communication and therefore interpersonal effectiveness: information in this area is advantageous only to oneself, and negative information about oneself is withheld from others. There are some kinds of information that people may not share simply because they are apathetic. More often, however, information is withheld in the interest of gaining or keeping power and control. Region 4, *the Unknown,* represents information known neither to oneself nor to others. This area contains the greatest potential for creativity if one is willing to work with others to discover information.

The Organizational Level

The Johari Window can be adapted (see Exhibit 6.2) to the purpose of easing organizational change by enhancing communication. Consider, for example, that during an organizational change, such as a merger or an acquisition, senior

EXHIBIT 6.2. THE ORGANIZATIONAL JOHARI WINDOW.

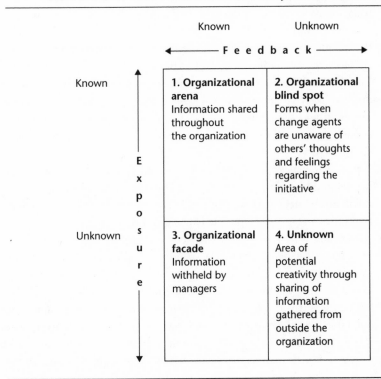

	Known	Unknown
	← **F e e d b a c k** →	
Known	**1. Organizational arena** Information shared throughout the organization	**2. Organizational blind spot** Forms when change agents are unaware of others' thoughts and feelings regarding the initiative
Unknown	**3. Organizational facade** Information withheld by managers	**4. Unknown** Area of potential creativity through sharing of information gathered from outside the organization

(vertical axis label: E x p o s u r e)

managers may try to keep information from people in lower-level positions for the same reasons that people in personal relationships keep information from one another: fear, power, and apathy. This kind of withholding creates a small organizational Arena and a large organizational Facade. A large Facade works to the advantage of the organizational change agents but puts everyone else at a disadvantage. As a result, people often distrust, dislike, and even sabotage change initiatives. In time, a Blind Spot may also form as the change agents remain unaware of others' thoughts and feelings. Therefore, it is important to expand the Arena both vertically, along the Exposure axis, and horizontally, along the Feedback axis.

Communication Models for a Merger

An effective communication plan for a merger is guided by several principles:

1. *Effective communication should be made a priority, and then all messages should be linked to the strategic objectives of the integration effort.* Suppose that one goal of the merger is to reduce costs. Any messages about the goal should communicate the reasons for the cost reductions, the specific reductions to be made, and the benefits of reducing costs. Messages should also identify the stakeholders—the people who will be most affected by the cost reductions.

2. *All communications should be honest.* It is best not to gloss over potential problems. People should be made aware of the realistic limits and goals. That way, they are less likely to jump to conclusions featuring worst-case scenarios. For example, if you tell people that the goal of an acquisition is a 30 percent cost reduction, then they probably will not worry that entire divisions will be shut down.

3. *The emphasis should be proactive rather than reactive.* Merger-related communications should be planned with ample lead time and disseminated early. Then it will not be necessary to take a defensive position when things start happening (for example, when people learn about the merger).

4. *All messages should be consistent and repeated through various channels.* The channels may include videos, memos, newsletters, and especially regular face-to-face meetings between managers and employees. In fact, if anything was learned about change management through the reengineering (that is, downsizing) era of the early 1990s, it is that the most effective change-management tool available to managers is face-to-face communication: employees want to hear it from the source. Face-to-face meetings also allow for real-time questions and answers. Unfortunately, however, face-to-face meetings are also the scarcest

change-management tool because of the time they require—but it is time very well spent. Because of their personal filters, people may easily misinterpret a one-time announcement from senior managers. They may not hear the whole message, or they may focus only on certain aspects. Most of the time, people care only about how changes will affect them—at least that's what they care about in the beginning. Multiple, consistent communications can help people absorb and internalize the true content of the messages.

5. *The organization needs to establish mechanisms for two-way feedback.* People should give and get feedback during the design, testing, and rollout of all change efforts. Effective feedback focuses on stakeholders' concerns, on the work areas and processes that will be integrated, on specific goals (such as cost reduction, reduced cycle time, or improved customer service), and on lessons that can be applied to future mergers and acquisitions.

As we know, many integration efforts are poorly managed, and managers may believe that withholding information ensures that people will get information only through the official channels. But the grapevine is always active.

When senior-level managers try to delegate ownership of the integration effort, they send a strong message that the effort is not worth their time. People then interpret this message as senior management's lack of commitment, and they too become reluctant to commit themselves. It is helpful, of course, to give a special department some responsibility for organizationwide communication. This department can help formulate messages, set up delivery channels, create opportunities for communication, and conduct communication events. To avoid the pitfall of low organizational commitment, however, senior managers should make it clear that final accountability for the integration effort still lies with them.

Another pitfall develops when communications contain unclear or incomplete descriptions of what is happening. Later on, implementation of the integration plans may break down as employees begin to question management's knowledge of the details.

Overall, when merger-related communications are poorly planned, the results may be unclear roles, insufficient follow-up, and lack of fine-tuning once implementation has begun. In particular, insufficient communication from top managers can lead middle management to stall the integration activities. A well-designed communication plan breaks down barriers to change and secures people's buy-in.

Once an integration effort is under way, it is important to keep the channels of communication open. By the time managers have set the direction of the effort, however, they probably have resolved their own personal concerns about it, and so they may be less likely to believe that they really have to communicate with others about what is happening. Nevertheless, open communication is what is needed more than anything else as the integration cascades down through all organizational levels. During rollout of the integration plans, people will have questions, and they will need to feel that they are being heard. They also may have helpful suggestions.

A Four-Phase Communication Process

Exhibit 6.3 depicts four phases of the communication process during an integration effort. In phase 1, the merger or acquisition is announced to all employees, and the details are explained. In phase 2, the focus is on identifying any issues that

EXHIBIT 6.3. FOUR-PHASE COMMUNICATION PROCESS.

Phase	Scope	Purposes
Phase 1: Awareness building "This is what is happening."	**Corporate-wide**	Link integration initiatives with strategic plans. Reaffirm the organization's values. Give specific information about the process. Announce senior management's involvement and support.
Phase 2: Project status "This is where we are going."	**Organization-specific**	Demonstrate senior management's commitment. Reaffirm the strategic rationale. Identify managers' and employees' issues. Provide the big picture.
Phase 3: Rollout "This is what it means to you."	**Integration-specific**	Continue to show senior management's commitment. Provide specific information on the changes being made and how they will affect people. Provide training in new roles, skills, and methods.
Phase 4: Follow-up "This is how we will make it work."	**Team-specific**	Continue to show senior management's commitment. Reaffirm the organization's values and strategic focus. Listen to and act on managers' and employees' needs to implement changes. Refine changes to ensure success.

may arise, such as employees' worry about possible layoffs. In phase 3, when the rollout occurs, communications should include information about the proposed changes. This phase also includes training in new skills, roles, and methods. Messages in phase 3 must be specific, focusing on the implications of the integration for all employees and for the organization as a whole. In phase 4, feedback is obtained, and the implementation of the integration plans is fine-tuned.

The communication process evolves as the integration effort takes shape, but some constants are necessary. The most important one is management's support. Another is the effort to keep people informed about how the proposed changes will fit with the organization's values and strategic focus. This effort helps people view the merger or acquisition as essential to business success.

A Communication-Strategy Matrix

A communication-strategy matrix (see Exhibit 6.4) can help clarify who does what and how things are done. The matrix defines stakeholders, objectives, key messages, vehicles of communication, timing of communications, and accountability for delivering or acting on communications.

The first step in using this matrix is to identify key stakeholders inside and outside the organization. This group may include senior and middle managers, lower-level employees, customers and suppliers, shareholders, and the community.

Once the stakeholders have been identified, it is important to discover exactly what their stakes or interests entail. Most people want to know what's in it for them. They want to know how their work will be affected, whether they will have to relocate, and so forth. When they know the particulars, they are more willing to listen to information about the broader issues (such as increased market share). For example, middle managers typically want to know whether they will manage the same people or report to the same boss. Shareholders want to know how changes will affect profits. Suppliers want to know whether their orders will be cut or whether their production efforts should be stepped up. Members of the business community may want to know whether jobs will be lost or new jobs will open up. If stakeholders' questions are not answered, the grapevine will provide its own answers, and these will often be less than accurate.

Early in the deal, it may not be possible to provide definitive answers to people's questions, because the details may not be settled. The details should be provided as quickly as possible, however, and their absence does not mean that communication should be held back until they are available. Regular, frequent communication should be continued, with content centering on the "fair process" (Kim and Mauborgne, 1997) being undertaken to develop the answers that people are asking for (such as information about the integration's core

EXHIBIT 6.4. COMMUNICATION-STRATEGY MATRIX.

Stakeholders (Who)	Objectives (Why)	Key Messages (What)	Vehicles (How)	Timing (When and How Often)	Accountability (Ownership of Delivery or Implementation)
Middle managers	Buy-in Understanding New skills	New roles New methods Personal impact	Meetings with the CEO and executives Training	Kickoff: week 1 Kickoff: month 1	CEO and other executives Training department
Employees	Buy-in Understanding New skills	New roles New methods Personal impact	Meetings with managers Training	Kickoff: week 1 Kickoff: month 1	Managers Training managers
Customers	Information Awareness	New methods Service impact	Meetings with sales reps	Kickoff: week 1	Sales reps
Shareholders	Information Awareness	Service impact Financial impact	Written information from CEO & CFO	Kickoff: week 1	CEO & CFO
Community	Information Awareness	Service impact Financial impact	News releases	Kickoff: week 1	CEO

team, its task force process, its timelines, and the expected deliverables). Kim and Mauborgne emphasize that people care not only about outcomes but also about the processes used to produce those outcomes. They also point out that "fair processes" have been found to positively influence attitudes and behaviors crucial to high performance.

"FRANK"

The following example of regular and consistent integration-related communication came to us from Kelly McCarthy, employee communications manager of a joint venture, Equistar Chemicals LP, between Lyondell Petrochemical (a $2.5 billion diversified petrochemicals and polymers company) and Millennium Petrochemicals (a $3 billion market leader in polymer products). Even before the deal officially closed, Equistar's senior managers saw the need to communicate openly with the workforce about the venture. In keeping with the communication format and process described earlier, the communications department was included as an integral part of the merger integration team, which was given responsibility by the officers of the company for coordinating the integration.

One very creative member of the department had the idea of creating a fictional character who, on behalf of the workforce, would monitor and report on the progress of the joint venture. This "person" was dubbed FRANK (see Exhibit 6.5). At least once a week, FRANK had access to the CEO and other senior managers. FRANK would also interview middle managers, lower-level employees, and customers, reporting on the progress of the joint venture and, most important, providing information to the workforce about the status of efforts to resolve their "me" issues. Feedback from managers and employees about the frequency, openness, and credibility of the FRANK communications was overwhelmingly positive. FRANK continued his reporting, not only throughout the planning phase but also well into the process of implementation—about eighteen months into the venture.

Knowledge Before New Skills

To help ensure the success of a merger or an acquisition, it is important to get stakeholders' buy-in. It is not enough just to tell people about the planned changes. Give people knowledge first, and then new skills; their willingness to change will follow.

All communications to stakeholders should describe the rationale for the integration effort, people's new roles, and the benefits that can be expected by employees, customers, shareholders, and the organization. It is also important to identify vehicles for communication: memos, speeches, face-to-face meetings, videos, newsletters, electronic message boards, training sessions, news releases, posters, and so forth. The more consistent communication is across those vehicles, the more credible it will be.

Even when communication is effective, the grapevine doesn't wither and die. But if you tell it like it is, you can trim the grapevine and keep it from growing wild.

EXHIBIT 6.5.

An electronic news service for employees. Updated weekly or more frequently as news becomes available.

HELLO, I'M FRANK. You and I will be getting to know each other in the coming weeks. First of all, you need to know that my name is no accident. In the days ahead, it will be my job, along with your supervisor, to communicate with you openly, frequently, and candidly about the changes under way at our company.

I'll be giving you information as early as I can—information you need to make better decisions. I'll tell you what I know about any aspect of the new venture. And if I don't know, I'll say that and get back to you as soon as I can. I'll tell you the good news and the bad. I'll help you tell the difference between rumor and truth.

I won't promise that you will always be satisfied with what I have to say, but I am committed to talking to you plainly, without any corporate doublespeak. In short, I'll treat you with respect and honesty.

CHAPTER SEVEN

DON'T LET THEM JUMP SHIP: RETAINING YOUR KEY PEOPLE

A career today represents more a collection of assignments than a collection of seniority pins and gold watches. Work, especially at managerial levels, is increasingly an activity more than a place. With the extinction of twenty-year stints at patriarchal corporations has come a reciprocal erosion of employees' loyalty toward their employers.

One result of this development is the greater difficulty of retaining key top performers. Often during a merger or acquisition, even when key personnel stay on board, they lose their commitment, especially when the environment becomes unstable, uncertain, or changes dramatically, as is inevitably the case during M&As.

It is no surprise that people often leave organizations, or "decommit," during M&As. When a company is in turmoil because of a merger or an acquisition, people's thoughts turn inward, away from their jobs and customers. "Me" becomes the most important issue as the focus on personal issues becomes paramount—my job, my pay, my security, my career—and headhunters and recruiters from other companies step up their efforts because a company in M&A turmoil provides a feeding ground for search firms and recruiting departments. Recruiters provide answers to personal issues—a job offer, higher pay, security, a career change.

A rerecruitment plan requires three key steps:

1. Identifying key people or groups
2. Understanding what motivates them
3. Developing and executing an action plan to address what motivates them

Identifying Key People

The key people and groups are those whose loss would have the most detrimental effect on the organization. People or groups can be considered key for various reasons, but the business impact of losing them should be the factor that identifies them as essential.

Make a list of all the employees and groups in the areas of the enterprise that are affected by the merger or acquisition. Then determine the impact that their loss would have on the business. Would their absence result in the loss of a key client or customer? the loss of critical skills in innovation or thinking? loss of knowledge about a core product or service? loss of crucial skills in project management? If the answer is yes, then the person or group should be considered key.

Many organizations have documented succession plans that identify how key vacancies should be filled. These plans can also serve as checklists for ensuring that all the key people have been identified for rerecruitment efforts. The rerecruitment plan should probably include everyone in the succession plan in addition to others.

Understanding What Motivates People

Abraham Maslow defined a hierarchy of general human needs. Executives, managers, and employees in a corporate setting likewise have a set of personal needs. The Rerecruitment Needs Pyramid (see Exhibit 7.1) is similar to Maslow's hierarchy in that it depicts the personal needs of managers and employees during organizational change.

Security

Often when people think of mergers or acquisitions, they think of potential job loss. They ask themselves such questions as "Will the companies consolidate my area? Are my skills outdated? Will I be let go? Can I learn the new company's methods?" Job security becomes a very basic issue at all levels of the organization

EXHIBIT 7.1. THE RERECRUITMENT NEEDS PYRAMID.

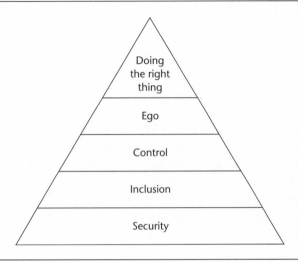

Doing the right thing

Ego

Control

Inclusion

Security

at such a time. For employees who have been identified as key, it is important to address the need for job security early—the same day the merger announcement is made, if at all possible.

Key people need to realize that they are integral to the success of the merger work. These people should be told that they have been identified as having an important role to play in the future success of the Newco organization and will, as a result, be kept in the organization. Deliver this message in person, and in private. Acknowledge that at this early stage the environment is uncertain, and much is still unknown.

Another element of security is its financial aspect. People who are staying with the company will wonder about their pay, benefits, and potential for increases. They should be told what is possible. Often, solid answers will be unavailable early in the process, but the answers should be developed as soon as possible—within days or weeks, not months.

"Stay bonuses" can be offered, as necessary, to protect against the loss of key people until initial reactions to the merger or acquisition have settled down, or until questions can be answered more clearly. Initially, stay bonuses can buy decision makers some time to determine the dynamics of the new organization and the roles that people will fill. Longer-term bonuses, pay raises, and incentive contracts can be used later on as further inducements for the key people to stay. A stay bonus should be tied to some type of performance measure or deliverable for the period during which the key people are needed; otherwise, there may be a temptation to sit and wait out the period of the bonus while offering no real productivity.

Inclusion

Especially in organizations, people have a very basic need to feel that they are in on things. They want to know what's going on. To maintain the loyalty of key people during an M&A transaction, the company should keep them in the loop by involving them in key meetings or in the integration process, for example, or by sharing information with them on a regular basis. Employers make a big mistake when they do not share information just because no decisions have been made. Letting essential people know about the alternatives being considered and asking for their input are great ways to make them feel a part of things. If people are considered good enough to rerecruit, they must also be considered good enough to add value to the difficult decisions being made, or at least good enough to be kept informed of progress.

Control

As time goes on, key managers and executives develop a certain addiction to control over how things are handled, and they want to maintain that control. For many, in fact, a strong sense of self-worth is derived from their range of control.

Key people's need for control can be satisfied if some of the merger-related decisions are left to them. First, during integration, the company should set criteria and boundaries for decisions: "Integration decisions should be based first on customer needs" or "All integration decisions must be supported by a business case." Second, the company should stress the need for upward communication about integration decisions that key people have taken or are considering, but then the company should give people the latitude to make those decisions.

Ego

An employee's or a manager's "work ego" begins with the belief that he or she plays an important role in the success of the company, and this belief is often fueled by the status symbols that organizations provide people. At the executive level, for example, status symbols often take the form of administrative assistants, large offices, and first-class travel. At the managerial and employee levels, the symbols are different—awards banquets, mention of achievements in the company newsletter, bonuses for major accomplishments, and the like—but they fuel people's work egos in just the same way. People's egos can be maintained during integration by the same types of rewards: inclusion in the integration process, recognition for the accomplishment of difficult integration tasks, and the like.

Doing the Right Thing

After their other needs have been met, people need to feel that they are doing the right thing. Whether for their careers, their families, or their employees, people want to do what's right.

Difficulties arise when what seems right for one party appears to be wrong for another. To be more specific, many times the key personnel in a company that is immersed in a merger or an acquisition are introduced to a new set of stakeholders, among whom are new colleagues, investors, analysts, and new customers. During an M&A transaction, the question is not only "Am I doing the right thing?" but also "Who am I doing the right thing for?" The answers to these questions are of paramount importance in making the integration successful.

How key people feel about decisions and whether they will commit themselves to the change effort during integration are particularly important issues. Again, giving people a sense of control and some say in decisions will reinforce their belief that making a particular change is the right thing to do.

It is usually impossible to involve all the key personnel in the decisions that are being made. Therefore, the company needs to create an environment that allows key personnel to feel that they are doing the right thing. Clearly communicating the reasons for decisions will help people answer the question "Who am I doing the right thing for?"

Often decisions are based not on what is immediately and directly right for the company's personnel but on what is right in the longer term for the company's customers, shareholders, and profits. Ultimately, doing what is right for customers, shareholders, and profits will have a positive effect on personnel, an effect that shows up in higher sales and greater market share. By offering this rationale for decisions, the company helps people see that the right thing to do is to stay and commit themselves to making the integration successful.

Developing and Executing an Action Plan

Once management understands what motivates key people, actions can be developed to rerecruit specific individuals and groups. One straightforward, organized approach uses a simple rerecruitment matrix (see Exhibit 7.2). This matrix is very helpful in organizing rerecruitment activity and retaining and revitalizing key people during a major change.

EXHIBIT 7.2. RERECRUITMENT MATRIX.

Targets	Impact of Loss	Issues	Rerecruitment Strategy	Responsibility and Timing
Top ten names	Key product delayed ($1.6M) Leadership lost May lure others away	Recognition Career control Financial independence	Promote Stay bonus Involve, raise Make VP of new division	T.G., 11/20 B.G., 11/22 D.R., 10/16
Other key employees by name	Customer relationships	Pay, benefits	Stock options	T.P., 10/20
Key Groups XYZ facility Sales	Production loss Revenue impact	Security Security	Communication Communication	Merger team, 10/16 B.C., 10/14

In the first column, individuals or groups key to the organization's future success are identified. In the second column, the business impact of losing each key person and group is stated. The business impact should be quantified whenever it is possible to do so; that way, it can be weighed against the cost of the identified retention actions. In the third column, people's motivators are identified: the general categories listed in Exhibit 7.2, or more specific motivators, such as promotion and involvement. In the fourth column, retention and recruitment actions are listed. If more than one action is implemented for each person or group, the company will increase its chances of retaining them. In the fifth column, the people who are responsible for implementing the actions are listed, and their deadlines are noted. With the matrix complete, what remains is the most important step: actually implementing the plan.

The human resources function can be of assistance here, but senior managers must be the ones who complete the matrix and own the rerecruitment actions for their areas of the enterprise. Exhibit 7.3 outlines a manager's guide to rerecruitment. It can be used by executives, middle managers, and supervisors alike to quickly assemble a plan for retaining and rerecruiting key people. Once the questions in the guide have been answered, the rerecruitment matrix shown in Exhibit 7.2 is essentially complete.

Rerecruitment efforts should include measurements of how effective the actions are. Many companies already measure overall turnover rates on an annual basis, but during integration, when rerecruitment becomes paramount, measuring yearly overall turnover is not sufficient. More frequent turnover assessments need to be done, perhaps monthly. Historical turnover data should be converted to the same frequency, for purposes of comparison. Turnover can be tracked in a way that allows early identification of trouble spots in specific groups, such as top executives or people and groups targeted by the rerecruitment matrix.

In addition, exit interviews should be performed with employees who have announced their impending departures. Because an integration environment accelerates the time frame in which information must be gathered, it is probably wise to conduct an exit interview before the employee's last workday. Exit interviews can be a valuable tool in understanding how the integration that the company is undertaking is affecting employees' motivation to stay.

Retention and rerecruitment should not be limited to pay and benefits. Pay and benefits do meet the basic needs that people have and cannot be ignored—they set the foundation for retention—but true rerecruitment of people into the Newco organization often requires more creativity. For example, when Lyondell Petrochemical wanted to transfer significant numbers of crucial managers and employees from Philadelphia to Houston during the integration of ARCO Chemical, the company employed a "visit Houston" rerecruitment plan. The plan consisted of bringing small groups of twenty-five managers and employees, and their spouses, to Houston for a three-day visit. Many people had never even been to Texas before and had some deep rooted preconceptions about not wanting to live in the Lone Star State. The groups were flown down on a Thursday, and that evening there was an informal welcome dinner and reception. The groups spent a few hours on Friday morning listening to talks by a Lyondell executive and by a representative from the Houston Chamber of Commerce, who spoke about housing, schools, neighborhoods, and recreation. Then they watched a short video about the Houston area. The groups were taken in vans to visit various sights around Houston and see some of the neighborhoods and communities. Many of those who had said they would never move to Houston decided to do so, and several actually purchased homes during their visits. The small-group trips were conducted over several weeks, and the retention rate for these high-priority people was well over 50 percent, whereas it had originally been predicted to be almost zero.

During the turbulence of an M&A integration, attrition will go up; there is no avoiding it completely. And the best people can—and will—find new jobs first. To stem the rising tide of workforce turnover during a merger or an acquisition, it is vitally important to enact a comprehensive "rerecruitment" strategy to retain and revitalize the company's valued human capital. The time it takes to develop and execute a rerecruitment plan is richly repaid as key people are won over. And one thing is certain: if you don't win your key people over, someone else will.

EXHIBIT 7.3. A MANAGER'S GUIDE TO RERECRUITMENT.

Use of this guide

Among the best ways to rerecruit people are involvement and communication: regularly explaining what is going on and why decisions are made. Ongoing rerecruitment in all areas of the organization is a tangible way to begin and to continually apply our vision and values. In short, we need to make our people feel a part of the new company.

This guide is designed to assist managers in their integration-related retention and rerecruitment efforts. It lays out a straightforward seven-step process that can be applied to all areas of the enterprise. If you have any questions about the use of this guide, please stop by the integration team office located at

_____ , or call _____ .

Rerecruitment

The term *rerecruitment* applies to efforts aimed at retaining people, as well as to actions that help keep people from mentally checking out. Loss of interest and commitment can be at least as devastating to performance as actual loss of people to competitors or other organizations.

I. Why rerecruit?

- Loss of key people

- Greater openness to headhunter calls

- Safety risks increase

- Productivity drops

- Poor quality of work

- Those who don't leave get discouraged by those who do

- Loss of organizational knowledge, talent, and resources

- Search, hiring, and training costs increase

List other reasons you can think of for your area or the company in general:

_____

_____

_____

II. What has been the impact so far?

We already currently have _____ open positions.

Numerous people have not accepted offers to be a part of the company.

In my area:

_____ (number exits/notices of leaving to date)

These are only the actual resignations so far. How many people are mentally checking out or may be part of a second wave of exits?

III. What do people want?

Place a check mark next to the items below that you feel may still be concerns for at least some of the people in your area.

_____ Security (a job, pay, benefits)

_____ Inclusion (timely knowledge of what's occurring, involvement in task forces/initiatives, ability to ask questions and get timely answers, access to managers' time and attention)

_____ Control (ability to make or influence decisions, latitude to make the call without multiple approvals)

_____ Recognition (recognition of achievements, pats on the back, thank-yous)

IV. Who am I concerned about?

List the people or groups in your area who you may be concerned are not rerecruited into the company yet:

People/Groups	*People/Groups*
_____	_____
_____	_____
_____	_____
_____	_____
_____	_____
_____	_____
_____	_____

V. What if they leave?

For the people/groups you listed what will be the impact on your area if they leave, or if their organizational commitment is not what you need it to be?

People/Groups	*Impact of loss/lack of commitment*
_____	_____
_____	_____
_____	_____
_____	_____
_____	_____

(continued)

VI. What have I done so far?

List *the actions that you have taken* to date to rerecruit your people into the company.

Rerecruitment actions to date	*Approximate completion date*
_____	_____
_____	_____
_____	_____
_____	_____
_____	_____
_____	_____
_____	_____

VII. What more can I do?

List *the actions that you will take* to further rerecruit your people into the company.

People/Groups	*Rerecruitment actions*	*Date/timing*	*Help needed/ from whom?*
_____	_____	_____	_____
_____	_____	_____	_____
_____	_____	_____	_____
_____	_____	_____	_____
_____	_____	_____	_____
_____	_____	_____	_____
_____	_____	_____	_____
_____	_____	_____	_____
_____	_____	_____	_____

Remember: We can spend the time, effort, and money now to rerecruit current knowledge and talent, or we can spend more time, effort, and money later to try to replace that knowledge and talent.

Rerecruitment suggestions, ideas, and thought starters:

Security (a job, pay, benefits)

- Tell people they have a job, *and* paint a bright/important vision of their role in the future of the company.

Inclusion (timely knowledge of what's occurring)

- Involvement in task forces/initiatives, ability to ask questions and get timely answers, access to managers' time and attention).

- Conduct *many* face-to-face team discussions with you, regularly schedule them (e.g. every Tuesday morning), include Q&A two-way dialogue, discuss company information, discuss your management style, discuss expectations of your area (productivity, financials, safety).

- Tell people why decisions are being made the way they are, "what's the rationale."

- Set a specific two-hour "open door" office time each week when you will be available for people to have access to you, and keep the scheduled time.

- Hold timely special meetings to communicate/discuss "hot news" (organizational announcements, and so on).

- Fly people to the new location for "community visits"; include family/spouse activities.

- Conduct spouse-to-spouse activities, have spouses communicate with each other to "sell" the community and the move to a new locale.

Control (ability to make or influence decisions, latitude to make the call without multiple approvals)

- Clearly tell people what decisions you want to be involved in, and let them make decisions and inform you later about everything else.

- Discuss learning opportunities from mistakes made, "what you would have done differently" or "what we should do the next time."

Recognition (recognition of achievements, pats on the back, thank-yous)

- Hold formal recognition events/meetings.

- Include recognition comments at the beginning or end of each of your team meetings.

- Give people something (a lunch, awards).

- Tell people when they do something well, *when they do it,* not days after the fact.

- Use the element of surprise; unexpected recognition demonstrates a leader's interest and initiative.

Special Notes:

- *Be creative* in your rerecruitment actions.

- *Involve others* (officers, spouses) to help you rerecruit, as necessary.

- *Don't delegate* rerecruitment: your actions/presence have a greater impact than the actions/presence of those below you.

- *Follow up* your words with actions; actions do speak louder than words.

- *Be persistent;* remember that just because you have done something once doesn't mean you shouldn't do it again, and again.

CHAPTER EIGHT

SETTING THE ORGANIZATION CURES MANY ILLS: STRUCTURE AND STAFFING DECISIONS

Nothing much happens in a merger integration until the organization is set.

J. HEMMER, VICE PRESIDENT, CUSTOMER SUPPLY CHAIN, EQUISTAR CHEMICALS LP

Robert Half International conducts a periodic survey to determine the top concern of senior executives in the nation's thousand largest companies. The perennial winner should come as no surprise: by an almost two-to-one margin, the number one fear is "loss of job due to a merger or acquisition."

This fear is not irrational, nor is it based on a misperception. On the contrary, an overwhelming body of anecdotal evidence and common experience indicates that few organizations both understand and apply effective processes for structuring and staffing during merger integration.

Union Pacific Corporation is a dramatic case in point. In 1996, Union Pacific attempted the biggest railroad merger in history by acquiring Southern Pacific Rail Corporation for $3.9 billion and a promise to merge the two systems into a seamless link between the West Coast and the Midwest. What happened instead was the organizational equivalent of a train wreck:

- Federal transportation regulators accused the company of a "fundamental breakdown in operations."
- The route system west of the Mississippi was in a state of gridlock for months, with thousands of freight cars routinely backed up.
- Union Pacific's chairman was forced to apologize publicly to the company's customers.

- Three fatal crashes occurred within three months.
- Service had become so bad, according to customers, that the company could not account for millions of dollars of shipments for weeks at a time: the company literally could not locate rail cars loaded with customers' products.
- Customers lost hundreds of millions of dollars through plant closings, unrealized revenues, and extra expenses, and they filed millions of dollars' worth of lawsuits in response.
- The company handed business over to its competitors just to alleviate the backlog.
- The congestion in Union Pacific's twenty-three-state operating area is said to have cost the U.S. economy $4 billion in stalled production and higher transportation expenses.
- Union Pacific reported substantial losses in revenues and in earnings per share.

The causes of the fiasco were many: corporate arrogance and overconfidence, cultural differences, and, principally, failure to do effective planning and post-merger staffing. According to Machalaba (1997, p. A1), "Company officials concede that they badly underestimated the number of crews and locomotives they would need; in part, they relied on their past success in acquiring other railroads. Those mergers allowed Union Pacific to lay off great numbers of employees . . . but at a time when freight shipments were booming nationwide, the company was offering buyouts to more than 1,000 workers at a time." The buyouts on the part of Union Pacific, combined with cultural conflicts, also provoked an exodus of many Southern Pacific executives and managers, whom industry officials later credited with unique context skills for keeping the acquired company running. Union Pacific, in its arrogance and immediate push for staffing synergies, cut too deep, showing very little regard for prevailing business conditions. The company lost far too much institutional knowledge, seriously damaged its core operational capability, and forever tarnished its previously outstanding image.

Common Problems

Union Pacific is not alone in having failed to do effective planning and staffing for a postmerger organization. This is one of the most important integration work streams; in all fairness, however, it is also one of the least effectively managed, for a host of reasons. The following issues may resonate with your own previous experience.

Synergy WAGs

WAG is an acronym for "wild audacious guess." Back-of-the-napkin synergy estimates are always dangerous; the area of selling, general, and administrative overhead is one in particular that is commonly miscalculated or overtly "buffered" to drive further cost cutting. Moreover, staffing estimates rarely take account of the risks involved in stripping out organizational capability. Staffing synergies should be part of every good deal, of course, but the real value must come through revenue-enhancing synergies—and those require headcount, talent, operational effectiveness, and customer service.

The Cost of Cutting Costs

Even valid staffing synergies have an implementation cost, but failure to perform due-diligence analysis in this area is rampant. Severance costs, "stay bonuses" and other such packages, plant-closure costs (such as continued insurance and tax payments on a closed facility) are often underestimated or omitted altogether. International labor laws and employment restrictions further complicate matters. Stories abound of deals made on the assumption of closing or consolidating facilities in a given country, with the discovery coming too late that the country in question does not allow broad reductions in force or that country-specific severance liabilities are prohibitively high.

Failure to Link Staffing with Strategy

In a classic cart-before-the-horse scenario, strategic business planning often fails to catch up with current decisions about structure and staffing until the next fiscal year. Senior leadership must rewrite this scenario by first revising fundamental elements of the business plan in light of the Newco organization's requirements and opportunities and then factoring this into initial structure and staffing plans.

Incompetence About Competencies

In another failure of senior leadership, there is very little initial validation of the organization's core competencies or of the individual competencies that will be required in maintaining them. Fundamental discussions regarding "why customers buy from us" and "what we do better than our competitors" will help in identifying essential strengths and capabilities that must not be gutted.

Failure to Establish a Process for Structure and Staffing

Three traditional staffing patterns all tend to have unfavorable results:

1. *The acquirer makes all staffing decisions unilaterally.* In this scenario, many capable people are never considered—they are "unknown commodities"—and there is no mechanism to prevent talent from being overlooked. Cronyism and favoritism, left unchecked, can quickly overcome good intentions. A Newco organization staffed primarily with managers from the acquirer is unable to capitalize fully on the acquired company's assets.

2. *The organization takes a "wait and see" attitude.* Managers may be initially unwilling to spend the time required to make difficult decisions about structure and staffing. Press announcements further compound this tendency by creating unrealistic expectations. (Does anyone really believe the oft-repeated statement that "no personnel changes are anticipated"?) Over time, however, more knowledge about the acquired company and its executive staff will inevitably reveal opportunities or problems that can be remedied only by staff changes. A second wave of disruption may then be triggered, and it may bring even more difficulties than the first one did.

3. *The acquirer "cleans house."* Except perhaps in the case of small consolidating acquisitions, this option is usually too costly, in terms of both severance and the loss of institutional knowledge. In today's tight market for leadership talent, this choice is no longer practical.

Zero Tolerance for Process

You've heard the pushback before: "The hiring manager knows who she wants in that role anyway, so why go through the process?" or perhaps "We don't have time to fill out forms; we just need to reduce our headcount." A merger tends to thwart an organization's ability to use processes that were formerly considered normal and customary. Most organizations have sufficient, sometimes sophisticated, routines for recruiting and staffing during times of normal business operations, but they fail to use these routines during the time of greatest need. Or worse, they fail to adapt their normal and customary processes sufficiently to match the speed and rigor required by merger integration.

Bartering for Executives

In many mergers, ironically, the job assignments that will have the greatest strategic and organizational impact are made with the least rigorous rationale. In this practice, which we call "bartering for executives," the CEO's direct reports, instead of being selected through an objective process designed to find the best talent, are treated like chits on the negotiating table. Unfortunately, however, "four for me and three for you" does not qualify as targeted selection.

Clandestine Operations

Some organizations treat postmerger staffing decisions as if they were top-secret military initiatives. This kind of behavior only fans the flames of unproductive paranoia and encourages qualified "keepers" to bail out early.

Ten Principles

Structure and staffing decisions will always be difficult, politically charged, and emotional in nature, but the following ten general principles have been proved to help:

1. Begin the decision process for structure and staffing with a due-diligence analysis of human capital and the organization in general.
2. Base decisions about structure and staffing on strategic considerations and on a determination of the Newco organization's business plan.
3. "If you build it, they will come."
4. The sooner, the better.
5. Triangulate, validate, and assess.
6. Communicate openly about the process for making decisions on structure and staffing.
7. Train hiring managers on the steps and responsibilities of the selection process.
8. Catch and correct mistakes.
9. Capture results and retain knowledge.
10. Start the development and team-building process now.

Structure, Staffing, and Due Diligence

As discussed in Chapter Two, due diligence should be the basis of structure and staffing decisions. This is not a new concept. For example, as Leighton and others (1969, p. 94) point out, "We cannot overestimate the importance of getting to know the president and his key personnel. Evidence indicates that the more fully the parent company understands their emotional and personal needs, their weaknesses and strengths, their fears and apprehensions, the more effectively it will be able to help with the acquisition and to manage the company later on" (cited in

Pritchett, Robinson, and Clarkson, 1997). A formal process should be used to discover, compare, and contrast organizational structures, depth of talent, management processes, and individual styles. International operations require even more attention to detail, and experienced counsel should be used to evaluate the regulatory requirements for anticipated changes in the workforce. Various scenarios for reductions in force and consolidation should be developed, and their costs should be estimated, so that an approximate range of total staffing synergies can be provided in addition to an idea of what it will cost to implement them.

Structure, Staffing, and Strategic Planning

While the deal is being closed, and while the initial integration-planning activities are being launched by the core team and the task forces, senior leaders should be defining and communicating the Newco organization's overall strategy and business plan. The better-defined the key parameters of the deal, and the more clearly articulated the subsequent operations, the more effective the process for making decisions about structure and staffing. The strategic template should identify facilities to be closed or consolidated, products to be rationalized or exploited, research initiatives to be funded or discontinued, new computing systems to be adopted or legacy systems to be maintained, and other business processes to be used in the Newco organization. Each unit, function, or task force then needs to clarify major elements of its mission and scope or of the other directions from which it will feel an impact. Only after this strategic translation process has taken place will it be possible for units, functions, or task forces to determine exact work requirements, structures, role descriptions, and staffing needs in order to carry out their specific parts of the Newco organization's mission. As one aspect of this process, each business unit should conduct a risk assessment of the potential impact of the requested staff reduction or consolidation. Contingency plans should be established and, as necessary, a transition organization and a timeline should be created to ramp up or down to the ultimate "to be" organization.

The next step is for each unit to verify its own core competencies required to support its strategic role and to identify critical positions, as well as specific competencies required for each position. Only then is the business unit ready to begin the thought process of actually designing the organization and its jobs and staffing those jobs with the best candidates.

The human resources function or the organization design function can play an important role in this process by providing tools, counsel, and facilitated discussions for business-unit partners. We saw an excellent example of this role in action during the merger integration of Lyondell Petrochemical and Millennium Petrochemicals. The assistant project manager of this integration, a self-described "reformed CPA" named Eric Silva, had expert knowledge of the business process and was leading Lyondell's organizational effectiveness function. Before the due-diligence phase, Eric developed and approved a set of organization design processes and templates, and a competency model that was ready for deployment when the merger integration got under way. Meetings were conducted with each business unit and task force, to help determine the organizational implications of the business strategy and the functional goals. Specific organizational capabilities were identified that were mission-critical to the success of each unit. A gap analysis was then conducted, to determine needs and options for closing the gaps. As part of this planning process, Eric gave each executive officer and business-unit head a primer on principles of effective organization design. Key parameters, definitions, and desired set-points were established, to guide the leadership team through the delicate process of creating a low-cost, high-performance organization with no loss of core capability. An abbreviated version of Eric's primer is shown in Exhibit 8.1.

An emerging strategic issue that senior leaders must begin addressing is the changing composition of the workforce and the pending consequences of this shift for organizational structure and staffing decisions. A research initiative conducted by Watson Wyatt Worldwide (1998b) focused on the strategic HR implications of dramatically changing workforce demographics. In it, William J. Miner, F.S.A., senior consulting actuary, observes that

> The human resource practices and policies that have worked well at many organizations for years will not survive in this new era. . . . The workforce has grown at 1.5 percent per year over the last 20 years—and at 2 percent per year before that. Contrast this with the reality that in 1995 the U.S. labor growth rate was slightly less than 1 percent and projected to steadily decline to a negative .15 percent in 2025. In an environment where the labor force is barely growing or even shrinking, and competition for these employees is likely to be intense, the retention of employees will become a major strategic objective well into the future.

Exhibits 8.2 and 8.3 show these demographic shifts and projections.

Effective Preparation

"If you build it, they will come." One reason why Eric Silva's approach was so successful is that he was ready to go when the time came. This key principle is lost on many acquirers. In the middle of a deal, there is no status quo; things move too fast and are too unpredictable. Chaos will ensue unless the organization is prepared and has defined processes for conducting strategic analysis, guiding

EXHIBIT 8.1. ORGANIZATION DESIGN PARAMETERS.

Design Parameter	Definition	Considerations
Strategic business focus	The specific strengths, capabilities, or business drivers that uniquely distinguish a particular department or unit from another.	Is the strategic business focus of the organization sufficiently clear to indicate the specific responsibilities, tasks, deliverables, and resources required of this particular function or job?
Reporting structure	The formal reporting relationship or arrangement for an individual, process team, or function.	Is a process activity "owned" by as few managers as possible? Is process completion established to cut across as few organization boundaries as possible?
Departmentation	The process of clustering work activities into business unit or departmental areas of responsibility.	Activities performed by a subunit or individual should directly contribute to that area's mission/purpose. Have all possibilities for grouping fundamentally similar work been considered? (For example, standardized tasks, redundant tasks, opportunities to reduce decision-making cycle time, economies of scale.)
Staffing level	The quantity of personnel (FTEs) occupying the same job, same process, same team, same function, and so on.	Have strategic and customer value-added processes been staffed sufficiently to ensure no risk of poor work quality or service gaps? Have essential support processes been staffed sufficiently to avoid bottlenecks/service gaps? Have all nonstrategic and administrative services been outsourced?
Depth of control	The number of levels in the organizational structure. The number of levels or steps of review, endorsement, and approval in an organization.	Has the number of levels been minimized, to the extent practical? Have jobs been designed so that the distance between information generation and decision making is minimized?
Span of control	A reflection of the number of individuals who report to a manager or supervisor.	Has the number of direct reports been maximized to support the manager's breadth of responsibilities? Have adequate processes and protocols been established so that managers can effectively operate larger spans of control?
Job content—vesting	The degree to which the responsibility for completing an activity is specified, understood, and accepted by an individual, team, or function.	Has responsibility for completing an activity been vested in one (and only one) individual (a single point of accountability)?

(continued)

EXHIBIT 8.1. (*continued*)

Design Parameter	Definition	Considerations
Job content—breadth	The degree to which an individual performs a broad array of activities.	Have jobs been optimized to allow individuals to perform the broadest possible array of activities within an area of responsibility or skills? Has the number of individuals performing activities within any one process been minimized?
Alignment of responsibility and authority	The degree to which the level of authority granted to an individual, team, or function is sufficient to accomplish the majority of tasks.	Have unnecessary review, endorsement, and approval steps been eliminated? Have the jobs been provided sufficient level of authority to enable the work to be completed as quickly as possible, without major interruptions for review steps? Have sufficient oversight processes been established?
Geographical location	The specific physical location of a job, process, or location and the people performing the work.	Has work been organized to maximize face-to-face communication? Is work location planned to facilitate adjacent or linear process steps by those nearby?
Integration	The extent to which business units, departments, or individuals share information, gain cross-functional involvement/responsibility, and coordinate decision making with other units.	Have we optimized jobs that will benefit from cross-functional collaboration and open access to communication between units, departments, or individuals? Have we identified processes or mechanisms to maintain effective cross-functional coordination and communication, even when work is not in the same geographical area?
Personnel capabilities	The set of competencies and skills required to perform the job.	Have we identified an objective staffing process with sufficient structure and parameters to ensure jobs are actually filled with individuals with the skills and competencies needed to successfully perform the work?
Bench strength	The degree to which individuals with the right skills or competencies are available to back up or fill positions in both a short-term and a long-term need.	Have we provided sufficient job rotation, cross-training, flexibility, and developmental "stretch" assignments to broaden skills?

EXHIBIT 8.2. GROWTH RATES IN THE U.S. WORKFORCE.

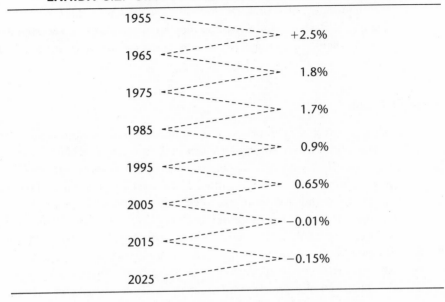

1955	
1965	+2.5%
1975	1.8%
1985	1.7%
1995	0.9%
2005	0.65%
2015	−0.01%
2025	−0.15%

EXHIBIT 8.3. AGE-RELATED DEMOGRAPHIC CHANGES IN THE U.S. WORKFORCE.

Age of Worker	1970–1980	1996–2006
16–19	+30.6%	+14.3%
20–24	50.0%	14.0%
25–34	72.4%	−8.8%
35–44	23.6%	−3.0%
45–54	0.0%	25.1%
55–64	5.3%	54.0%
65+	−6.1%	9.2%

discussions of structure, and making actual staffing decisions. Effective preparation requires detailed policies, process maps, templates, and user-friendly tools that can be deployed quickly when they are needed. An officer from the executive staff should be assigned to manage these processes and ensure adherence to them; they should not be regarded as optional exercises.

Prompt Action

According to Jeff Hemmer, vice president, customer supply chain, of Equistar Chemicals LP, a Houston-based leader in the specialty and commodity chemicals business, "Nothing much happens in a merger integration until the organization is set." This is a reliable observation. To gain full understanding of the important relationships and realities of the Newco organization, people need to see an organizational chart. Far more than a "pretty picture," the organizational chart serves an essential clarification and instructional role, helping to improve the effectiveness of communication and decision-making processes and fostering an atmosphere of common courtesy.

For example, during a particularly difficult integration meeting with a newly acquired company in Brazil, Millennium Inorganic Chemicals senior vice president Don Abbott skillfully brought about an important breakthrough. The Brazilian executive staff and task force leaders were having extreme difficulty grasping the concept of a global matrix organization. Detailed verbal explanations were only confusing the issue; nevertheless, because much of the structural decision making was yet to be formally approved, there was little more that could be communicated. During a lunch break, Don hurriedly sketched out a best-guess model that illustrated the complex interrelationships. A draft of Don's quick sketch was faxed to staff members in the United States, who immediately created a clean diagram and e-mailed it back to the core team in Brazil. When this preliminary model was distributed to the Brazilian partners, they connected with it immediately. A subsequent discussion of how to communicate and manage in the global matrix yielded specific action plans, events, and descriptions of responsibilities that everyone understood with respect to who would be involved, when, and in what issues. Exhibit 8.4 shows one task force's discussion model.

GE Capital also advocates a fast process for determining structure and staffing (Ashkenas, De Monaco, and Francis, 1998). Remember, the pace of integration affects outcomes; a good rule of thumb in many cases is that decisions should be carried out as quickly as possible after the deal closes. Doing so buffers the inevitable psychological letdown of those managers who are not joining the Newco organization, and it helps reassure other employees that there is no other shoe

EXHIBIT 8.4. EFFECTIVE COMMUNICATIONS MATRIX: FINANCE FUNCTION.

	Functional Management	Geographic Management
Who	Direct manager ————————————→ Global functional Team Direct employees	Geographic business team
What to communicate	Core functional work and ————→ reports Advisories/requests for ————————→ information (for example, financial impact of strike; items having financial impact on business) Information sharing/best- ————————→ practice networking	
How to communicate/ what format	E-mail ————————————————→ Voice mail ————————————————→ Conference calls ————————————→ Video teleconferences ——————————→ Face-to-face meetings ——————————→ Paper reports ——————————————→	
Timing/frequency	Reports (monthly) ——————————→ CFO meetings (monthly) Biweekly conference calls (regional controllers)	
Notes/comments Primary role distinction	Technical expert	Business adviser/consultant to team

about to drop. When key staff are needed in transitional roles but will not be joining the Newco organization, specific bridging arrangements should specify precise performance expectations, length of stay, and nullification or cancellation provisions if these terms are not met.

Triangulation, Validation, and Assessment

A seasoned executive recruiter once passed along this pearl of wisdom about making the best possible selection decisions: "I always follow my gut instincts, but I never trust those instincts until I've made sure I've gone through all the rigorous homework possible." Similarly, in a merger integration, it is folly to trust one hiring manager's instincts without soliciting other input. Each organization will need to determine its own optimal level of involvement and assessment, of course. Nevertheless, the baseline process should always include, at the minimum, input from the candidate's current organization, input from the Newco organization and the current hiring manager, and data from an external assessment tool or an interview with an outside professional. With regard to the external assessment, many organizations rely on one or more proprietary tools that are commercially available. It should be emphasized that any assessment tool is to be used only as a means of bringing data into the decision process, not as the sole basis of a unilateral staffing decision. Nevertheless, consistent use of the same assessment tool across an entire organization or business unit can provide very useful information as a complement to the selection process itself. Most assessments are capable of analyzing and reporting on an entire team of managers, or on the entire leadership structure of the company, and these analyses can highlight group strengths, gaps, and methods to help maximize the effectiveness of teams and the individuals on those teams.

Open Communication About Structure and Staffing Decisions

Research and practical experience have shown that most employees want the truth and can respond to it far more effectively than they can to uncertainty, ambiguity, delay, and prolonged agony. A recent study (Watson Wyatt Worldwide, 1997) found that 30 percent of executives who were surveyed said that the greatest barrier to change was the organization's lack of communication about tough structural or staffing decisions. This barrier was reported more frequently than the usual culprits: employee resistance (reported by 15 percent of the executives) and inadequate change-management skills (reported by 13 percent). Once the organization has defined the steps of the process that will be followed in making structural and staffing decisions, this information should be widely disseminated throughout the organization. It will also be necessary to communicate more specifically with certain groups of stakeholders who will experience the strongest impacts of these decisions:

- People who have received (or will be receiving) offers of employment with the Newco organization
- People who definitely will be needed in short-term transitional roles but not in the Newco organization
- Individuals who are currently in limbo, with no job offers and no news about future full-time or transitional roles with the Newco organization
- Individuals who are currently in outplacement or awaiting notification that their jobs have been eliminated

Timelines for making these decisions should also be established and published, to drive accountability for managers completing the process and to set expectations and keep the rest of the organization updated. One client's staffing calendar is shown in Exhibit 8.5. Each level of the organization was given an aggressive but achievable deadline for making decisions and getting them approved by its immediate boss; business units and functional areas were given some flexibility, as necessary, in keeping with the complexity of the restructuring and with competing priorities on other integration issues.

Training the Hiring Managers

Because of the overwhelming number of their other commitments, managers will fight to get out of every possible meeting. Therefore, in order to work effectively, they will need tailored instructions, and this is a time to pull out all the stops. For some organizations or functions, it may be appropriate to provide a comprehensive classroom-based training program, including an overview of the hiring process, role clarification, instructional walk-through of specific hiring tools and forms, thorough discussion of legal requirements and risks, and skill-building exercises related to techniques of structured behavioral interviewing and common rating biases to be avoided. For other organizations, it may be appropriate to provide various tools, resources, and reminders (a help line, for example, can be established or made available on request). One of our clients, a frequent acquirer, has trained all hiring managers over the past twenty-four months and continues to publish periodic refreshers and resources during the staffing process for new deals. Exhibit 8.6 shows one such periodic reminder, which was customized to the particular challenges and complexities of the current deal.

EXHIBIT 8.5. STAFFING CALENDAR MATRIX.

Direct report to:	Business Unit 1	Business Unit 2	Business Unit 3	Business Unit 4	Business Unit 5	Business Unit 6	Business Function 1	Business Function 2	Business Function 3	Business Function 4	Business Function 5
CEOCOO (Level 1)	28 Jul	28 Jul	28 Jul	28 Jul							
Director/ Manager (Level 3)	07 Aug	07 Aug									
Depart- ment Unit											
Organi- zation											
Total Head Count											
Prior to JV											
After JV											
Variance											

EXHIBIT 8.6. RECRUITING TIPS FOR MERGER STAFFING.

- Develop Summary Position Descriptions

    Verify compensation and benefit plan specifics with HR rep.

    Take your best shot—don't overnegotiate must-haves.

    Outline and review your offer conversation.

- Strategic Fit and Professional Context

    Watch out for the forest-for-the-trees syndrome.

    People need to be reminded of the compelling business opportunity and the fact that they are an important part of that.

- Interpersonal and Reporting Relationships

    People want to like their boss/those they will be working with.

    Do something for the family, especially if relocation is involved.

- The Schmooze Factor

    People want to be wanted . . . this is a "fraternity rush."

    Give a realistic job preview, especially now; people need to know what it's really like (for example, "Will have typical plant level discretion").

    Don't mislead or dangle unrealistic future possibilities.

- Coach Candidates Through the Issues

    Get their concerns on the table, and deal with them honestly.

    Share your personal insights and encouragement, but stay out of getting them embroiled in your personal agendas.

- Close the Sale

    Every marketer knows you have to follow up hot leads while they're hot. The longer you wait with no contact, the more likely they are to lose interest.

    Know your "wiggle room," and be creative with extras.

- Surround 'em with Allies

    Pull out the stops—ask other colleagues to tactfully reinforce your offer/the opportunity.

    Be prepared for second-guessing.

    Do anything to keep the conversation going if they start to vacillate or back out.

- Tailor Your Efforts

    Recruiting and management efforts should be customized to preferences/needs of individuals. What's most important to them? (Secure retirement, location, influence and authority, professional development, respect and recognition, and so on.)

Catching and Correcting Mistakes

Bauman, Jackson, and Lawrence (1997) tell the story of merger integration at the global pharmaceutical firm SmithKline Beecham. After much work and painstaking effort to ensure that all structure and staffing decisions worldwide would actually be made according to the desired values and performance-based principles, the company demonstrated that it meant what it had said. As soon as news broke that the hiring manager for the leadership team in one country's business unit had composed a new management team entirely of his old colleagues, the vice president of human resources, Peter Jackson, was on a plane. With only a day's notice, Jackson flew in to speak directly with managers from both partner companies, to gain an understanding of how the staffing decisions had been reached. After hours of one-to-one meetings, Jackson learned that the violation had been more an error of judgment than a blatant attempt to protect former colleagues. The country manager had based his decisions on the short-term sales objectives, which were largely driven by existing products most familiar to the present team, rather than considering who had the best ability to grow the business over the long term. Given the enormous potential for negative fallout from this apparent high-level disregard for the stated cultural and business objectives, Jackson had the country manager reconsider his recommendations and worked closely with him to redefine the new team, this time with more of a strategic composition for longer-term business requirements. It is this kind of responsiveness that will be required in setting and delivering on expectations for fairness and objectivity.

Capturing Results and Retaining Knowledge

In a merger integration there will be the disappointing reality of not getting or not keeping certain key managers or technical talent desperately needed by the Newco organization, so if you don't get the "sale," get the lesson instead. Surprisingly few organizations are effective at continuing their normal and customary practices of exit interviews or debriefings with candidates who reject job offers. Without this feedback, however, the organization is doomed to repeat its mistakes. Likewise, when a business unit places a key candidate or achieves certain staffing milestones, this information should be captured and publicized as a part of the organizational staffing announcements communicated to relevant portions of the organization.

Many active acquirers are also intent on capturing organizational knowledge, especially from key employees who are leaving. For example, one company with an innovative solution to this issue is Harvard Pilgrim Health Care. To prevent institutional knowledge from walking out the door with departing employees, it pays a "knowledge bounty." Further, to prevent the perception that it rewards people for leaving, and to demonstrate that knowledge is a valuable commodity that should be shared, it pays incoming and departing employees alike for what they know. Upon entering or leaving the company, employees fill out a job workbook, with key job components, knowledge, techniques, secret code words, processes that they use, and learning needs. Each person presents his or her answers to a panel of managers and peers, who pay the individual between $1,000 and $5,000 for the knowledge shared.

Early Development and Team Building

The selection process, correctly designed and administered, will yield important information that the hiring manager needs in order to lead and develop the new direct reports effectively. Specific process tools and steps should be in place for capturing this information and linking it to developmental plans and processes aimed at improving the effectiveness of the new team.

One mechanism that has had great success is the Newco managers' meeting. This meeting, conducted immediately before or immediately after the deal closes, has the purpose of getting the top leaders of the company, or specific functions or business units, together as quickly as possible to help with the necessary steps of formulating and establishing an identity. This meeting is a good time to promote clear understanding of and commitment to the Newco organization's strategy and business plan and to its core values and cultural objectives. It is also a good time to verify and assign key day 1 or early-transition business-process instructions and to focus the team's problem-solving efforts on essential short-term breakthroughs that will have the maximum potential impact.

Fair Processes

When the stakes are high and levels of stress are even higher, organizations must implement and adhere to objective processes for making decisions about structure and staffing. Just as important, however, is that these processes be widely perceived as fair. Kim and Mauborgne (1997, p. 65) illustrate this corporate reality with the following story:

> A London policeman gave a woman a ticket for making an illegal turn. When the woman protested that there was no sign prohibiting the turn, the policeman pointed to one that was bent out of shape and difficult to see from the

road. Furious, she decided to appeal by going to court. Finally, the day of her hearing arrived and she could hardly wait to speak her mind. She had just begun to tell her side of the story when the magistrate stopped her and summarily ruled in her favor. How did the woman feel? Vindicated? Victorious? Satisfied? No, she was frustrated and deeply unhappy. "I came for justice," she complained, "but the magistrate never let me explain what happened." In other words, although she liked the outcome, she didn't like the process that had created it.

As a general rule, managers must remember that people care about more than just outcomes; above all else, they must know that fair processes have been used, and that all the factors involved in decisions have been considered fairly. This truth becomes even more important when the outcome of a decision is loss of a job, derailment of a career, and the consequent disruption of a life. Adherence to fair processes has also been found to have a significant influence on whether people will exhibit the attitudes and behavior (such as trust, innovation, and knowledge sharing) that are essential to achieving a high-performance organization. Conversely, the absence of fair processes yields attitudes and behavior that can seriously disrupt integration proceedings and permanently mar employees' perceptions of the company, its management, and their own need for personal commitment to the enterprise. For example, during the initial kickoff meeting of an integration project, the vice president of a German pharmaceutical company made the following remark: "It's clear to me now that when we did our last acquisition, three years ago, we basically did everything wrong. Those employees and managers never forgave us, and the performance of that division never regained its former level."

Kim and Mauborgne (1997) offer three guiding principles for establishing fair process:

1. Engage the people involved or potentially affected by asking for their input and allowing them to debate the validity of the ideas and assumptions informing this decision.
2. Offer explanations so that everyone affected by a decision actually understands not only what is going on, and why it is going on, but also the steps, roles, and responsibilities leading to the decision, as well as the rationale that underlies the specific outcomes.
3. Be clear about expectations so that the decision can be carried out and its implications can be discussed openly and honestly.

Especially when a merger-related staffing decision is to be made, the organization must identify and explain a rational process, gain meaningful input from those affected by this process, announce an objective rationale and the resulting decision, and make clear that the decision will be implemented not just with expediency but with respect and due regard for the dignity of those affected by it. This lesson was powerfully demonstrated by one manager's impassioned feedback during a focus-group session for employees that was part of a recent integration:

> It's been six months since the merger was announced. The trade journals have said there will be at least a 10 percent reduction, but the company hasn't said anything. We see interviews and meetings taking place, but nobody seems to know who's in charge, or what the next step is, or when it will happen. And even if they did know, you can be sure they wouldn't be able to make a decision. It seems like every last detail has to go all the way to [the] corporate [level] for review and approval. A friend of mine got a job offer the other day, and the hiring manager said that pay, benefits, and incentive plans hadn't been approved yet! How do they expect us to have confidence in a new organization or a new boss, when all we see is "dumb and dumber"?

Staffing Process Models

To reinforce and support its good intentions and general principles, the organization should provide a variety of process maps, tools, and templates for managers and employees to use when candidates are to be rated and interviewed and staffing decisions are to be made.

A Streamlined Model

One successful acquirer, noted for speed to market and fast decision making, chose to implement a very brief, streamlined process for staffing decisions, a process that would be consistent with the way its managers were used to operating. Senior executives began the process by outlining their desired objectives, which included the following items:

- Use this opportunity to build a higher-performance organization.
- Create an organization with fewer and more productive people than the competition's (a goal to be achieved in part through fewer organizational levels and wider spans of control).
- Settle the Newco organization quickly through reassurances that the right people with the right skills have been placed in the right jobs and are doing the right things.

- Ensure integrity in decision making through objective consideration of people and their abilities and of the business needs.
- Make sure that people who have not been offered roles in the Newco organization are handled sensitively and provided assistance.

The human resources function was then asked to define a process for delivering these objectives in an expedient, low-impact way. (Exhibit 8.7 illustrates the model that was used to ensure fast, objective consideration of all viable candidates.) The following specific process instructions were provided via live briefings, e-mail, and individually facilitated staffing meetings:

1. *Get strategic clarification.* Gain a quick understanding of the purpose of major work activities your department is to perform in the new organization.

2. *Develop summary position descriptions.* In the context of the Newco role for your function, department, or unit, create summary position descriptions [see Exhibit 8.8]. This information is essential to gaining the right candidates and establishing appropriate pay ranges.

3. *Identify and rate candidates.* Develop a list of incumbents from both companies and high-potential candidates (if any exist) from other functions. Rate each candidate on each dimension [of the rating form shown in Exhibit 8.9] according to how well he or she matches with the summary position description. Ratings should be provided by current managers.

4. *Select candidates.* Interviews should be conducted with top candidates. Consider multiparty interviews, to ensure that objective data are gathered. (The HR generalist could provide this support. In tie-breaker situations, you also have the option of recommending an

EXHIBIT 8.7. STREAMLINED STAFFING PROCESS MODEL.

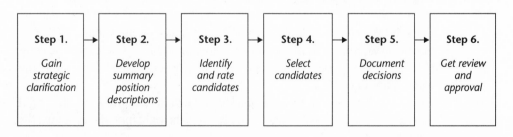

Step 1.	**Step 2.**	**Step 3.**	**Step 4.**	**Step 5.**	**Step 6.**
Gain strategic clarification	*Develop summary position descriptions*	*Identify and rate candidates*	*Select candidates*	*Document decisions*	*Get review and approval*

EXHIBIT 8.8. SUMMARY POSITION DESCRIPTION.

Position Title: _____

Supervisor's Title: _____

Department: _____

Location: _____

BASIC FUNCTION: A brief statement indicating why the job exists. Clearly define the specific role of the position in the organization.

JOB SPECIFICATIONS: Define the typical knowledge and experience required for the job. Include technical or specialized knowledge and experience, supervisory or managerial skills, human relations skills, and any professional certification or licensing required.

RESPONSIBILITIES AND ACCOUNTABILITIES: Please state the key responsibilities and accountabilities of the position.

-
-
-
-
-
-
-

DIMENSIONS: Provide any appropriate indicators of the scope of the position. Dimensions should relate to the business results the job affects. Data should be current. It need not be exact—estimates are fine.

Annual Operation Budget	$ _____	Employees Supervised _____
Revenues Produced	$ _____	Product Volumes _____
Capital Expenditures	$ _____	

REVIEW:

Line Manager	Date
Human Resources Consultant	Date

EXHIBIT 8.9. NEWCO RATING FORM.

CANDIDATE PROFILE RECORD: For each dimension, please rate each candidate as follows: H = High Match; M = Medium Match; L = Low Match.

CORE COMPETENCIES:

Communication: Demonstrates effective oral and written communication skills that enable others to clearly receive and act upon the message. Provides input/feedback in a timely, direct, and candid manner. Uses active listening to enhance understanding of information or direction given.

Initiative: Proactively seeks opportunities for continuous improvement in order to meet and exceed business objectives. Moti-

vated and interested in the success of the company as well as in professional development. Takes on challenging assignments and is willing to work on long-range objectives. Maintains high standards to ensure customer satisfaction and excellent business performance. Demonstrates honesty and integrity in all actions.

Work Planning: Determines what needs to be done and how it can be achieved in a logical, systematic, and cost-effective way.

Core Competencies

Candidate's Name	Years of Experience	Overall Knowledge and Skills	Communication	Initiative	Work Planning

Notes:

Completed By: _____

Evaluates priorities and coordinates required resources, actions, and methods to ensure successful completion. Measures progress/effectiveness of actions against plan.

Problem Solving: Employs sound, creative thought processes to arrive at innovative solutions or breakthroughs. Bases recommendations on facts and logical assumptions, balancing customer needs with business priorities. Displays a bias for action.

Leadership: Takes charge and leads in a facilitative manner. Achieves desired results while balancing the needs of the company, group, and individuals. Collaborates with others to accomplish organizational goals. Acknowledges and communicates appreciation to others for their contributions.

Core Competencies

Problem Solving	Leadership	Historical Work Performance	Historical Supportiveness of Change	Willingness to Relocate	Overall Evaluation	Selected?

Date: _____

independent managerial assessment by a certified industrial psychologist or a consultant.)

5. *Document decisions.* Note the rationale for each of your selections, and use a separate list to identify candidates who were not selected. Coordinate salary range, salary offer, and EEO analysis with HR.

6. *Get review and approval.* The functional vice president will review and approve the analysis [step 1] of departmental purpose, structure, and headcount before any staffing decisions are made. The hiring manager's manager will review and approve individual staffing decisions and hiring decisions.

A More Comprehensive Model

Other organizations may have success with a more comprehensive staffing process model (see Exhibit 8.10). In this model, steps 1 through 5 constitute the "Analyze" phase. Step 1 is the workforce planning and forecasting module, where a comprehensive plan for rationalization and consolidation is developed. The strategic business plan and the major parameters or "givens" of the deal are combined with specific due-diligence information and cost projections to provide a variety of scenarios to senior managers. Step 2 includes a structured process for assessing the mission-critical jobs needed in carrying out the business plan of the Newco organization and keeping its primary focus. Steps 3 and 4 establish the specific competencies required in the mission-critical jobs. (Existing data are to be used whenever it is possible to do so, but new data may also be required, given the new roles required by the Newco organization). In step 5, the final competencies are defined and "wordsmithed" so as accurately to portray the specific behavior, attitudes, and actions that the organization perceives as essential to success in these particular roles.

Steps 6 through 8 constitute the "Focus" phase of the model. In step 6, the company compiles a complete list of incumbent candidates from both parent companies and provides an opportunity for other interested candidates to present themselves for consideration. Employees are given a biographical data form, and process instructions are distributed electronically to all interested candidates. The form captures basic employment data in addition to information about the candidate's education, certifications, special training, relevant work experience, skills, specialized knowledge, and expertise. A narrative portion gives the employee an opportunity to list particularly noteworthy career accomplishments and comment on specific aspects relevant for consideration. A copy of the form is returned to the local HR representative and forwarded to the hiring manager. In step 7, multiple raters are asked to complete a survey (see Exhibit 8.11) and to

EXHIBIT 8.10. COMPREHENSIVE STAFFING PROCESS MODEL.

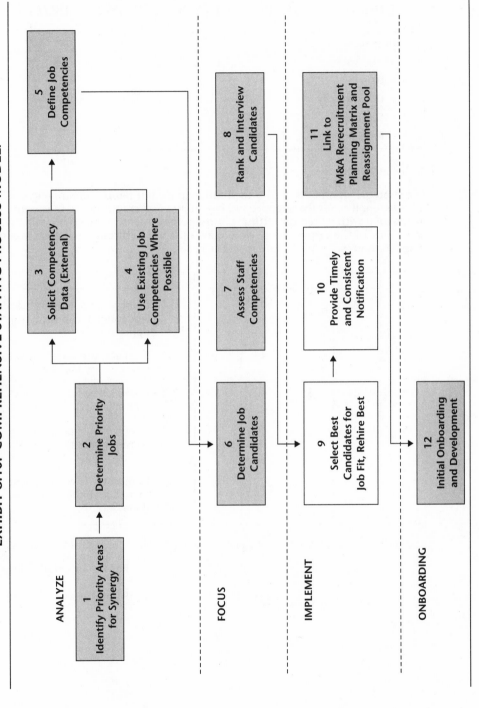

EXHIBIT 8.11. SAMPLE PAGE FROM ASSESSMENT SURVEY.

Rating Scale:

5 = Always

4 = Usually

3 = Occasionally

2 = Seldom

1 = Rarely, if ever

7. Results-Oriented

The strategic vision of Newco is the road map for our people, identifying our destination. It takes the support and ingenuity of all employees to reach our destination with a "can do" attitude and a commitment to the vision, mission, and values of the organization. Newco lives the vision through our actions and decisions and by keeping our eye on the road.

1	2	3	4	5	7.1	Recognized potential challenges and turns them into opportunities.
1	2	3	4	5	7.2	Connects the vision to daily job activities and decisions.
1	2	3	4	5	7.3	Demonstrates a "can do" attitude.
1	2	3	4	5	7.4	Leads by example, showing consistency between words and actions.
1	2	3	4	5	7.5	Demonstrates commitment to and celebrates organizational success.

Add the columns cumulatively (if you have circled three 2s, then they total 6).

_____ + _____ + _____ + _____ = **Results-Oriented Total**

(Total ÷ 5) = **Results-Oriented Average**

assess each candidate against set competencies. Among the raters are the current incumbent's manager and an internal customer who is selected by the manager from a list submitted by the employee. Then the current managers and a staffing consultant attend a meeting where all the assessment surveys are reviewed, validated, and scored; the rating team tries to reach consensus as often as possible. Candidates' names are listed in rank order on a scoresheet matrix (see Exhibit 8.12), which gives summary information about all the candidates being considered. In step 8, team interviews are conducted by the incumbents' managers and by the supporting HR generalist or the staffing consultant assigned to the particular business unit. A competency-based interview guide is then used to determine specific evidence of the candidates' behavior and achievements in each major competency area (see Exhibit 8.13).

Steps 9, 10, and 11 constitute the "Implement" phase of the model. In step 9, the rating team meets to discuss the slate of candidates and recommend final rankings. Specific details are discussed with respect to creating the best offers and opportunities for all candidates involved. In step 10, a communication plan is completed. Before the successful candidates are notified of their selection, all recommendations are reviewed and approved with the functional executive officer, and they are also validated by human resources. In step 11, any candidates not initially selected are maintained in an available talent pool for a period of thirty to sixty days. To ensure that desired key talent is retained, managers are reminded of the rerecruitment process and of the tools available for their use.

Step 12 constitutes the "Onboarding" phase of the model. In this step, the hiring managers meet individually with the successful candidates to plan approaches to key issues, work out details of the transition to the Newco organization, set priorities, and define developmental opportunities. For acquired employees joining the Newco organization and for relocating employees, additional orientation and transition briefings are provided.

EXHIBIT 8.12. SAMPLE PAGE FROM SCORESHEET MATRIX.

FIRST RANKING CORE COMPETENCY ASSESSMENT MATRIX

SUPERVISOR: _____

DEPARTMENT: _____

COMPANY: ☐ Company A ☐ Company B

DATE: _____

CONSULTANT: _____

CONSENSUS RATING

R A N K	EMPLOYEE NAME	JOB TITLE	1	2	3	4	5	6	7	8	AVERAGE SCORE	COMMENTS/ JUSTIFICATION

Competencies:

1 = Agility
2 = Business knowledge
3 = Communication

4 = Customer focus
5 = Decision making
6 = Human energy

7 = Strategic vision
8 = Teamwork

EXHIBIT 8.13. SAMPLE PAGE FROM INTERVIEW GUIDE.

4. Customer Focus

Serving the customer is the heart of XYZ. The core of our business is to make our customers happy both in and outside of XYZ. Employees who are committed to satisfying the customer are enterprising, making that extra effort to provide quality service. It is the right thing to do.

Interview Questions:

1. Tell me about a time when a customer (internal or external) was dissatisfied with your service. What was the situation, and what did you do to remedy the situation?

2. What process have you used to determine your customer's expectations?

3. How would you define quality customer service?

Look for evidence that candidate:

- Contributes to improving processes for better satisfying customers

- Demonstrates a commitment to providing high-quality products and services to both internal and external customers

- Seeks to exceed customers' expectations

Situation	Action Taken	Result/Outcome

Competency rating: Circle the number that best describes the candidate's competency.

5 = Exceptional

4 = Usually demonstrates competency

3 = Occasionally demonstrates competency

2 = Seldom demonstrates competency

1 = Not exceptional; rarely, if ever, demonstrates competency

CHAPTER NINE

KEEPING TRACK OF SUCCESS: MERGER MEASUREMENT SYSTEMS

Organizations have to keep their head in the clouds but their feet on the ground. The best measurement process strikes a balance between metrics focused on synergies and those focused on the day-to-day operations.

J. HEMMER, VICE PRESIDENT, CUSTOMER SUPPLY CHAIN, EQUISTAR CHEMICALS LP

During a client engagement, we presented the company's executive staff with the rationale and strategy for a comprehensive process of measurement and feedback. After our meeting, the vice president in charge of merger integration teasingly chided us for "messing up a pretty comfortable arrangement." "Until now," he explained, "our executive team has had a 'don't ask, don't tell' policy surrounding mergers. I don't ask what the next deal is going to be, and they don't ask me how this one is going." Here's a toast to simpler times—may the memories be pleasant. Now, on to a more effective process for focusing the organization's efforts in the heat of battle.

The unfortunate reality is that many organizations, as our client pointed out, have failed to establish sufficient mechanisms for tracking and reporting on the results from a variety of distinctly different types of merger integration measures. As a consequence, right when the organization and its people need the greatest amount of focused, effective performance-related feedback, they typically get the least.

Marks and Mirvis (1992, p. 282) articulate the need to capture information about "how things are going and people's reactions" through a combination of surveys, focus groups, interviews, and the like. They conclude that a formal tracking process is of benefit because it serves the following functions:

- Determining whether the transition is proceeding according to plan
- Identifying "hot spots" before they flare out of control
- Ensuring a good flow of communication
- Highlighting the need for midcourse corrections
- Demonstrating interest in the human side of change
- Involving more people in the combination process
- Sending a message about the new company's culture

Marks and Mirvis's recommendation is good counsel, and in today's fast-paced, merciless merger environment, companies need even more direct, timely feedback. We believe that there are actually four areas for which separate but interrelated measurement processes must be continually managed during merger integration (see Exhibit 9.1):

1. *Integration measures* are necessary in assessing specific integration events and mechanics and thereby determining whether the overall integration approach is accomplishing its mission of leading the organization through change. Examples of such measures would be brief surveys of task force members and employee focus groups, or feedback received via a confidential hotline.
2. *Operational measures* are necessary in tracking any potential merger-related impact on the organization's ability to conduct its continuing, day-to-day business. Examples of such measures would include statistics that reflect sudden changes in health- and safety-related incidents or that indicate more than the normal number of productivity- or quality-related issues or that reveal an inability to process accounts receivable in a timely manner.
3. *Process and cultural measures* are necessary in determining the status of merger-driven efforts to redesign business processes or elements of the organizational culture. Examples of such measures would include reports (in terms of percentages) on the completion status of task forces' integration plans, specific surveys of the internal customers of a given process (to spot bottlenecks or new disruptions that are due to the merger), and periodic feedback identifying pressure points with respect to how things are being done in the Newco organization.
4. *Financial measures* are necessary in tracking and reporting on whether the organization is achieving the expected synergies of the deal. Examples of such measures would include ongoing summaries of the actual synergy projects in process and the economic value of those already captured, plus some kind of synergy-related communications.

EXHIBIT 9.1. FOUR AREAS FOR MEASUREMENT.

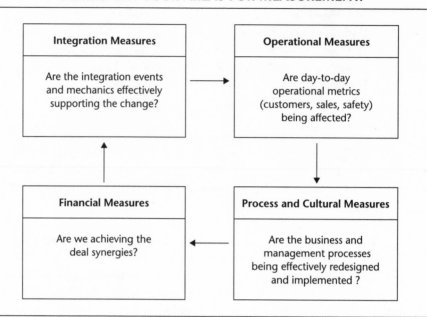

Only when these four separate kinds of measures are sufficiently developed and linked will the executive staff be able to gain an objective understanding of how the merger is going, and of the impact that the merger is having on the relevant stakeholder groups.

Integration Measures

Merger measurement systems need to evolve as the integration evolves into each successive phase. Typically the first measure taken is an assessment of the integration process as perceived by the task force leaders, the core team members, and executive staff members. Exhibit 9.2 shows a simple tool for conducting this assessment.

An initial assessment covering the first eight questions can be conducted during the kickoff meeting for task force leaders. Initial baseline data will be useful in comparing subsequent follow-up assessment results. More important, an early initial assessment will invariably provide some pointed feedback regarding the need for faster information transfer or more attention to "me issues." This assessment

EXHIBIT 9.2. INTEGRATION PROCESS ASSESSMENT.

In general, please indicate how well you believe the integration of ABC Co. and XYZ Co. has progressed in the following areas. To date . . .

	Extremely Inadequate		Adequate			Extremely Adequate	

1. *Overall employee communications* about the process have been . . .

    1   2   3   4   5   6   7

Comments/Suggestions: _____

_____

2. The amount and quality of *personal information transfer* from managers to their respective direct reports have been . . .

    1   2   3   4   5   6   7

Comments/Suggestions: _____

_____

3. The understanding of Newco *vision, values, and business strategy* by management and employees has been . . .

    1   2   3   4   5   6   7

Comments/Suggestions: _____

_____

4. The progress of the *operational integration* (how effectively we have merged our business practices) has been . . .

    1   2   3   4   5   6   7

Comments/Suggestions: _____

_____

5. The processes used for making and managing Newco *staffing, rerecruiting, and relocation decisions* have been . . .

    1   2   3   4   5   6   7

Comments/Suggestions: _____

_____

6. The way *"me issues"* (benefits, pay, job responsibilities, reporting relationships) are handled has been . . .

    1   2   3   4   5   6   7

Comments/Suggestions: _____

_____

(*continued*)

EXHIBIT 9.2. (*continued*)

	Extremely Inadequate		Adequate			Extremely Adequate

7. The focus on preserving/enhancing *safety, ongoing operations, sales, and customer service* has been . . .   1   2   3   4   5   6   7

Comments/Suggestions: _____

_____

8. The effectiveness of processes for *making decisions and knowing whom to go to* has been . . .   1   2   3   4   5   6   7

Comments/Suggestions: _____

_____

The next series of questions pertains to the mechanics of the task force integration process and various project management disciplines used.

9. Please rate the effectiveness of the following integration events and processes:

	Extremely Inadequate		Adequate			Extremely Adequate

A. Deal announcement/initial planning   1   2   3   4   5   6   7

Comments/Suggestions: _____

_____

B. Task force kickoff meeting   1   2   3   4   5   6   7

Comments/Suggestions: _____

_____

C. Weekly conference calls and meeting notes   1   2   3   4   5   6   7

Comments/Suggestions:

_____

D. Task force report/deliverables   1   2   3   4   5   6   7

Comments/Suggestions:

_____

EXHIBIT 9.2. (*continued*)

	Extremely Inadequate			Adequate			Extremely Adequate
E. Timeline/project plan	1	2	3	4	5	6	7
Comments/Suggestions:							
F. Task force follow-up meetings	1	2	3	4	5	6	7
Comments/Suggestions:							
G. Toll-free hotline	1	2	3	4	5	6	7
Comments/Suggestions:							
H. Day 1 events and process	1	2	3	4	5	6	7
Comments/Suggestions:							
I. Other	1	2	3	4	5	6	7
Comments/Suggestions:							

10. What other ideas or recommendations do you have for ensuring the success of other potential integration efforts in the future? (What else worked well and should be used again? What are new ideas or processes we should try? What did not work and needs to be deleted or upgraded?)

_____

_____

_____

_____

should be documented for the executive staff and task force leaders, to reinforce the need for each senior manager to do his or her part in the change-management communications. Questions 9 and 10 involve a different line of questioning, intended for later in the integration process. These questions are intended for task force leaders, subteam members, members of the core team, and others who have been directly involved in the process of integration planning and implementation. Near the end of the project, it is essential to capture feedback, learning, and process upgrades that can be used to build an ongoing institutional knowledge base regarding the integration process itself. As one part of this step, a specific effort should be made to consult with the combined group of task force leaders and collect documentation formats, reports, customized tools, and templates that have potential for reuse in subsequent deals.

Automated Feedback Channels

Another very important process for capturing integration-related feedback includes the use of various electronic technologies to establish safe and convenient methods for ventilating, asking questions, and offering suggestions. E-mail, confidential toll-free hotlines, and bulletin boards on a Web site are three tools that are very effective in gauging the types and intensity of employees' concerns. In one of our recent engagements with a client, all three tools were used by the task force responsible for communications and measurement, and their availability was widely publicized at the time of the initial internal announcement of the deal. During the first two weeks after the announcement, data from all three sources were "swept" daily. Comments were tallied and analyzed according to type of issue and were then sorted according to urgency and importance. When there was clear ownership of an issue and the need for a direct response, the task force leader submitted a confidential, "sanitized" list of issues to key executives, functional department heads, and other managers. The team worked directly with the subject-matter experts in each category of issue, to craft appropriate responses. By the next day, the previous day's issues and concerns were being answered through a variety of channels, which included the integration e-mail newsletter, departmental meetings, and presentations by senior executives. After this initial two-week period, the daily process of analyzing and responding to feedback became a weekly cycle that was continued through the end of the full integration project.

Shoe Leather

Even with the best technology-based feedback, executives and task force leaders still have to get out into the organization. There is simply no substitute for first-hand asking about, listening to, and observing what is going on. In spite of well-intentioned efforts in this area, it is understandable that many organizations still fall short, given the time crunch and the overwhelming nature of the urgent priorities. One technique that can accommodate this reality is the use of very fast, highly targeted telephone surveys. To test the miscellaneous feedback encountered in the field and to create the clarity needed for formulating an organizational response, the task force responsible for communications and measurement, or members of the core team themselves, should conduct brief, structured telephone interviews with stakeholders who can provide additional information.

For example, one recent integration effort was flooded with a variety of comments about the two organizations' perceived differences in communication and decision-making style. Because this feedback was trickling in from various people and various parts of the organization, each new comment offered a particular interpretation, and so it was virtually impossible to isolate the real issue, let alone the root cause. Rather than allow these issues to fester, a senior-level group of core team members came together to address the problem directly. Two dozen key stakeholders from both organizations were identified as individuals who were directly enough involved, and who were candid enough, to offer valuable insights. A structured interview guide was drafted so that the team members collecting the data would be defining issues and asking questions in a consistent manner. The team members were given one day to work the phones and bring their data back in summary form. The next day's meeting was charged with enthusiasm: the team, no longer perplexed by frustratingly diffuse comments, had been able to gather enough detail to understand the root cause of the issues being reported and to formulate potential solutions. At the end of this meeting, the team members were prepared to meet with the executive committee. They presented their consolidated findings, discussed the implications, and led the executive team through a series of action items intended to remedy the situation. The executive staff responded by commissioning and directly helping to implement a variety of action items grouped into three categories of urgency:

1. Things we will do this week
2. Things we will do in the next thirty days
3. Things we will do throughout the remainder of the integration project

Operational Measures

Mergers mean chaos, and chaos means that some desired processes may be temporarily disrupted or ignored, but the company's ongoing process for measuring operational results should not be one of them. As we have been saying, merger integration is the ultimate change-management challenge, in large part because the business must continue in the midst of the most disruptive, frustrating conditions conceivable. This point bears repeating here because organizational difficulties are compounded by the weight of personal stress, exhaustion, and uncertainty. When these pressures are left unchecked, a common psychological response is to be consumed by one's own internal, personal concerns, to the detriment of a focus on external, customer-related concerns. The establishment of the Newco organization's basic operational metrics should be an urgent short-term priority, to be implemented as quickly as possible after day 1. Specific metrics will need to be determined by each company on the basis of business requirements, but integration task forces can recommend initial measures for the Newco organization's basic operations.

Exhibit 9.3 shows the development process used by one acquirer to engage subject-matter experts from each function and process area in deciding what to measure and how measurement should be conducted, during the initial transition state as well as in the eventual "to be" state. In this example, an initial briefing was given to all task force leaders, to establish the overall objectives and expectations of the measurement initiative. Task forces compared the "as is" measurement processes from their respective companies and drafted initial recommendations for Newco measures that could be implemented in the short term. Functional officers reviewed and approved the recommendations, and the integration team developed an overall process to track, consolidate, and report summary business measures, a process that would begin in the first week of Newco operations. Subsequent measurement processes were phased in at various intervals as determined by specific task forces' needs or recommendations.

Another fundamental but often overlooked approach to measurement and tracking relies on establishing and communicating the critical success factors. Don Abbott, senior vice president of Millennium Inorganic Chemicals, has used this process very effectively to focus integration efforts, reinforce accountability, and celebrate results. As one part of the core team's initial planning for each new integration project, a set of factors critical to success is defined. These factors summarize the essential strategic business outcomes that must be achieved. For example, in one recent integration, a global acquisition, the following success factors were initially perceived as mission-critical:

- Delisting the company from the local country's stock market
- Retaining the key managers and the sales force
- Integrating the Millennium safety, health, and environmental programs into the new organization
- Achieving efficiencies in the manufacturing process

EXHIBIT 9.3. DEVELOPMENT PROCESS FOR MEASURING

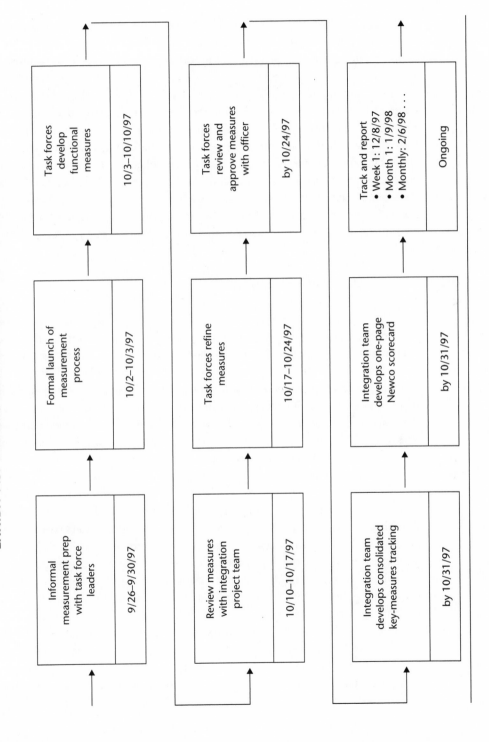

- Integrating the Millennium manufacturing technology into the new company
- Gaining positive reactions from customers, and retaining customers
- Maintaining and improving Millennium's reputation in the local community

Each of these broad objectives was supported by specific goals and desired outcomes, which were validated and refined by senior executives and task force leaders early in the process of planning the integration. The final list of critical success factors then became an integral part of the continuing communication and status-checking activities. A more formal process of accounting and reporting was conducted at each major project interval (on day 1, at completion of the hundred-day plan, at completion of the first year, and so on). Reported results were then quickly summarized and published throughout the organization, as a means of recognizing the work of the integration teams and the subject-matter experts.

Process and Cultural Measures

In addition to creating overall change-management mechanisms and processes for continuous measurement of operational results, the organization should create some kind of formal process for measuring the effectiveness of major merger-related redesign and cultural integration efforts. The consolidated project plan (see Chapter Five) provides a foundation for determining the status of all project milestones and tasks. Specifically targeted surveys, focus groups for internal customers, and other techniques can also be used to solicit more detailed comments and probe for additional issues related to major business processes that are undergoing rationalization or integration.

Given the high failure rate of mergers because of cultural factors, the organization must be in a position to accurately assess and respond to the inevitable bumps in the road toward creation of the Newco organization's desired culture. Exhibit 9.4 shows a representative sample of one organization's assessment of progress in this area. In this case, as one part of a comprehensive process for cultural integration, an extensive communication and training campaign launched the values, behavioral guidelines, and performance expectations for the Newco organization throughout the organization. At intervals during the first year of the merger, and periodically until full integration was achieved, a similar survey was conducted among representative groups of managers and employees. The data were captured, tabulated, and analyzed according to which of the original parent companies the respondent was from, and to minimize the inherent "we-they" bias, the results were always summarized and publicly communicated as a single

EXHIBIT 9.4. CULTURAL PROGRESS CHECK.

Please circle the previous employer organization you are from:

XYZ Co.   ABC Co.

Instructions:

1. Briefly review the "Newco Way" document (attached), which outlines the future desired culture, values, and strategic focus for our organization.

2. Rate each cultural dimension listed below according to how effectively this "lever" is currently being used to drive the desired culture.

3. Note any specific examples, concerns, major discrepancies, or suggestions in the space provided.

Cultural Dimensions

1. Information Transfer

To what extent is information readily disseminated throughout the organization? (*Considerations:* Financial performance? Operating performance? Meeting notes and outcomes? What is routinely communicated? held back? Employee perceptions of open information sharing and access to news?)

| 1 | 2 | 3 | 4 | 5 | 6 | 7 | 8 | 9 | 10 |

| Lesser Extent | | Greater Extent |

Comments/Suggestions:

_____

_____

2. Feedback and Interpersonal Communication

To what degree do individuals receive appropriate feedback regarding objectives, instructions, and performance? (*Considerations:* Regularly scheduled meetings or informal conversations? Sufficient two-way dialogues? Open access to higher levels of management for communication and assistance?)

| 1 | 2 | 3 | 4 | 5 | 6 | 7 | 8 | 9 | 10 |

| Inadequate | | Adequate |

Comments/Suggestions:

_____

_____

(continued)

EXHIBIT 9.4. (*continued*)

3. Decision-Making Processes and Authority

To what degree are decisions made through streamlined and effective processes? (*Considerations:* Are responsibility and authority provided for the appropriate individuals/groups? Are decision processes well defined and understood? Is there agreement on what types of decisions should be directed versus delegated? To what degree are consensus building/multiple inputs expected?)

| 1 | 2 | 3 | 4 | 5 | 6 | 7 | 8 | 9 | 10 |

| Ineffective | | Effective |

Comments/Suggestions:

_____

_____

4. Leadership and Managerial Behavior

To what extent do managers consistently demonstrate desired behaviors and values? (*Considerations:* What percentage of time do managers lead through a coaching/facilitative approach versus an autocratic approach? How is desired leadership behavior factored into decisions for selection, rewards, and advancement?)

| 1 | 2 | 3 | 4 | 5 | 6 | 7 | 8 | 9 | 10 |

| Inconsistent | | Consistent |

Comments/Suggestions:

_____

_____

5. Policies, Rules, and Procedures

To what degree are policies, rules, and procedures appropriately defined? (*Considerations:* What level of detail is optimum? What protocols are required for low-risk procedures—other than compliance, safety, and the like? What degree of flexibility do supervisors have in applying policies?)

| 1 | 2 | 3 | 4 | 5 | 6 | 7 | 8 | 9 | 10 |

| Less Structure | | More Structure |

Comments/Suggestions:

_____

_____

EXHIBIT 9.4. (*continued*)

6. *Time-Based Advantage*

To what degree are speed and a sense of urgency considered essential to success? (*Considerations:* Controls on length of meetings? Short review/approval processes? 80/20 principle? General expectations?)

| 1 | 2 | 3 | 4 | 5 | 6 | 7 | 8 | 9 | 10 |

Lesser Degree   Greater Degree

Comments/Suggestions:

_____

_____

7. *Customer Focus*

To what extent is the organization focused on meeting the needs of customers (internal and external)? (*Considerations:* Customer satisfaction goals and measures that are widely known and communicated throughout the organization? Customer satisfaction metrics linked to broad performance rewards and incentives?)

| 1 | 2 | 3 | 4 | 5 | 6 | 7 | 8 | 9 | 10 |

Lesser Extent   Greater Extent

Comments/Suggestions:

_____

_____

8. *High Performance*

To what degree are employees sensitized and committed to continuous improvement in organizational and personal performance? (*Considerations:* How are organizational goals/objectives set and cascaded down to the team and individual levels? How are employees linked to these goals through rewards/recognition, communication, development/advancement opportunities?)

| 1 | 2 | 3 | 4 | 5 | 6 | 7 | 8 | 9 | 10 |

Lesser Degree   Greater Degree

Comments/Suggestions:

_____

_____

(continued)

EXHIBIT 9.4. (*continued*)

9. Employee Involvement

To what extent is employee involvement used for productivity improvements and/or positive employee relations? (*Considerations:* How widespread are employee teams? What roles and responsibilities do employee teams have, and at what levels? Are employees able to get involved with planning and managing activities like communications, social events, sports, or special committees and task forces?)

| 1 | 2 | 3 | 4 | 5 | 6 | 7 | 8 | 9 | 10 |

| Less Involved | | | | | | | More Involved |

Comments/Suggestions:

_____

_____

10. Training and Continuous Learning

What degree of importance has the organization established for development, training, and continuous learning? (*Considerations:* Actual use of training programs, learning resources, structured curricula, access to outside training, and educational reimbursements?)

| 1 | 2 | 3 | 4 | 5 | 6 | 7 | 8 | 9 | 10 |

| Lesser Degree | | | | | | | Greater Degree |

Comments/Suggestions:

_____

_____

11. Customs, Norms, and Ceremonies

To what extent has the organization defined ongoing events or processes to support the desired culture? (*Considerations:* What recognition processes exist to reinforce values-based behavior? What opportunities exist for the organization to celebrate successes and key learning?)

| 1 | 2 | 3 | 4 | 5 | 6 | 7 | 8 | 9 | 10 |

| Lesser Extent | | | | | | | Greater Extent |

Comments/Suggestions:

_____

_____

12. Other: Please specify. _____

_____

score for the Newco organization. The survey results were further validated with input from focus groups in areas of the organization where the survey had not been conducted. Soliciting this input allowed the results to be cross-checked and verified, and it served as a means of gaining the maximum practical amount of employee involvement. The integration core team and the task force for cultural integration then consolidated the combined findings and drafted specific action items for review and approval by the members of the executive staff.

The Merger Integration Scorecard

When Lyondell Petrochemical Company merged with Millennium Petrochemicals to form Equistar Chemicals LP, Jeff Hemmer, vice president, customer supply chain, of Equistar, served as project manager for the integration. He recognized that the two organizations had to have a convenient, expedient method for summarizing and reporting all the critical measures during the transition process.

"Organizations," he says, "have to keep their heads in the clouds but their feet on the ground. The best measurement process strikes a balance between metrics focused on synergies and those focused on the day-to-day operations. Before the merger, both organizations had very sophisticated, balanced-scorecard types of measurement processes, with a variety of cockpit charts, dashboards, and other displays to keep the respective companies focused. In our situation, it was impossible to redesign or consolidate those processes in the short term, but what we could do was to take the concept of the balanced scorecard and apply it immediately to those issues that were most susceptible to being disrupted during the merger."

The resulting "merger integration scorecard" (Exhibit 9.5) was an immediate hit with the executive officers, who could now get a quick "snapshot" type of status update for the most important critical success factors in key measurement categories. The scorecard used a nonthreatening rating scale (ahead of plan, on track, or behind plan), along with graphical icons, to indicate the status of each factor. Explanatory comments for each item were provided on the summary form, to facilitate detailed discussion and planning at the executive level. Because one objective of this process was to keep things simple, a streamlined data-gathering and data-rating process was used, to avoid placing additional significant time demands on task force leaders and senior managers. What this meant was that each category and each item was assigned a "process owner," who was responsible for capturing the data from the appropriate source or subject-matter expert. (Specific data sources, reports, and feedback sources were mapped to each item on the scorecard, to ensure that the right information

EXHIBIT 9.5. MERGER INTEGRATION SCORECARD.

	Indicators	Rating	Comments
Customer	Relationship with key accounts	◖	For polymers, system breakdowns initially forced internal versus external focus. The "simpler" petrochemical allowed for more frequent customer contact.
	Effectiveness of our order and delivery services	○	Breakdown in our transactional order-fulfillment process quickly noticed by our customers. Seeing results from actions initiated in 3/98.
Financial	Timely receipt of cash	◖	Trends (average days late, total past-due dollars) increased 11/97–3/98, with April showing improvements. Pulled together cross-functional team to address pricing issues.
	Organization's focus on capturing all identified synergies	◖	Ahead of budget. Concern Newco II may delay business-case development on petrochemical and feed-stock projects.
	Timely and accurate performance reporting	○	Lack of SAP datamart resulting in manual calculations for close. Business not getting concise information for decision making because systems not understood.
	Disbursements made to vendors on timely basis	◖	On-time payment rate averaging 85% versus industry best of 90%.
Operational	Accessibility to partner company's legacy system	◖	Complexity of MPC systems underestimated. Move to one box improved efficiency. Still at fragile stage. Pricing biggest gap. Unexpected downtime has caused delays.
	Are we purging the nice-to-haves? (Are we doing what is important and urgent?)	○	Business process and infrastructure gaps creating inefficiencies, resulting in work overload.
	Personnel permanently relocated?	◖	Physical relocations complete. New approach expected to improve feasibility, schedule, cost on construction schedule.
	Integration timelines meeting original schedule?	◖	77% of items completed. Remaining items relate to communicating how we work and to improving processes.
	Is SAP implementation on schedule for 10/5?	◖	All modules finalized design for 4/1. Tabletops highlighting gaps. Rollout communication and training needs nearing completion.
	Ability of infrastructure to handle workload	○	Lack of automated systems caused delay in 4/1 salary-adjustment timing. Large number of uncommitted IS requests.

EXHIBIT 9.5. (*continued*)

	Indicators	Rating	Comments
People	Number of second-wave resignations	●	In Nov.–Dec. had 8; 2 R&D and 2 sales during 1998.
	Training being completed on a timely basis	○	Focus needs to be on completing transition-related training only; learning curve still steep. Many started out knowing only 50% of the jobs.
	Are we rewarding and recognizing what we said we would?	◐	Too early to judge.
	Number of site-to-site transfers	●	Manufacturing actively working opportunities.
Organizational	Number and frequency of "Frank" and other communication vehicles	●	"Frank" and monthly employee meetings well received.
	Dialogue and information transfer flowing up, down, and across organization	○	Too "siloed." Problem resolution will improve with use of more cross-functional workout groups.
	Are we creating the Newco Way?	◐	We are bridging cultures.
	Are we involving enough employees in the process?	◐	Time to drive synergy work lower into organization.
	"How we work" process broadly understood by the organization?	◐	Materials Management and IS roadshows big help. Planning process next on the list.
	Critical business processes well documented?	○	Beginning to double back and do this.
Indicator Rating Scale		● Ahead ◐ On track ○ Behind	

would be consistently evaluated when ratings were made.) Once the data had been collected and summarized, the core team met to review this information, assign ratings, and prepare the scorecard document for executive officers' review.

Financial Measures

Effective measures of synergy must be based on a comprehensive process of planning and verifying the achievement of the expected synergies. Among the many synergy-measurement elements that the organization will need in order to ensure that it identifies and accomplishes its essential objectives, the following four components are recommended:

1. An education process
2. A verification process
3. Document templates for submitting, tracking, and summarizing the achievement of synergies
4. A process for reporting and communicating the achievement of synergies

Education

Given the highly charged emotions and the uncertainty surrounding any deal, it is a safe bet that most employees understand the term *synergy* to mean only one thing: "I'm going to lose my job." Therefore, the entire organization must start with a common and clear understanding of what this term means, what the targets of the deal are, and what employees' roles are with respect to verifying or capturing all-important synergies. Each company must interpret the term *synergy* for itself, but most companies use the term to designate some measurable reduction in costs, increase in revenues, or avoidance of capital outlay that comes about as a direct result of the combination of two operations into one company and would not have been realized had the companies remained separate. A variety of tools can be used to educate the organization about synergies (for example, classroom training, an e-mailed "synergy kit," or a self-instruction module posted on the company's intranet).

When synergies are explained, they can be organized according to their timelines, their impacts on profits and losses, and their sources. For example, Mike Pulley, vice president of synergies and purchasing at Oxy Vinyls LP, helped educate his task forces and gave them a fast start on the synergy-capture process when he established a one-page project plan for each synergy. This plan, or "synergy charter," included a description of the synergy project, listed its owner, gave a statement of its value and the basis for the valuation, and set key milestones for it. Because the plan was further broken down into "triage" categories of priority and resource allocation, the task forces knew from the very first planning meeting which synergies were urgent (a timeline of up to six months), important for the short term (a timeline of six to twelve months), desired by the time of full integration (a timeline of twelve to eighteen months), and important for the longer-term (a timeline of more than eighteen months).

The education process should also distinguish among the various types of synergies, for example, one-time or recurring synergies that impact financial statements ("P + L") and those related to avoiding or reducing previously planned capital expenses.

- One-time "P + L" synergies, by definition, are those that occur only once and that will be recognized only once on financial statements.
- Recurring "P + L" synergies result from adjustments to the fixed-cost structure, from ongoing contracts, or from revenue enhancements that create multiyear returns.
- "Capital avoidance" synergies are those that do not have a direct impact on income statements, but that do have an impact on future cash flows.

The sources of various synergies will also need to be made clear. As already mentioned, synergies are typically derived from income generation, expense reductions unrelated to reductions in staffing expenses, avoidance of capital outlay, and expense reductions related to reductions in staffing expenses:

- Income-generation synergies are those that produce efficiencies whereby increased production is achieved via changes to processes, new or different equipment, new products, new channels for sales or distribution, enhanced quality, new management techniques, or best practices.
- Expense-reduction synergies include opportunities, due to the integration, for both avoidance and reduction of costs. Examples include (but are not limited to) lower prices for products and services currently used, lower expenses in connection with processes or contractual arrangements, and expense reductions from agency buying. (Each company will need to determine its own best practices in the area of accounting for price fluctuations during the synergy window and calculating total cost.)
- Capital-avoidance synergies are those that involve any reduction in planned use of capital, or in the scope of capital projects, that is made possible by improvements in plant use or by the sharing of resources.
- Staffing-related synergies involve the elimination of redundant roles, positions, or units when these reductions are attributable to the integration. (Note, however, that any costs for contractors or outsourcing will have to be charged against the total staffing-related synergies that are projected.)

Verification

A specific process is needed for verifying and approving actual synergy capture projects. Some organizations create an executive staff role to focus entirely on

EXHIBIT 9.6. STREAMLINED SYNERGY VERIFICATION PROCESS.

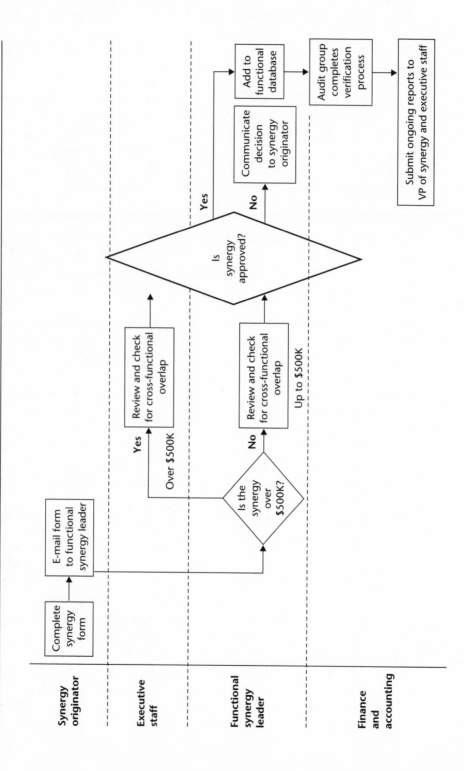

managing the complete synergy process. Others create a dedicated integration task force to lead the effort or a steering committee composed of senior people from a number of functions. Regardless of the method used, there should be specific steps, roles, and responsibilities that clearly set out the instructions for validating and approving various synergy projects. For example, Equistar Chemicals LP created a streamlined process (see Exhibit 9.6) that gave functional leaders the authority to approve any synergy projects under $500,000. In this approach, the individual or task force began the process by submitting a proposal for a synergy project via a form. The functional leader reviewed and validated this synergy project and, as necessary, submitted the proposal to the executive staff for review. A careful determination was made regarding cross-functional overlaps, potential conflicts, or resource constraints in connection with internal service providers whose involvement would be required in the achievement of the synergy. After the project was approved, the synergy-related data were entered into a tracking database and forwarded to the audit group, where an economic verification was conducted.

Documentation

As the preceding discussion implies, a brief form should be designed and implemented for the submission of synergy projects consistent with how the organization defines the term *synergy* and with the organization's synergy categories and verification process. The key components will often include those mentioned in connection with the "synergy charter" used at Oxy Vinyls LP (see "Education") and may also include the name of the synergy project's sponsor, a description of the type and category of the synergy project being proposed, a listing of any requirements for cross-functional support, specification of any capital investments that may be required, and supporting documentation. A master tracking spreadsheet will be necessary for listing specific synergy projects by business unit, timeline, value, and category; Exhibit 9.7 shows a sample of such a spreadsheet.

Reporting and Communication

At regularly scheduled intervals, the status of each synergy project should be summarized and reported on a graph or matrix. It is suggested that this summary report include the total number of verified synergies, the total number of synergy projects currently in process, the number of new synergies (or those pending verification), the total dollar value of synergies already captured, and a listing of key issues or of actions needed from executive staff members or other key business leaders. Exhibits 9.8 and 9.9 show samples of summary reports.

EXHIBIT 9.7. MASTER SPREADSHEET FOR SYNERGY TRACKING.

DIVISION NAME

(All amounts in millions of dollars)

Near Term (pre-12/99)

Synergy Description	Proba-bility	P&L One-Time	P&L Recurring	Non-P&L	Total
Business Unit 1	Low	—	2.0	—	2.0
Business Unit 2		—	1.5	—	1.5
Business Unit 3		—	0.2	—	0.2
Process 1	High	—	1.0	—	1.0
Process 2	Medium	—	1.5	—	1.5
Process 3	Medium	—	0.1	—	0.1
Process 4	High	—	0.1	—	0.1
Staff Function 1		—	0.6	—	0.6
Subtotal		—	7.0	—	7.0

Long Term (post-12/99)

Business Unit 1	Low	—	5.0	—	5.0
Business Unit 2	Low	—	4.0	—	4.0
Process 1	High	—	1.0	—	1.0
Process 2	Medium	—	10.0	—	10.0
Process 3	Medium	—	2.0	—	2.0
All Others	High	—	0.3	—	0.3
Sales force approach to market		—	1.0	—	1.0
Subtotal		—	23.3	—	23.3
Total Task Force Synergies		—	30.3	—	30.3

SYNERGIES ACHIEVABLE IN QUARTER						Total	Total
3/98	4/98	1/99	2/99	3/99	4/99	Pre 12/99	Post 12/99
—	—	—	—	—	—	—	—
—	—	—	—	—	—	—	—
—	—	—	—	—	—	—	—
—	—	—	—	—	—	—	—
—	—	—	—	—	—	—	—
—	—	—	—	—	—	—	—
—	—	—	—	—	—	—	—
—	—	—	—	—	—	—	—
—	—	—	—	—	—	—	—
—	—	—	—	—	—	—	—
—	—	—	—	—	—	—	—
—	—	—	—	—	—	—	—
—	—	—	—	—	—	—	—
—	—	—	—	—	—	—	—
—	—	—	—	—	—	—	—
—	—	—	—	—	—	—	—
—	—	—	—	—	—	—	—

EXHIBIT 9.8. MONTHLY SCORECARD FOR SYNERGY PERFORMANCE.

		Amount (millions of dollars)					
Total number	Plan	1998			1999	2000
		YTD	Remaining	Total		
Synergies verified						
Synergies awaiting verification						
New synergies (verified since last report)						

Synergy Issues List

Key Issues	Synergies Affected	Action Taken

EXHIBIT 9.9. CUMULATIVE SYNERGY CHART.

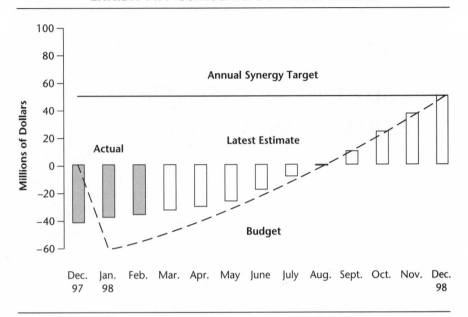

As a complement to the summaries that are reported regularly to the executive staff, it will be necessary periodically to remind the entire organization about key elements of the synergy process and to communicate the results achieved to date. One very effective tool for doing so was created by Kelly McCarthy, employee communications manager at Equistar. An electronic newsletter, *Equi-Flash,* was published under her direction and disseminated to the entire organization. It contained summary scorecards, described synergy projects, and gave recognition to teams that had completed their projects. The newsletter kept the organization informed and motivated, and the practical examples and illustrations that it featured inspired employees and managers to suggest even more possibilities for synergy.

CHAPTER TEN

"BUT THEY'RE SO DIFFERENT": CULTURAL INTEGRATION

Achieving and sustaining the strategic goals of a merger or acquisition will be difficult at best—and, for many organizations, seemingly impossible. Most integration initiatives fall short of reaching their goals when the rubber hits the road—that is, during implementation and follow-up. Lasting organizational integration requires that the operations, systems, and procedures of the newly formed enterprise be clearly connected to the cultures of the organizations that have come together to form the new company. A clear connection between the new enterprise's business needs and the parent companies' cultures not only enables effective integration but also embeds a strong new culture in the day-to-day life of the new organization. To sustain the desired strategic outcomes of a merger or an acquisition (lower costs, higher revenues, improved customer service, fewer errors, quicker processes, and so on) requires managers to begin with the strategic goals of the Newco organization. Once these have been articulated, they should become the cultural foundation of the new company.

Defining Organizational Culture

The components of organizational culture can be isolated, and yet no one component by itself fully accounts for the culture of any one organization. This is because organizational culture is a mosaic of interrelated elements, or *organizational processes.* When a culture is viewed as segmented into these processes, it becomes possible to establish an *operational description* of the culture—it becomes possible, that is, to describe a culture that can be actively managed.

A company's culture is created and continuously reinforced by processes that take place in ten areas:

1. Rules and policies
2. Goals and measures
3. Rewards and recognition
4. Staffing and selection
5. Training and development
6. Ceremonies and events
7. Leadership behavior
8. Communications
9. The physical environment
10. Organizational structure

As the processes connected with these ten areas are brought into contact during each workday, they collectively make up the environment that surrounds the workforce; this organizational environment in turn builds and reinforces the organization's culture. Consider, for example, a company with a strategy that includes "service excellence," a strategy aimed at the desired outcome of higher revenues through high levels of service. Most if not all of the company's organizational processes should reinforce a culture of service excellence. The company should hire and promote service-oriented candidates, train the workforce in techniques of service and in service-oriented behavior, set goals that are based on service, measure people against those service-based goals, reward and recognize people for high levels of service, and establish rules and policies that support a strong service orientation throughout the organization. Likewise, managers who refer to these ten discernible areas of culture-related processes are also able to determine which tangible elements can be put to use in achieving the cultural integration of two organizations. Nevertheless, just as no one of these ten areas uniquely defines organizational culture, no one set of processes can individually support the desired organizational integration.

Discovering, Inventing, and Delivering Cultural Integration

The primary motive for addressing the question of cultural integration should be to accelerate and sustain the desired strategy of the Newco organization. Too often, however, senior leaders struggle during integration because they do not understand how to make the strategy and the required changes important to the managers and employees of the Newco organization.

For example, during the acquisition of one major retailer by another large retail chain, managers of the acquiring company identified a clear difference between the two companies' orientations to and valuing of customer service as a major driver of revenue growth. The acquired company's service was not horrible, but a quick analysis indicated that it had no service goals, measures, or training in place; the company simply expected its sales employees to provide good service. Managers in the acquiring company tried to improve the situation by declaring to the workforce of the acquired company that excellence in customer service was important, and that poor service would not be tolerated. The company also spent a significant amount of money, in addition to managers' and employees' time, on training in new service-oriented behavior. Unfortunately, however, these two actions were not enough to bring about the desired changes in behavior and make them stick. There was a brief rise in service ratings, but the ratings fell soon after the training ended. Clearly, management of the processes in only one or two of the ten organizational areas (in this example, the areas of training and development and communications) is not enough to bring about or sustain cultural integration.

How could the acquiring company have done better? It could have embedded service excellence in the culture of the acquired company in the same way that it had done in its own organization: by driving and reinforcing the desired culture through the use of processes in as many of the ten organizational areas as possible. Exhibit 10.1 illustrates a three-phase approach to accelerating and sustaining cultural integration.

It will not always be necessary to use processes in all ten of the organizational areas to bring about sustained integration, but processes in as many of the ten as possible should be leveraged to achieve the greatest impact on the integration effort. During the merger of two large manufacturing companies, for example, a proposal was put forth to combine the two organizations' purchasing processes in order to lower costs and improve the accuracy of tracking. At first glance, the implementation of this proposal did not appear particularly complex; the new, integrated process was easy to understand, and it looked good on paper. Nevertheless, when the new purchasing process was presented to employees from both companies, they were equally unenthusiastic about making the required changes. Exploration revealed that the companies' old purchasing processes were being reinforced by the companies' current processes in the areas of training and development, goals and measures, and leadership behavior, as well as in other areas. When the merging companies analyzed the proposed purchasing process in light

EXHIBIT 10.1. THE DISCOVER-INVENT-DELIVER APPROACH TO CULTURAL INTEGRATION.

	4 Weeks		4 Weeks	Ongoing	
Timing					
Phases	Phase I DISCOVER		Phase II INVENT	Phase III DELIVER	
	Step 1 Needs analysis	Step 2 "As is" assessment	Step 3 Process design/redesign	Step 4 Implementation	Step 5 Tracking and refinement
Steps for each of the ten organizational processes					
Core questions/information needs	Based on the business strategy, our cultural anchor . . . • Low-cost operations • Profitable growth • Value to customers • Productivity of employees • Safety and reliability What process philosophy do we need . . . For the enterprise? By business unit, function, and organizational role?	What is our current process philosophy? "As is" assessment (for both companies) . . . • What is done? • Who does it? • How? • Where? • Resources? • Costs? • Measures? Alignment/gap analysis . . . Which process components/activities (from step 1) fit/do not fit our desired process philosophy?	Based on our desired process philosophy (from step 1) and what we currently do (from step 2) . . . • What process components/activities should we keep/continue? • What process components/activities should we eliminate? • What process components/activities need to be redesigned? • What are our priorities? Which process components/activities need to be addressed/redesigned first? • What do the re-designs look like?	• What are the process implementation time frames/milestones? • What communication about the process changes needs to occur? • What education about the process changes do we need to do? • For management? • For employees?	• What should our success measures be for the redesigned process? • How do we collect the measures? • Who collects them? • How often? • Who reports progress? • How do we make needed adjustments?

of current processes in all ten organizational areas, they found six areas—rules and policies, goals and measures, rewards and recognition, training and development, leadership behavior, and communications—in which the development of new processes would contribute to making the purchasing changes stick and to reinforcing the new purchasing process. These new processes, once developed and put into motion, enabled the merging organizations to implement the new purchasing process within sixty days and to achieve the goals of lower costs and improved tracking.

Once the core components of the Newco organization's strategy have been defined—when the cultural anchor, so to speak, has been cast—and organizational processes have been reviewed, with any gaps identified between current and desired states, specific actions aimed at redesign and implementation should be determined for each process. (Examples for organizational processes in each of the ten areas we have been discussing are shown in Exhibit 10.2.) Moreover, when organizational processes are being redesigned to drive cultural integration, some key design principles should be adhered to. The following redesign actions should be taken with respect to each organizational process:

- Eliminate legacy activities from the process that are not pertinent to the goals of the desired, "to be" organization
- Keep the costs of the redesigned process low
- Make the redesigned process easy to implement
- Make the redesigned process easy to use
- Make the redesigned process easy to measure

Answering Key Questions

During redesign, the answers to key questions will help to create organizational processes that both reinforce the desired strategy of the Newco organization and drive cultural integration. The following questions are examples of those that can be asked about processes in six areas: rules and policies, rewards and recognition, staffing and selection, training and development, leadership behavior, and communications:

- *Rules and policies* should consistently reinforce our strategy and desired culture.
  What rules and policies are needed to drive the business strategy and influence the development of the desired culture?
  What rules and policies does the enterprise need in order to influence the development of the desired culture?

EXHIBIT 10.2. DRIVING CULTURAL INTEGRATION WITH REDESIGNED PROCESSES.

Rules and policies

- Eliminate rules and policies that will hinder performance of integrating methods and procedures.
- Create new rules and policies that reinforce desired ways of operating the Newco organization.
- Develop and document new standard operating procedures.

Goals and measures

- Develop goals and measures that reinforce desired changes.
- Make goals specific to operations. (For example, establish procedural goals and measures for employees involved in processes that are to be integrated, rather than financial goals that are a by-product of changing the process and that employees cannot easily relate to their actions.)

Staffing and selection

- Establish a staffing, hiring, and promotion process that sources and promotes the type of people needed to drive the Newco strategy. (For example, identify and hire people with proved sales and service experience and orientations.)

Training and development

- Eliminate training that reinforces the old ways of operating. Replace it with training that reinforces the new.
- Deliver training "just in time" so people can apply it immediately.
- Develop training that provides real-time, hands-on experience with new processes and procedures.

Ceremonies and events

- Establish ceremonies and events that reinforce new ways of doing things (such as awards ceremonies and recognition events for teams and employees who achieve goals or successfully implement changes).

Leadership behavior

- Develop goals and measurements that reinforce the desired behavior of management and supervisors in the Newco organization.
- Provide leadership training that focuses on the new, desired behaviors.
- Publicly recognize and reward managers who change, by linking promotion and pay rewards to the desired behaviors.
- Penalize managers who do not change behaviors. (For example, do not give promotions, pay increases, or bonuses to managers who do not demonstrate the desired behaviors.)

(continued)

EXHIBIT 10.2. (*continued*)

Rewards and recognition

- Eliminate rewards and recognition that reinforce old methods and procedures. Replace them with new rewards and recognition that reinforce the desired ways of operating the Newco organization.
- Make rewards specific to the integration goals that have been set.

Communications

- Eliminate communication that reinforces the old ways of operating. Replace it with communication that reinforces the new.
- Deliver communication in new ways to show commitment to the Newco way of operating.
- Use multiple channels to deliver consistent messages in a continuous, relentless manner.
- Make communications two-way by soliciting regular feedback from management and employees about the changes being made.

Physical environment

- Establish a physical environment that reinforces the Newco way of operating. (For example, relocate management and employees who will need to work together to make the company successful.)
- Use "virtual offices," to encourage people to work outside the office with customers, and telecommunications, to connect people who need to interact from a distance.

Organizational structure

- Establish an organizational structure that will reinforce operational changes. (For example, set up client service teams, eliminate management layers, centralize or decentralize work as needed, combine overlapping divisions.)

What different needs, in terms of rules and policies, have been identified in the business units? in the functions? in different organizational (managerial, employee-level) roles?

What are our current rules and policies?

What kinds of rules and policies should be eliminated?

What kinds of rules and policies should be added?

What are the most cost-effective rules and policies?

Who should administer rules and policies?

Who is responsible for outcomes in this area?

Who must implement rules and policies?

What time frames are appropriate in this area?

How can we best measure and track our success in this area?

- *Rewards and recognition* should consistently encourage our strategy and the development of our desired culture.

  What kinds of rewards and recognition are needed to drive the business strategy?

  What kinds of rewards and recognition does the enterprise need?

  What different needs, in terms of rewards and recognition, have been identified in the business units? in the functions? in different organizational (managerial, employee-level) roles?

  What kinds of activities do we currently conduct in the area of rewards and recognition?

  What kinds of rewards and recognition should be eliminated?

  What kinds of rewards and recognition should be added?

  What are the most cost-effective kinds of rewards and recognition?

  Who should administer rewards and recognition?

  Who is responsible for outcomes in this area?

  Who must implement rewards and recognition?

  What time frames are appropriate in this area?

  How can we best measure and track our success in this area?

- *Staffing and selection* should identify, hire, and promote people who embody our strategy and desired culture.

  What kinds of staffing and selection are needed to drive the business strategy?

  What kinds of staffing and selection does the enterprise need?

  What different needs, in terms of staffing and selection, have been identified in the business units? in the functions? in different organizational (managerial, employee-level) roles?

  What kinds of processes do we currently have in the area of staffing and selection? internal moves? external hires?

  What kinds of activities should be eliminated from the area of staffing and selection?

  What kinds of activities should be added to the area of staffing and selection?

  What are the most cost-effective kinds of activities and processes for staffing and selection?

  Who should conduct staffing? sourcing? screening? interviewing? hiring?

  Who is responsible for outcomes in this area?

  Who must implement staffing and selection?

What time frames are appropriate in this area?

How can we best measure and track our success in this area?

- *Training and development* should be designed to provide consistent support to our business strategy and the creation of the desired culture.

    What kinds of training and development are needed to drive the business strategy and influence the creation of the desired culture?

    What kinds of training and development does the enterprise need in order to influence the creation of the desired culture?

    What different needs, in terms of training and development, have been identified in the business units? in the functions? in different organizational (managerial, employee-level) roles?

    What kinds of training do we currently conduct?

    What kinds of training should be eliminated?

    What kinds of training should be added?

    What are the most cost-effective kinds of training?

    Who should design training?

    Who should conduct or deliver training?

    Who is responsible for outcomes in this area?

    Who must implement training and development?

    What time frames are appropriate in this area?

    How can we best measure and track our success in this area?

- *Leadership behavior* should continuously drive our business strategy and desired culture.

    What kinds of leadership behavior must all managers and supervisors demonstrate to drive the business strategy and influence the development of the desired culture?

    What kinds of leadership behavior does the enterprise need in order to influence the development of the desired culture?

    What different needs, in terms of leadership behavior, have been identified in the business units? in the functions?

    What are our current leadership-related processes and activities?

    What kinds of leadership-related processes and activities should be eliminated?

    What kinds of leadership-related processes and activities should be added?

    What are the most cost-effective processes for developing leadership behavior?

    Who is responsible for outcomes in this area?

    Who must implement leadership behavior?

What time frames are appropriate in this area?

How can we best measure and track our success in this area?

- *Communications* should constantly reinforce our business strategy and the development of the desired culture.

  What communications are needed to drive the business strategy and influence the development of the desired culture?

  What communications does the enterprise need in order to influence the development of the desired culture?

  What different needs, in terms of communication, have been identified in the business units? in the functions? in different organizational (managerial, employee-level) roles? internally? externally?

  How do we currently conduct our communication-related processes, both internally and externally?

  What communication-related processes and activities should be eliminated?

  What communication-related processes and activities should be added?

  What are the most cost-effective communication processes?

  Who should deliver communications?

  Who is responsible for outcomes in this area?

  Who must implement communications?

  What time frames are appropriate in this area?

  How can we best measure and track our success in this area?

Sticking to the Implementation Plan

After integration-reinforcing key actions have been identified for each organizational process, a specific implementation plan should be developed. It should focus, as appropriate, on organizationwide or function- or unit-specific implementation. An effective implementation plan will take account of the people involved, the key milestones, the time frames, and the resources that will be needed, but implementation itself will depend on adherence to all facets of the plan. Failure to stick to the plan will send a strong message to the new organization—that management is not serious about creating and sustaining cultural integration—and the commitment needed from the workforce will be lost. For example, during the merger of two large information-systems companies, processes in eight areas—rules and policies, goals and measures, rewards and recognition, staffing and selection, training and development, ceremonies and events, leadership behavior, and communications—were redesigned to expedite and sustain cultural integration. The Newco integration team developed action plans for each of the eight processes. When implementation began, however, schedules slipped, senior managers did not show up for rewards presentations, events were canceled, and little of the planned communication occurred. The implementation went poorly, and the desired outcomes of the integration were never realized.

Continuous Management of Cultural Integration

To help ensure that the goals of cultural integration will be not only met but also sustained, it is essential to continue managing organizational processes with an eye to reinforcing the changes and embedding them in the day-to-day operations of the Newco organization. Two merging retailers, for example, while changing stock-replenishment procedures, learned from employees' feedback that communication had to be improved between the buyers and the stores. Therefore, management moved the buyers into stores so that they could customize inventory for the local markets.

Taking your eye off the ball after a change has been implemented can cause the change effort to slip—and an integration effort that is not managed continuously will not yield sustained results. For example, one acquiring company wanted to increase sales in a newly acquired division by changing the new division's sales process. The company had conducted excellent training for all the employees who would be using the new process. Frequent communication had been offered through multiple channels, and processes had been realigned in the areas of goals and measures and rewards and recognition. The new sales process was kicked off, and an initial increase of 10 percent was achieved across the newly acquired division. But management failed to follow through by continuing to manage the new processes that had been implemented for setting goals, measuring results, and recognizing and rewarding success. As a result, the goals achieved within the first two months were short-lived, and after six months, sales volume returned to preacquisition levels.

Many organizations ignore cultural integration because it appears so difficult to manage. Instead, they focus on the supposedly more tangible kinds of integration, those that involve operations, equipment, systems, and procedures. But achieving and sustaining full integration requires clear connections to be made among changes in organizational culture, strategy, and operations. When a company can leverage processes in the ten organizational areas we have described in this chapter, it can accelerate its achievement of a tangible and pragmatic organizational integration.

CHAPTER ELEVEN

PUTTING IT ALL TOGETHER: HUMAN CAPITAL INTEGRATION AND THE HUMAN RESOURCES FUNCTION

If the greatest difficulties in most mergers are people and cultural issues, the human resources function . . . has the greatest ability to influence integration results.

We are often asked about the role of the human resources function during merger integration. Sadly, there are two distinctly different answers: first, what should be expected; and, second, what is typically delivered. Although there are no easy roles in merger integration, there are some functions that bear more responsibility for overall integration success. With respect to the human resource function, Exhibit 11.1 illustrates why this role is more difficult. Not only must HR integrate its own shop, it must also perform two other demanding roles simultaneously—specifically, a strategic role for enterprisewide integration, and a support role for business units in transition.

This is no excuse for poor performance, however. The fact remains that the greatest difficulty in most merger deals has been consistently found to be people and cultural issues—those areas over which HR can and should be able to exert some positive influence, if not the outright power to effect change.

In some deals, senior management is squarely to blame for this failure. For example, we recently read the account of one well-known merger in which the senior leadership team was selected primarily through barter and horse trading, during lavish dinners that led to the preliminary agreement for the transaction. Company A had a well-respected and strategic human resources function focused on delivering outstanding internal customer service and innovative consultative solutions to its business partners. Company B had a traditional human resources function focused on administrative work and policy enforcement. As could have

EXHIBIT 11.1. INTEGRATION ROLES FOR THE HUMAN RESOURCES FUNCTION.

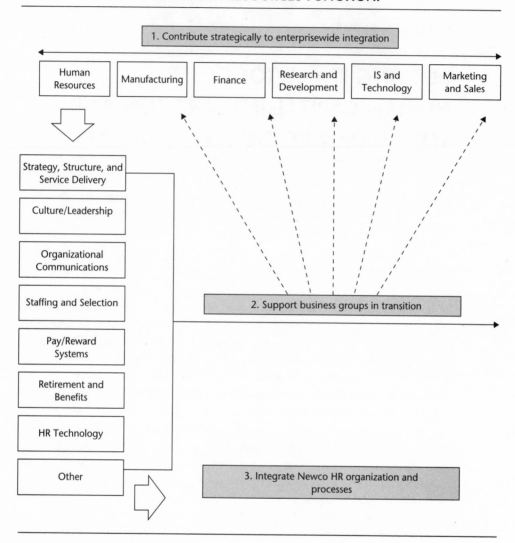

been expected, the vice president from company B got the top HR job as a means of balancing the senior team with executives from both parent companies. The arrangement lasted one year, during which time HR was minimally involved in anything other than such core fundamentals as payroll processing and benefits administration. As this company learned, defining and integrating a human resources function begins with the first HR decision.

In other deals, the human resources function never seems to get out of the blocks. Integration planning is weak and haphazard. Deliverables are late, inaccurate, and out of scope. Leaders are so busy fighting fires, they are never able to engage with the prevailing issues.

In still other deals, HR staff members do not have enough knowledge about the core business to be able to provide objective counsel, and in others they effectively address the basics (compensation, staffing, and benefits) but end up providing unimaginative and highly tactical solutions that do not take account of the new strategic realities of the Newco organization.

If the greatest difficulties in most mergers are people and cultural issues, the human resources function, backed by a supportive and proactive senior leadership team, has the greatest ability to influence integration results in a positive direction—if the people in HR know how and are allowed to perform that vital work.

Perhaps more than most other functions involved in merger integration planning, human resources has priorities that fall clearly into two distinct phases. The initial transition responsibilities include organizational structure, selection/deselection and staffing, compensation, benefits, and retention. The responsibilities for full integration include rationalization and alignment of all the acquired company's organizational and HR processes to more directly support the business objectives of the Newco organization. Even HR departments that are fully and effectively engaged in the tasks of the first phase are usually not able to make a meaningful impact through the tasks of the second phase. Increasingly, however, organizations are implementing a more strategic human resources focus and discovering the far-reaching impact of HR on merger integration and on organizational results.

The "Making Strategy Work" Model

In order for HR to deliver a more strategic business impact during M&A integration, the organization must realign its influence systems in order to change actual behavior. One way to view these opportunities and relationships is depicted in Exhibit 11.2.

EXHIBIT 11.2. THE "MAKING STRATEGY WORK" MODEL.

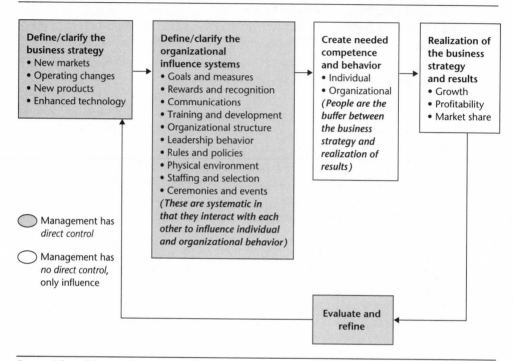

Source: Adapted from Galpin (1997, p. 17).

In the past, management tried to control people's actions by applying stringent rules and policies or issuing edicts. Some employees respond to this approach; in general, however, this kind of management has met with little success. The reality is that people are not actually under anyone's direct control; they are influenced only by the makeup of their work environment. In the military, for example, when a sergeant gives an order to a group of privates—"Paint that fence!"—the privates usually respond quickly by painting the fence. Some would call that control, but a closer look reveals the obvious: the privates are responding to their organizational environment. Soldiers have rules that are clearly communicated to them; the negative consequences of not painting the fence are understood, and the positive consequences—if they paint enough fences and paint them well—are also clear (for example, promotion to the next rank). They also receive training, rewards, recognition, and other positive feedback. Likewise, people in all kinds of organizations are really influenced only by the systems that make up their environment. To achieve new, different, or more strategic business outcomes during an M&A integration, HR must adapt the organizational influence systems more skillfully, to yield the specific kinds of behavior required for producing those outcomes. Further, it is important to emphasize that "integrated sets" of influence systems (Galpin, 1997) must be deployed (rather than one or two isolated practices, such as a new pay program) in accomplishing the intended effect:

> Several single-industry and cross-industry studies have identified that integrated sets of human resources practices create multiple reinforcements for motivation and skill development (see MacDuffie, 1995; Berg and others, 1995; Arthur, 1994, Huselid, 1995; and Ichniowski, 1995). Moreover, each of these studies found that interconnected work and human resources practices lead to improved company financial performance, and that new work organization coupled with human resources management practices can have major positive effects on productivity and quality. Collectively the findings also suggest that peripheral changes to singular practices have marginal or no impact on company performance. Furthermore, no single collection of practices leading to higher company performance has been identified to date.
>
> In addition to the research data, several case examples exist to support the application of integrated groupings of the twelve influence systems. For instance, one widely publicized strategic shift is the transformation taking place at Sears under the direction of CEO Arthur Martinez. He has refocused Sears on the core retail business and has been improving the look and service of the stores as key growth strategies. To implement the strategy, Sears has realigned at least eight of the twelve influence systems. For example, it has redesigned its performance management approach. Managers now receive 360-degree feedback, and bonuses for the top two hundred executives are no longer based solely on financial measures. Revenues, return on assets, and operating margins are the basis for only half of executive incentives. The other half is equally dependent upon customer satisfaction measures and employee ratings of management. Additionally, the physical environment has been changed by converting the store offices of individual department supervisors into a shared team space, which encourages supervisors to spend more time out on the selling floor providing feedback and coaching to sales associates about sales behaviors and techniques. Sears has also employed the communications and ceremonies and events influence systems. Their rules and policies have been revamped by replacing the old Sears policy manuals with a "Freedoms and Obligations" booklet. Training on customer service has been provided to management,

supervisors, and employees across the company, and new job descriptions and operating structures have been implemented to place decision making closer to the customer (Dobrzynski, 1996).

Another example of realigning integrated sets of the influence systems comes from the Royal Nedlloyd Group, a $3.5 billion shipping company based in Rotterdam, the Netherlands. To accomplish the company's turnaround strategy, Nedlloyd's management redesigned no fewer than seven of the influence systems. Management realigned the organization's structure and rules and policies, making the corporate logistics unit the coordinator of the company's operating units. It also realigned goals and measures and rewards and recognition to focus on accountability and profitability. The information systems and knowledge sharing and the operational/process changes influence systems were put in place in the form of a database that allows the entire company to identify which of Nedlloyd's units is doing business with certain clients, and to identify gaps on which the company can capitalize. Meetings are held every month among the account managers of the various operating units to share customer information. Additionally, communications and training were employed that focused on the new operating procedures being put in place.

Similarly, management at Southwest Airlines has employed most of the influence systems to implement a strategy of quality, flexibility, and superior customer service. The workplace has few rigid rules, and the company rewards employees through a profit sharing plan and emphasizes customer service in performance appraisals and communications. Additionally, extensive training is provided to the entire workforce. The mechanics, customer service, operations, reservations, and other divisions all provide their own technical training, and all employees participate in courses on customer service, decision making, safety, and career development (Gephart, 1995).

The Competitive Advantage Model

As another means of identifying key organizational processes to align for maximum impact, one acquirer based its initial analysis on recent research using a survey of employees' opinions. Using Watson Wyatt's competitive advantage model, this company categorized the myriad factors that determine employees' behavior and organizations' performance into four major areas: enablers, influencers, motivators, and navigators. (These dimensions and sample constructs are illustrated in Exhibit 11.3.) The term *enablers* refers to factors that largely determine how work gets done in an organization. These include job design, the way work is organized, staffing, flexibility, training, the ability of the organization to capture and

EXHIBIT 11.3. SAMPLE ALIGNMENT PROJECTS.

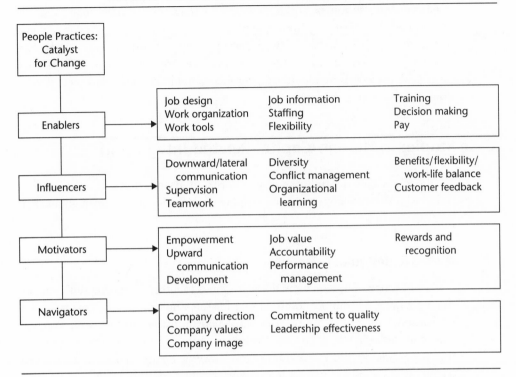

People Practices: Catalyst for Change			
Enablers	Job design Work organization Work tools	Job information Staffing Flexibility	Training Decision making Pay
Influencers	Downward/lateral communication Supervision Teamwork	Diversity Conflict management Organizational learning	Benefits/flexibility/ work-life balance Customer feedback
Motivators	Empowerment Upward communication Development	Job value Accountability Performance management	Rewards and recognition
Navigators	Company direction Company values Company image	Commitment to quality Leadership effectiveness	

leverage institutional knowledge, and effective decision-making processes. The term *influencers* refers to factors that can have a significant impact on the day-to-day experiences and perceptions of employees, prompting people to be either more or less effective. These factors include the quality of supervisory relationships, the skills of the team and its effectiveness in carrying out its objectives, the ability of the organization to support diversity and resolve work-related conflicts and grievances, regular and direct customer feedback, and work/life flexibility opportunities. The term *motivators*, obviously, refers to the overt aspects of eliciting peak results through such mechanisms as compensation, benefits, performance management, and incentive and bonus programs. Also included among the motivators are the more qualitative aspects of improving performance: employees' general perceptions of empowerment, the formal and informal developmental processes to ensure professional growth, recognition, and accountability processes. The term *navigators* refers to the more intangible factors necessary to ensuring essential focus and strategic direction for all employees. This dimension includes overall perceptions of leaders' effectiveness and credibility, clarity about essential strategic objectives and individuals' roles in them, bona fide commitment to company values, and the company's image in the marketplace and the community. In the case of this acquirer, data from both the parent company and the target company were reviewed during a comprehensive "as is" study conducted by the HR task force. On the basis of the resulting gap analysis, specific alignment projects were identified, prioritized, and implemented in each of these four major areas.

Case Studies in Human-Capital-Related Integration

As the following case studies indicate, more and more acquirers are successfully using M&A transactions to create significant strategic change throughout their organizations.

Total Rewards Redesign at Conectiv

"The challenge of human capital integration is to integrate several different cultures into one reasonably common one for the whole company," explains Ben Wilkinson, manager of compensation and benefits for Delaware-based Conectiv (cited in Arapoff, 1998, p. 20). Wilkinson, having just completed the utility merger of Atlantic Electric and Delmarva Power to create Conectiv, says the new company is a good example of how communication can lead to a successful integration: "We purposely designed all of our new HR policies and processes— structure, staff, and services—during human capital integration, in order to harmonize with the new company."

It is a unique story. Because the two utilities merged at a time when deregulation had greatly expanded, Wilkinson and his team had to contend with a host of issues unrelated to the actual merger. "In the human capital arena," he says, "the biggest challenge for us right now is the industry in general. There has to be a sense of urgency about business that was not necessarily present when we were highly regulated—an urgency about getting new customers and keeping old customers. Now we have to refocus our customer care operations."

There was also a shift in workforce incentives. Deregulation has meant more chance for turnover, which means different hiring practices. "The new initiatives include hiring experienced workers, competing in the open market for hi-tech people, and having programs in place that are going to keep and motivate these employees," Wilkinson says. "So as we began the merger process, looking at these people issues—and communicating with our employees about them—became a priority."

With these new initiatives, as well as the typical dilemmas inherent in a merger or acquisition, Conectiv had to take steps to ensure that all aspects of the workforce were integrated. Employees were involved through numerous focus groups and informal discussions, but integration of the human capital area was facilitated primarily through the work of Conectiv's Total Rewards Team. Made up of equal numbers of Atlantic and Delmarva employees, the team concentrated on compensation and benefits work. Cochaired by the managers of compensation and benefits from both companies, the team was able to put together an action plan and deliver messages about its findings to the entire workforce.

"The team selected Watson Wyatt to help us through the integration," Wilkinson says. "Working together, we tried to create an atmosphere of cooperation because we knew there were going to be a lot of challenges ahead. Within just a couple of months after the announcement was made, we also developed a plan with one of our key audiences: the unions. We wanted to make sure that we gathered their input as the programs and processes were designed for Conectiv."

As ideas were put on paper and concepts were developed, Conectiv used an internal newsletter, *Emerging Times,* to document developments. Published for approximately one year, the newsletter explained new overtime policies, gave an overview of the new facilities, defined terms like *shared services* and *targeted voluntary separation,* and announced the official date of the merger.

In addition, Conectiv intentionally redesigned its entire benefits and compensation package to reflect a more modern pattern and to serve the new unified workforce. Finding a plan that served all entities took some time, but Wilkinson believes that the sooner a plan can be communicated and implemented, the more receptive employees will be: "We tried to be as open as we could with our intentions," he says. "As we got to the final phases of design, we went from the . . . newsletter format to one-page fact sheets with the new company logo on them to communicate internally. These fact sheets were very well received."

It's important for everyone in an integration, from senior management to newly hired entry-level employees, to have realistic expectations. Wilkinson believes that this is one of the most important lessons he's learned: "I would have paid more attention to the old saying 'The devil is in the details' if I had it to do over again. We ended up administering former Atlantic benefits, former Delmarva benefits, Conectiv benefits, Delmarva pensioner benefits, Atlantic pensioner benefits, and three different unions. So, be prepared. Lock in your key people early. And remember that there will be surprises." Conectiv's unexpected challenges came in the form of jargon differences, data-entry system upheaval, and overcoming the mind-set of a utility monopoly. But once these obstacles were dealt with, the company was able to move forward with the integration process.

"In broad terms, and given the amount of change in practice and policy that we experienced," Wilkinson says, "we're glad to have that part of the merger experience behind us. There were bumps in the road, but I think at the end of this year, Conectiv employees will be able to look back over the last nine months or so and say, 'Wow, we really accomplished a lot.'"

Building an HR Service Center at a Major Banking and Financial Services Firm

Formed through the merger of three major banking and financial services firms, this organization found itself with sixty thousand active employees, twenty thousand retirees, and a need to drive cost out of the benefits service-delivery process and, at the same time, improve internal customer satisfaction. As a result of the merger, service delivery was very fragmented and confusing. One company used regional service centers. Another used local HR generalists. The third partner used a call center. After studying various options, a strategy team developed a proposal for delivering all HR services through a single call center to create both a common business process and a common identity for the newly formed company. During the research effort, the study team identified a number of potentially favorable outcomes of this approach:

- Other organizations had significantly lowered the fixed costs of benefits service delivery, as well as the cost per transaction.
- The center created a much simpler and easier-to-manage process, with a single source of up-to-date information for all customers.
- Callers would be assured consistent answers to difficult technical questions because key information would be provided to customer service representatives via an electronic knowledge base.
- The center would reduce "answer shopping" by employees hoping to get a more favorable response from a different representative, and it was a more effective use of time because calls could be made after hours and on weekends.

In order to accomplish these objectives and leverage the Newco's HR organization to a more strategic level, it was decided to create a call center platform and process that ultimately would be able to respond to inquiries, solve problems, and provide service on a wide variety of issues. Initially, the following potential applications were determined:

- Benefits
- HR policies and procedures
- Payroll

- Leaves of absence
- Workers' compensation
- Exit/retirement
- Educational and developmental information and enrollment
- Forms distribution
- Employee records/employee verification
- Job posting

An integration task force was created and staffed to manage three different but interrelated functions essential to the success of the center: process redesign, technology, and people.

The process-redesign team analyzed the current state of processes and identified objectives and desired characteristics for the "to be" processes. These included the following considerations:

- Elimination of manual processing
- Emphasis on service delivery through automated voice-response technology
- User-friendliness
- A confirmation process for all transactions
- Automated document-fulfillment capability
- Reduced cycle time

New processes were designed, mapped, and documented for review and approval and were then presented to the full task force and executive staff for approval.

The technology team was responsible for designing and building the overall platform that would best support the desired call center environment. This project involved several key tasks:

- Database design
- Computer telephony integration
- Design of automated forms
- Design of the customer service representative's computer screen
- Development of an electronic scripted knowledge base, with all technical information in conversational hypertext, and "rapid look-up" features
- A case management system for ensuring effective follow-through to resolution of extended issues

To ensure that the design components would actually come together into a functional service organization, the people team was given responsibility for a variety of initiatives:

- Establishment of an organizational structure and facilities requirements
- Creation of a competency-based staffing process, and its integration with a comprehensive training program, to ensure that customer service representatives and managers would have a high level of skill in customer contact and the ability to use the automated tools in answering employees' questions
- Creation of a marketing and implementation plan, to ensure that the process would be effectively deployed and launched
- Creation of a measurement process for tracking a variety of metrics that included productivity/efficiency measures, measures of customer satisfaction, measures of call center employees' effectiveness, and measures of organizational effectiveness

This integration project took only eight months from approval to the "go live" state, but the results came even faster. The Newco company calculates that, as a result of the creation of the call center, transaction costs have dropped from approximately $8 to $4 per internal transaction. This increase in transaction-processing efficiency will result in savings of roughly $8 million over a five-year period (net of the initial investment to create the center).

The call center was also used to support its annual benefits enrollment process in 1998. In previous years, the annual enrollment process had been outsourced, at a yearly cost of more than $700,000. Expenses surrounding 1998's enrollment process were less than $300,000, and a much higher level of customer satisfaction was achieved. This was an especially important improvement because customer satisfaction had been a key strategic driver from the outset. Executives believed that improving satisfaction for internal customers would have a corresponding positive impact on both retention and external customer satisfaction. Using an existing baseline of customer satisfaction, as measured before the creation of the call center, overall satisfaction with benefits service delivery went from 48 percent to 73 percent in the first year of the center's operation, and on other measures of customer satisfaction (involving courteous and professional service, timely resolution of problems, ease of obtaining information, and accuracy of information) there was a net improvement on the order of 25 to 30 percent.

Organizations installing HR service centers have experienced another key result with specific relevance to merger integration and the ability to quickly drive change in an organization: the ability, once an effective, shared service-delivery platform has been developed, to introduce significant change within a matter of hours or days by making prompt and direct contact with each employee. When the company announced a stock split, for example, it was able to get important messages out to all sixty thousand employees within a few hours of the official announcement and was able to ensure that each employee got the same message.

Under the old service-delivery model, this communication would have taken weeks, and there would have been considerable inconsistency in its delivery.

Strategic Compensation Alignment at GE Capital Japan

GE Capital Japan is one example of an organization that is successfully integrating traditional Japanese human resources practices with state-of-the art Western approaches. In recognition of the sensitivities surrounding this shift, a multinational project team, including business leaders and HR professionals from GE Capital and GE Capital Japan, was assembled for one recent assignment. Before we discuss this assignment, however, it will be helpful to provide some information about the environment in which it was carried out. This information should be particularly useful in light of the financial crisis that has rocked Asia and the fact that our global economy has also provided an unprecedented opportunity for acquirers. Asian companies that are cash-strapped and reasonably valued have become timely targets as many global employers seek further expansions. In 1997, merger and acquisition activity in Asia totaled $52 billion, and in June 1998, Cox (1998) reported that Asian deal value was expected to "at least triple" during that year as an estimated 64 percent of all U.S. and European multinational firms announced plans to increase acquisition activity in Asia during the next eighteen months.

Many global acquirers are also discovering that these new opportunities bring with them a whole new range of human-capital-related integration issues. In addition to all the typical difficulties inherent in domestic deals, a global integration must take into account not only strong cultural differences but also sweeping societal and economic forces. Exhibit 11.4 illustrates one aspect of this complex transformation by showing how traditional Japanese compensation practices have begun to give way to Western-style performance-based pay arrangements.

As a general rule, the transition can be observed in pay components, pay determinants, and evaluation processes. Where *pay components* are concerned, the overall trend is from complex approaches to more simplified ones. In a traditional Japanese system, for example, the primary pay components include an age-based salary, an ability-based salary, and numerous allowances (including a family allowance, a housing allowance, and, in some cases, a commuting-distance allowance), combined with a seasonal bonus. Under performance-based arrangements, an annual base salary is combined with an annual performance bonus. Where *pay determinants* are concerned, the general trend is embodied in a shift from the individual to the individual's performance. For example, current compensation decisions are based on the employee's age and personality and on

EXHIBIT 11.4. TRENDS IN JAPANESE COMPENSATION.

Period	1960s	1970s	1980s	1990s
Type of system		*Shokuno-shikako* Skill-based pay		*Nenpo* Performance-based pay
Objective	Control cost of blue collar	Compensate lack of job posts		Secure high-potential individual Control cost of white collar
Component Example	Base: 6 grades by job, no maximum + Addition: base up + Family and other allowances	Skill-based: compensation tables by skill grades + Age-based: maximum at 45–50 years old Allowance of title: decided by job grade + Family and other allowances		Base: no base up no regular increase + Job responsibility–based: Increased/reduced by job responsibilities + Performance bonus
Evaluation	Not linked with evaluation	Decided by attitude, skill, and result evaluation		Decided by management by objectives, review

certain criteria that apply across the board to entire groups of people, or perhaps to everyone in the company. By contrast, more Asian acquisitions are beginning to implement criteria based solely on job performance, position level, attainment and demonstration of competencies, and other function-specific requirements. Conventions are also changing with respect to the *evaluation processes* being used, as more Japanese companies are moving from closed evaluation systems to open ones. Traditional evaluation systems were strictly confidential, with no official communication; more recent pay plans are implemented and maintained with official communication, and they include typical kinds of objective-setting and feedback exercises.

A number of major forces have been combining to drive Japanese companies toward a performance-based pay system. For one thing, there is an increasing need for autonomy and empowerment among line managers: deregulation has accelerated in many industries, and the fast-changing technological environment has shifted emphasis from factory productivity to white-collar productivity. For another, there is an increasing need for control over the costs of total compensation. The traditional "lifetime pay" system tended to create a lockstep mechanism whereby employees were paid less in their twenties and thirties and more in their late forties and fifties, and there was no way of altering this arrangement on the more reasonable basis of performance. Under this system, the large baby-boomer cohort began to push compensation costs significantly out of alignment with the value of this cohort's actual contributions. Now, however, changes are being driven by a changing HR market. Attitudes toward lifetime employment are shifting among the younger generation, and companies are increasingly hiring midcareer experts.

With that said, let us now return to our discussion of the change project at GE Capital Japan. After a study to fully define the issues and develop initial high-level concepts, a comprehensive human resources management strategy was developed on the basis of best-practice research and internal findings. As one part of this strategy, an overall human resources functional structure was proposed along with initial strategic directives and transition outlines for each major human resources subfunction.

Upon approval of the initial concepts, the multinational project team began the detailed program design of a new total rewards structure. The components included a new compensation band system, a new performance-based salary structure that would eliminate the traditional tenets of promotion by age and ever-increasing salaries, a redesigned program for retirement and health and welfare benefits, professional development processes for core employees, and a comprehensive communications process to ensure clear understanding of and effective transition to the new programs.

CHAPTER TWELVE

KEYS TO M&A SUCCESS

Bringing about a successful merger, acquisition, or joint venture is not easy. As we have seen, it is no simple undertaking to combine two or more organizations to form an entity that realizes its intended financial returns and meets its strategic goals.

Recommendations for Success

In creating a successful merger, ten key recommendations should be kept in mind. Following them is no guarantee of success, but they can increase the odds of a faster, smoother integration:

1. Conduct due-diligence analyses in the financial and human-capital-related areas.
2. Determine the required or desired degree of integration.
3. Speed up decisions instead of focusing on precision.
4. Get support and commitment from senior managers.
5. Clearly define an approach to integration.
6. Select a highly respected and capable integration leader.
7. Select dedicated, capable people for the integration core team and task forces.

8. Use best practices.
9. Set measurable goals and objectives.
10. Provide continuous communication and feedback.

Due Diligence

Due diligence is a key ingredient both of successful negotiation and of postdeal integration. Most companies do a decent job of financial due-diligence analysis but a dismal job of human-capital-related due-diligence analysis. Due diligence in the area of human capital can provide a picture of where two companies converge or diverge on such aspects as leadership, communication, training, performance management, and so on. Instead of learning about such aspects of a partner or target company after the fact, you can learn a great deal during the due-diligence process. In this way, the integration manager and others involved in the integration process can start gaining valuable information right from the start and do a better job of determining where the integration focus should be and where resources should be applied.

Required or Desired Degree of Integration

Will the integration be full? partial? limited? This determination helps greatly in letting people know how complex the integration will be and how much work will be required. Fully integrating two companies' processes, people, and systems requires a lot more effort and organization than only partial or limited integration.

Speedy Decisions

A focus on speed rather than on precision not only facilitates faster integration but also enables people to refocus more promptly on work, customers, and results. Moreover, reaching decisions quickly about pay, benefits, structure, staffing, reporting, and so on, will give people faster resolution of their "me issues" and, again, enable them to refocus more quickly on their work.

Support and Commitment from Senior Managers

Too often we have seen senior managers, while appropriately delegating integration management and tasks, inappropriately delegating their own roles in an integration. Senior managers should not and must not delegate decision making on items that involve large capital expenditures, or where an impasse has been reached at lower levels of the integration decision-making process. Moreover, the best change-management tool available is senior managers' "face time" with middle managers and employees. Face-to-face meetings provide opportunities for real-time, two-way information dissemination, feedback, questions, and answers.

Clearly Defined Approach

A clearly defined approach facilitates faster decision making and organizes the entire integration effort. Using an integration manager, a core team, and integration task forces will provide the infrastructure and resources needed in getting a huge job—integrating processes, people, and systems—done more quickly and more smoothly. Without a defined approach that includes clear deliverables, due dates, milestones, information flows, and so on, each function of the enterprise will be working on a different schedule and producing deliverables that vary widely in terms of quality and content.

Capable Leadership

The integration leader should be an excellent project manager with a broad view of the enterprise and good people skills. This is the person who will make or break the integration, overseeing its decision-making process, the achievement of milestones and deliverables, and the quality of the reporting process. Choose this leader wisely.

Core Team and Task Forces

Integration is not a part-time job. Therefore, many of the people serving on the core team and the task forces, especially the leaders of these groups, will have to delegate their day-to-day responsibilities in order to focus on the integration effort. If they fail to do so, the effort will bog down, and deliverables (such as integration plans) will be damaged.

Best Practices

Learning from others' mistakes is a great way to avoid making your own. Likewise, learning from others' best practices and integration successes can shorten your own learning curve.

Measurable Goals and Objectives

Measurable goals and objectives let people know what a successful integration will look like and how long it should take. Synergy targets, integration time frames, specific deliverables, and due dates all drive a faster, smoother integration.

Continuous Communication and Feedback

All the people involved in the integration effort should be given continuous communication and feedback, which will help them understand the progress that is being made. Gathering feedback from the organization also helps in identifying areas that need even more attention as the effort progresses. Constant communication and feedback are the oil of a well-run integration machine.

Developing a Sustained M&A Capability

Many companies do multiple deals but treat them as single, on/off events. Nevertheless, given the high frequency of merger and acquisition activity today and into the foreseeable future, organizations would do well to embed into their workforces the capability to conduct multiple efficient and effective integration efforts. Managers often wonder why they make the same mistakes, deal after deal, never realizing that if they installed the tools, processes, and techniques described throughout the previous chapters, they would provide the organization with a road map for future acquisitions. This is not to say that every deal is the same, but a valuable "how to" manual can be produced if managers define *and document* the organization's M&A processes by describing the following typical elements:

- Steps
- Activities
- Tasks
- Tools and templates
- Time frames
- Samples of deliverables
- Various parties involved along the way (for example, senior managers, the legal and finance departments, the human resources department, external consultants, and so on
- Their roles at each step

This kind of M&A process manual will help to drive an efficient, effective process each time the organization embarks on a deal. For example, Dow Chemical, GE

Capital, and Lyondell Petrochemical all have defined and documented M&A processes. Each of these companies conducts multiple deals (in the case of GE Capital, sometimes as many as dozens per year), and each has a set approach to M&A due diligence and integration, identifying all the tasks, parties involved, roles, and deliverables throughout a deal flow.

In addition to documenting the company's M&A process, it can be very helpful to train people in effective use of the materials, thereby also building a strong M&A competency for the organization. The training does not have to be long and involved; it can be as short as an "awareness" session orienting participants to the contents of the company's M&A documentation. Through this kind of training, all the people who will be involved in a deal can learn about their roles, the roles of others, and what the deliverables will be throughout the deal process.

Avoiding "Killer" Phrases

The phrase "a merger of equals" is an integration killer. With very rare exceptions, there is no such thing as a merger of equals. Even when the assets contributed and the size of the workforces and revenues are virtually the same, it is still not a merger of equals; just naming one of the two companies' CEO the head of the new entity sends signals about who is in charge. The greatest damage done by use of the phrase "a merger of equals" is the creation of a perception that decisions will be made in an egalitarian way. This perception is a misperception, however. It can only slow the integration down and cause infighting between the two organizations as they attempt to integrate their people, processes, and systems. Someone needs to make the call when an impasse is reached, give direction in such areas as the pay and benefits programs that will be used by the Newco organization, which information system will be used, which business processes will be used, and so on. This someone is usually found among the top executives and, eventually, may even have to be the CEO of the Newco organization, not a consensus-driven decision-making body.

"Take your time, and ease the changes in" is another integration killer. Managers often feel the pressure when the organization pushes back on the speed of integration. But this pushback is only a natural reaction to the changes taking place. As in any other kind of change process, people will try to hang on to the status quo—and, as in any other kind of change process, the longer management takes to make the changes, the longer the organization will retain an inward focus, and the longer organizational productivity will drop. Merger integration can be fast and painful, or it can be slow and painful. It is better to get the changes made quickly.

Another killer is the phrase "We'll tell them something only when there's something to tell." This is the wrong approach. We have seen companies go months at a time without sending any kind of merger-related communications because there was "nothing to tell." All the time, they could have been letting their people know about the integration process and the progress being made. Instead, the workforces of these organizations filled the dead air with rumors, falsehoods, and speculation.

Even worse, "killer" phrases often drive "killer" actions. Unfortunately, when managers use killer phrases, believe them, and act on their beliefs, they create the nemesis of positive integration. Instead of using such phrases, managers should spearhead quick, effective efforts to integrate the two organizations. Using the tools, templates, and techniques described throughout this text will facilitate a process that efficiently and effectively achieves the goal that motivates deals in the first place: value creation for the new company, its customers, and its shareholders.

RESOURCE A:
SAMPLE TASK FORCE CHARTER

Please complete each section with specific information relevant to your task force.

Team Name:

Overall Objective Statement:

Team Leaders:

I. Team Members

Please provide subteam resource names and contact information on the attached "Task Force Subteam Members" form. Please provide a final subteam organization chart on the attached form, indicating any subteams or special project teams you will establish.

Note: This sample task force charter can be used to ensure a clear understanding of each team's integration scope and as an initial planning guide to launch the team's effort.

II. Synergy Targets

Please list the initial synergy assignments for your task force, along with any new or prospective synergies you intend to pursue. Synergies that are dependent on two or more task forces working together should also be noted.

Synergy Number	Description	Value ($mm)	Time Frame	Other Task Forces Involved

III. Deliverables

Item	Due Date	Description
1. Final task force charter	Friday, November 6	Synergy targets; subteam resources; high-level issues list; task force meeting logistics; data or documentation needed for planning
2. Initial transition plans	Wednesday, December 2	Recommendations to achieve short-term operational functionality: how work will get done; organizational charts, roles; service agreement requirements; facilities/systems support needs; estimate of transition costs; timeline
3. Full integration plans and synergy project plans	Friday, January 29, 1999	Review of business plan for necessary changes; detailed synergy project plans; high-level identification of processes to align; policy/practices alignment; revised facilities/systems needs; revised transition costs; comprehensive timeline

IV. "As Is" Analysis

Integration planning must begin with a careful review of each partner's business and processes. In order to avoid bogging down early in the integration planning, we recommend that you start with a sufficiently high-level overview of key issues in your functional area and then ask each project team or subteam to get more detailed information, as appropriate.

A. Data Collection

Please list the relevant documentation/information to help your task force gain an appropriate understanding of each organization's "as is" status. The following list is only representative. Determine who will supply this information and when, and verify which items require legal counsel.

- ☐ Current operational plans and strategic direction
- ☐ Current long-range plans
- ☐ Budgets
- ☐ Number and locations of personnel
- ☐ Facilities (space, costs, locations, addresses)
- ☐ Organizational charts
- ☐ High-level process maps (outlining who makes key decisions and how, inputs/ outputs, organizational interdependence, and so on)
- ☐ Other: _____
- ☐ _____
- ☐ _____
- ☐ _____
- ☐ _____
- ☐ _____

B. Organizational Background

Please list relevant issues pertaining to how each organization conducts business. The following list is only representative. We recommend that you discuss the relevant issues with your task force leader and with your combined task force members as early as practical sometime during the first two weeks of the planning process.

- ☐ What are the key business drivers?
- ☐ What are the key elements of the business plan?

☐ What issues and barriers will have an impact on organizational performance?

☐ What major perceptions and obstacles will employees bring forward? What about managers?

☐ Is IS functionality required and provided?

☐ What major legacy systems and functionality exist? What access is needed to these systems?

☐ Are there performance goals and measures? Are baselines identified?

☐ How are metrics linked to rewards and incentives?

☐ How do staff and line units relate to each other/get services and deliverables from each other?

☐ How do people access units or resources outside their immediate function?

☐ What formal planning systems are in place and followed?

☐ What degree of consensus or autonomy is typically expected in formulating decisions?

☐ To what degree are policies, rules, and procedures prescribed and formal rather than flexible?

☐ How widespread are employee teams or other methods of involvement?

☐ How are formal and informal communications conducted?

☐ Do people gain an understanding of relevant policies and procedures?

☐ Do people gain an understanding of culture, values, and leadership?

☐ Other: _____

☐ _____

☐ _____

☐ _____

☐ _____

☐ _____

V. Initial Identification of Issues

To ensure thorough planning to provide sufficient direction for subteams, please provide a detailed outline of issues for integration/transition planning in each area. The following items are presented as thought starters only; an initial list of issues should be an output of today's working session.

A. Business Plan

☐ What changes to our function's or unit's business plan might be necessary because of the integration?

☐ What assumptions, competing priorities, or resource constraints might also need to change?

B. Transition Costs and Synergy Projections

☐ Create a plan or model documenting total financial impact of integration synergies and transition costs.

☐ What assumptions from the original synergy estimate may need to be revised?

☐ What new synergy opportunities have been identified that were not previously considered, and in what time frame?

C. Business-Process Analysis

☐ Short term: Define the processes to be used beginning on day 1.

☐ Longer term: Continue to explore and identify changes to key business processes that drive value. What processes should continue as stand-alones? What processes should one company or the other adopt? What processes should be redesigned altogether? What are the general timing and priorities for our recommendations?

D. Organizational Structure and Staffing

☐ What will be our near-term and longer-term staffing requirements? When are structure and staffing decisions due? What ramp-up/ramp-down process and plan will be used to get to the desired staff level without disrupting operations?

☐ What processes will be used to select/deselect, communicate, and implement decisions?

E. Policies and Practices

☐ What specific policies and practices will be used as we go forward?

☐ How and when will any revisions be endorsed and implemented?

F. Workstation/Facility Needs

☐ What specific requirements will the new unit/function have for computing and telecommunications?

☐ What needs exist for colocation? What specific facilities impact is projected?

☐ What are the estimated costs and necessary timing?

G. Information-Transfer Plan

☐ How will the department/function be informed of transition-plan issues?

☐ How will people be trained for any new or expanded responsibilities?

☐ What processes will be used to keep staff and other key internal stakeholders informed on an ongoing basis?

H. Integration Issues and Risks

☐ What issues could be showstoppers for our integration?
☐ What are our recommendations for dealing proactively with these concerns?
☐ What high-impact opportunities for major process redesign initiatives have been identified?

I. Other Considerations

☐ What worksheets, reports, or supporting data will be necessary to establish the business case for our recommendations?
☐ How will we keep our functional executive staff member(s) informed and involved during integration planning and implementation?

VI. Task Force Logistics and Communications

☐ How and when will task forces and subteams be launched?
☐ How and when will task force meetings be held?
☐ How will subteams update task force leaders for the weekly report?
☐ Who will manage and update the project plan's timeline?
☐ Are facilitation or support resources needed?

VII. Links to Other Task Forces

Please list other task forces to coordinate with, key issues, and contacts.

Issue(s)	Task Force	Primary Responsibility

Attachment: Task Force Subteam Members

Subteam/ Name	Location	Phone	Fax	Pager/ E-Mail

RESOURCE B:
INTEGRATION PLANNING TEMPLATE

An Outline for Task Force Initial Transition Plans

    I.   Overall Work Flow and Key Operating Rules
    II.   Synergies—"Quick Hits and Low-Hanging Fruit"
    III.   Initial Systems and Facilities Requirements
    IV.   Transition Costs Estimate
    V.   Transition Timeline
    VI.   Issues and Recommendations for Executive Staff Attention

We believe these categories represent the minimum business requirements for successful transition and initial synergy capture.

While each Task Force's requirements will be different, we ask your help with the following:

- Address each of the categories to the extent practical.
- Suggest other issues/areas needed for overall planning or for your specific Task Force requirements.

Note: A detailed outline of expected "deliverables," along with representative document formats and actual plans from previous integration projects, can be used to help task forces produce effective plans.

- Remember, the level of detailed planning is a key success factor.
- Be as specific as you can be given exchange restraints and lawful access to information. Be sure to contact counsel.
- Plans are iterative—will likely need further clarification as we move to full integration and synergy project planning.
- Use the format/documentation most helpful for your team.
- The attached samples are illustrations and possibilities only.
- We will be building a consolidated timeline/project plan in MS-Project.
- Our core team will support each task force in creating and periodically updating the document.

I. Overall Work Flow and Key Operating Rules

- Purpose: Capture specific instructions and transition process recommendations to ensure seamless operations.
- Three samples have been provided:
  - Note level of drill-down detail.
  - These documents summarize the task force agreement on how work will get done and also serve as essential communication tools for the functional staff involved.
- Process roles and responsibilities:
  - Where certain roles and responsibilities have substantially changed, be sure to document key highlights.
- While actual process alignment/redesign will come later, some brief summary of transition process steps may be needed.
- A contact roster of key staff members now involved, or added to the communications/chain of command may also be helpful.

BUSINESS GROUP 1
EXAMPLE TRANSITION PLAN
MAY 14, 1998

1. **Services Required:** The Transition Services and Systems listed below will not be linked to installation of SAP as an anticipated date for the termination of such requirements. The new system will operate relatively independent (at least initially) of the old system.

Service	FTE	Duration
• Supervisor for inventory management	.1	3Q98
• IS hardware & software support	.2	2Q99

—Connectivity to base via T-1 line as of 6/1/98

—Continued access to plant data via intranet

—Maintenance of SQL server

—Configuration and mapping of existing PC's to access legacy system until after system merger

—Passwords/drivers installed and maintained to allow efficient data transfer

—Transfer of software licenses

2. Systems Requirements:

Services by	Duration
• Access to SQL server for data base function	6/99
• LAN, WAN, e-mail, and Internet access	6/99
• Pricing data base with independent data entry PC	6/99
• Independent PC for connectivity with modems	6/99

(See attachment 1 for details of "Computer System Support")

Continuing Services by

• PC for connectivity with common drive

• Programming models licensed for each plant

• LAN, WAN, e-mail, and Internet access

• Pricing data base

• Phone and FAX access

3. Key Process Operating Rules

• During Phase I, systems will continue to operate independently

—Liberal use of phone, fax, and e-mail to gather product prices, to agree on inventory targets and to generate plans and case runs

—Ensure that common set of prices is being used for both systems

—Weekly product price inputs from managers and verification of inventory targets

—Runs generated for third week of the month to be used for input to plant outlook process

—Weekly meetings to share input and conduct meetings with other groups

—Hold first Case Review Meetings with supply managers

Conduct first Strategy Review Meeting with broad spectrum of Plant operations personnel and commercial functions

• Open communication encouraged, but focus product issues through Product "experts" and local plant issues through Plant Engineers

• Share ideas, successes, and failures openly for learning and validation.

- Develop common file of plant schematics; set aside time to cross train personnel in all plant configurations
- Routine plant linkages will involve frequent direct phone contact between the Analyst and Plant Engineer or the assigned plant contacts. In addition, routine plant operating information will be gathered as shown below (as implemented, there will be opportunities to streamline this data gathering process)
  - Shift notes via e-mail, plus phone contact
  - Daily calls; weekly summary via fax
  - Shift notes website, plus phone contact
  - Shift notes via e-mail, plus phone contact
  - Weekly phone contact
- Issue daily Break-even Reports
- New opportunities to be processed as follows:
  - Assay to B. Smith for initial classification
  - Sample to R. Peters for full composition analysis
  - Analytical results to T. Thompson
  - Plant review and acceptance, as required
  - Yield models run (both systems initially) and added to yield library
  - Relative values calculated, based on special or weekly case runs and reported back to initiator of process
- Conduct weekly case review with supply managers
- Conduct semi-monthly Product Strategy Reviews to include plant operations participation as well as supply and management functions. Initially alternate meetings between teleconference and rotating plant sites
- Issue monthly plant production targets to Plant Engineers for use in their operations outlook as follows:
  - Special emphasis on product price input and inventory analysis to be expected during the third week of each month
  - LP runs for third week each month to be used for key production targets communicated to each plant
  - Plant Engineers to generate a material balance for their site for the current month plus two, incorporated active plant constraints and known maintenance schedules
- Roll up plant outlooks into global production plan—monthly (rolling 3-month plan)
- Weekly meetings to coordinate activities, identify issues, and encourage teamwork
- Focus on identifying and capturing synergies

4. **Roles and Responsibilities:** See attached organizational charts, roles and responsibilities reviews, work flow chart, and contact directories.

Payroll Accounting

A. Key Process Operating Rules:

The following rules are based on former employees becoming employees on 6/1/98 (the transfer date).

- Until employee transfer date, all former employees will be paid under the new compensation plan.
- From 6/1/98 through 12/31/98 R. Jones will process the payrolls for all former employees moving to new location.
- R. Jones will process the payroll based on their current pay schedule and pay practices except for changes to the Short Term Disability, Relocation policy, and Transportation subsidy/deduction.
- J. Paul will utilize a separate payroll company within their current payroll processing system using the persons Employer Identification Number.
- Paycheck printing will occur in the same printing locations as are currently being utilized until 12/31/98.
- John Doe will utilize a bank account at First National to fund the payroll.
- Jane Doe will provide all the necessary signatory requirements to management.
- B. Smith will take the necessary payroll deductions for employees based on employee elections to support benefit plans.
- T. Ross will deduct the appropriate Federal, FICA, State, and Local taxes for employees.
- T. Ross will manually submit the periodic tax reports to ADP until the automated version is complete (estimated automation complete by end of June).
- Once the automation is complete J. Paul will send the periodic file to ADP with each payroll processing.
- S. Jones will provide the quarterly file to ADP within the month following the close of a quarter (schedules are currently being worked through).
- ADP will participate in testing of the periodic and quarter files.
- For the period from 1/1/98 through the date the employees become permanent employees S. Jones will produce the W2's.
- ADP will produce W2's for employees who are transferred from the old site as of the transfer date through 12/31/98.
- P. Paul will participate in the transition of employees to the ADP payroll system to enable ADP to begin processing pay on 1/1/99.
- P. Paul will participate in the migration of the identified population from the old site to the new site.
- Plant personnel will update their personnel and payroll systems with necessary employee changes including indicative data, salary changes, benefit deduction changes, benefit plan updates, etc.

- Plant personnel will continue to remit garnishments and third party payments on behalf of employees as deductions are taken.
- ADP will continue to perform electronic transmissions with encryption, computer check issue information and recording of all manual checks, cancels, and stop payments to the bank account at First National. The payroll account will be reconciled monthly by T. Jones and a copy of the reconciliation will be forwarded to the Treasury department.
- T. Jones will provide information regarding funding and forecasting of payroll to the Treasury department via fax.

B. Roles and Responsibilities: Payroll processing for former Company A employees will be performed in accordance with a service agreement between ADP and Newco. The service agreement is being finalized and will address the points outlined above.

C. Transition Timeline:

>5/98—Employees remain Company A employees and paid by Company A Payroll Department using Federal EIN and First Republic bank account.

>6/98—Employees become Newco employees and will be paid by Payroll Department using Federal EIN and First National bank account.

>10/98—Employees will be loaded into the system in preparation for "open enrollment" of benefits.

>1/99—Payroll Department begins paying former Company A employees.

Customer Service Transition Plan

- Build CSR staff from 7 to 24 by Nov. 30
- Train Newco CSR's on processes, systems, and customers by Jan. 15
- Maintains CS staff at 24 through Feb. 2 by supplementing with newly trained CSR's
- From Oct. 15 thru Nov. 15, communicate Newco changes to CUSTOMERS
- From Dec. 15 thru Jan. 15, communicate "Transition-to-Day 1" to CUSTOMERS
- From Oct. 1 thru Nov. 15, survey CUSTOMERS by application area to determine components of "Benchmark Service"
- From Jan. 1 thru May 30, survey CUSTOMERS to determine service level achieved during transition and after Day 1 using "Report Card" format
- From "close" (Dec. 1) thru Feb. 2, test Customer Service Center

- From "close" (Dec. 1) to Feb. 2, run legacy businesses on legacy systems
- From Feb. 2 thru Feb. 27, transition company A-based Customer Service business area by business area
- From Feb. 2 to April 1, run legacy businesses on legacy systems at location A
- April 1 and thereafter, run all Newco business on most current version.

Sample Attachment:
Group Roles and Responsibilities

Corporate Analyst Roles:

- Identify/develop/track synergies
- Calculate break-events
- Evaluate opportunity feeds
- Provide planning interface among Management, Supply, and Manufacturing organizations
- Perform model maintenance and structure changes
- Provide project evaluation and interface
- Support logistic activities (may include training of corporate transportation position)
- Maintain updates to global database
- Provide supply/demand forecasts—by plant
- Coordinate Case Study and hold Strategy meetings; communicate results
- Roll-up production forecasts and communicate
- Produce plant cost curves
- Interface with technology vendors

Plant Engineer Roles:

- Provide direction for updating the pricing model, based on plant operation and constraints
- Develop new operating targets as needed
- Provide coordination with day-to-day issues with the plant and with corporate functions
- Ensure optimum targets are implemented in the units
- Provide understanding of the sensitivities of operating parameters on the profitability of the new unit, including communication with plant operators
- Ensure that current operating limits/constraints are recognized and reflected in pricing models

- Provide understanding of the functionality/capability/limitations of the pricing models
- Maintain and enhance the plant's pricing models
- Maintain current incremental and product pricing as input
- Maintain current composition information as input
- Maintain the topology of the on-line system to accurately reflect the configuration of the plant
- Acquire support, as necessary, to ensure high on-stream time for the on-line system
- Monitor output of the models to ensure that targets remain stable and that both on-line models are consistent
- Manage the furnace analyzer to ensure corrected pattern information is provided to update the models
- Provide production outlooks and forecasts—define system for information flow and timing (joint effort with corporate function)
- Publish plant reliability report ("Actual vs. Attainable")
- Use model for troubleshooting
- Perform joint reconciliation (joint with corporate)
- Begin training in emerging role to handle plant online optimizer
- Provide coordination with local refineries regarding refinery streams
- Assist in developing supply emergency plans (joint with corporate and transportation)
- Document opportunity audits—yield verification
- Provide local project interface
- Coordinate operation of local, on-line systems

Sample Attachment: Liquids Purchased Under an Alternate P.O.

1. Manager-Domestic Supply or Manager-International Supply purchase feedstock for Newco.
2. Manager-Domestic Supply or Manager-International Supply creates P.O./contract and distributes to Plant Managers:
   a) Corporate group
   b) Transportation group
   c) Plant group
   d) Engineers
   e) Director Supply
   f) Supply Representative
   g) Accounting

3. Invoice received by Accounting
   a) Invoice data entered into Wire Log
   b) Pay date requirement (due date to Accounts Payable) assigned
4. Invoice routed to appropriate supply manager by fax
   a) Supply manager verifies price
   b) Supply manager assigns P.O. number
5. Invoice routed to Accounting by fax
   a) Invoice matched against accruals
   b) Ledger codes added to invoice
6. Invoice routed to Accounting
   a) Invoice checked for completeness
   b) Invoice held until pay date
7. Invoice routed to Accounts Payable

II. Synergies—"Quick Hits and Low-Hanging Fruit"

- Purpose: Focus short-term actions on immediately achievable synergies, and start the high-level planning on longer-term, high-impact projects.
- Sample:
  - Follow the general format provided.
  - Remember, the initial assignments are just a starting point.
  - Each needs to be verified, and further idea generation is highly recommended. Use your creativity and expertise to help us maximize the value of the deal.
  - Project plans for complex synergies need to include timelines, persons responsible, etc.
  - Consider the cost effectiveness of solutions.
  - Where exchange restraints limit access to sharing information, assign "homework" to an individual(s) from one partner company to independently start as much planning as possible.

DATE:	SYNERGY NO.	AREA	VALUE	REV
10/4/98	10	MANUFACTURING	$2.13	0

SYNERGY: Supply all raw material for Site A and Site B from Newco Site C by Pipeline.

DESCRIPTION: Newco Site C capacity exceeds raw material need to Produce Product Z. Better coordination of pipeline use and raw material logistics to other locations will improve overall cost.

VALUE: Initial analysis targeted savings of $2.13 MM.

PRIMARY RESPONSIBILITY: Business Management—Logistics—P. Smith.

SUPPORTING FUNCTIONS:
- Business Management—Logistics.
- Management—Plants.

APPROACH/MILESTONES:
- Establish the raw material supply chain from the raw material Plants to customers constraining the Site D and Site A Plants to use all pipeline supplied raw material.
- Study the true capacity of the pipeline between Site E and Site A assuming close coordination of use.

- Study the raw material fleet size and rationalize the number of railcars accordingly.

VERIFICATION:

- Establish the cost basis for supplying Site B the way it was done in 1998 (raw material freight; rail car lease, maintenance, and storage; fixed cost for unloading and maintaining the unloading facility).
- Compare actual experience of Newco to that of the base (adjusted for needed capital and increased volume).
- Key Measures—raw material freight cost; railcar lease, maintenance, and storage costs; Plant fixed cost; size of raw material rail fleet.

III. Initial Systems and Facilities Requirements

- Purpose: Minimize the disruption of relocations and new assignments by providing fast connectivity when and where it is needed.
- Sample:

    Focus on who, what physical location (especially new people coming to Newco location), when they will arrive.

    Indicate basic connectivity needs (LAN connection, telephone, and all applications required).

    Indicate colocation or adjacency needs by department or team name.

ACCOUNTING DEPARTMENT
INFORMATION SYSTEM REQUIREMENTS

Name: *Please list specifically who the user names will be.*	Location: *Specific physical location. For example: Site A, which floor, etc.*	System Access: *Indicate which systems will need to be accessed*
		OPBS; MSA G/L; NIC1CSP; NIIMSP; NITSO; RDS; Keymaster; CC:mail; TM1; all PC current desktop software
		OPBS; MSA G/L; NIC1CSP; NIIMSP; RDS; Keymaster; CC:mail; TM1; all PC current desktop
		Operations Cost Accounting System; MSA G/L; RDS; TM1, N1CICSP; NIIMSP; NitSO; CC:mail; all PC current desktop software
		MSA G/L; MSA A/P; Operations Cost Accounting System; RDS; NITSO; TM1; CC:mail; NIIMSP; OPBS; all PC current desktop software
		OPBS: MSA G/L, NICICSP; NIIMSP; NIIMSP; NITSO; RDS; Keymaster, CC:mail; TM1; and PC current desktop software

IV. Transition Cost Estimate

- Purpose: Provide finance with best estimates for planning and conduct the business transition in a cost-effective manner.
- Sample:
    A general spreadsheet format has been identified to facilitate easier data roll-up.
    Please indicate overall categories and line items appropriate to your function.
    Please note basis for estimate.

FUNCTIONAL AREAS ONE-TIME FORMATION COST ESTIMATE	Responsible Person	Cost ($000)	Basis for Estimate
Office Set-Up Remodelling/build out Furniture Rewiring, phone, systems Office phone/computer reconfigurations Stationary/supplies			
Severance Expenses Plant personnel Company A headquarters personnel Company B headquarters personnel			
Relocation Expenses Plant personnel Company A headquarters personnel Company B headquarters personnel			
Plant Expenses Data Systems set-up/connectivity Emergency communications system set-up Re-permitting			
Legal Expenses Registrations to do business Copyright/Trademark registrations			
Marketing/Sales Packaging/labelling modifications Customer notifications			
Purchasing/Supply Chain Vendor notifications Develop/print purchasing policy manuals Company A PO's with new terms and conditions			

(*continued*)

FUNCTIONAL AREAS ONE-TIME FORMATION COST ESTIMATE	Responsible Person	Cost ($000)	Basis for Estimate

Finance
   Consolidated reporting systems set-up
   Cash collection system set-up
   Payables system set-up
 	
Compensation/Benefits
   Consultant assistance
 	
Corporate Structuring/Start-Up
& Integration Planning
   Consultant assistance			

Total			

V. Transition Timeline

- Purpose: Input to consolidated project plan. Will be used to communicate accountabilities to specific individuals/teams and track project status.
- Sample:
    - –A representative MS Project Plan is provided. Note outline format and approximate level of detail for key milestones, rather than all tasks required for each action item.
    - –Specific transition and synergy project teams may choose to create their own overall detailed task lists.
    - –An MS Word format is also provided. The Integration Core Team is available to support Task Forces by converting various timeline formats to our consolidated plan.
    - –Please list start/finish dates and persons responsible for each item.

Transition Timeline:

- *Prior Day-1*
    1. Define interim business process. 4/23 (All)
    2. Determine common reference price inputs and mechanism for Product Manager weekly price input. 4/24 (Team A)
    3. Meet with Supply and Product Managers to determine deliverables and expectations. 4/28 (All)
    4. Review plant specifications for each site. 4/29 (Team A)
    5. Share plant constraints and impacts for each site. 4/29 (Team A)
    6. Determine list of common products and develop yields for same under both and complete yield modeling systems. 4/30 (Team B)
    7. Review Plant Engineer position descriptions with plant management personnel. 5/1 (Team B)
    8. Communicate organization, description of roles/expectations of individuals and the group. 5/5 (Team B)
    9. Move Corporate personnel from site A to Newco Site. 5/7 (Office Services)

- *Day-1*
    1. Gather product prices from Product Managers. (All)
    2. Get inventory and production strategy from Product Manager. (Team C)
    3. Develop Cost of curves for each plant, based on common prices. (All)
    4. Begin comparison process of cost curves; determine if major discrepancies need to be addressed. (All)

ID	Task Name	Start	Finish	% Complete	1999 J J A S O N D J F M
1	HSE	Wed 7/1/98	Fri 6/30/00	32%	32%
2	Purchased Safety Services	Wed 7/1/98	Fri 6/30/00	28%	28%
3	Complete detailed analysis and prioritization of current	Wed 7/1/98	Fri 8/14/98	100%	100%
4	Generate updated synergy target based on above	Wed 7/1/98	Tue 9/1/98	40%	40%
5	Consolidate purchases identified in target—as contracts permit	Wed 7/1/98	Fri 6/30/00	25%	25%
6	Provide functional support to achieve target—ongoing	Wed 7/1/98	Fri 6/30/00	25%	25%
7	Corporate Safety Consolidation	Wed 7/1/98	Mon 2/1/99	41%	41%
8	Develop organization plan and headcount recommendation	Wed 7/1/98	Tue 9/1/98	100%	100%
9	Review above with appropriate Officers	Tues 9/15/98	Tue 9/15/98	100%	100%
10	Modify and finalize plan as necessary	Thur 10/1/98	Thur 10/1/98	85%	85%
11	Develop consolidated safety management philosophy end	Thur 10/1/98	Mon 2/1/98	10%	10%
12	Implement	Wed 7/1/98	Wed 7/1/98	50%	50%

ID	Task Name	Start	Finish	% Complete	1999 (J J A S O N D J F M)
13	**Regional Safety Consolidation**	Wed 7/1/98	Tue 9/1/98	60%	60%
14	Confirm organization plan and headcount recommendation	Wed 7/1/98	Tue 9/1/98	20%	20%
15	**Gain Approval and Implement**	Wed 7/1/98	Tue 9/1/98	60%	60%
16	Corporate Safety consolidation in place	Wed 7/1/98	Tue 9/1/98	100%	100%
17	Common philosophies adopted	Wed 7/1/98	Tue 9/1/98	30%	30%
18	Current synergies achieved	Wed 7/1/98	Tue 9/1/98	50%	50%
19	**Regional Plant Safety Consolidation**	Wed 7/1/98	Tue 9/1/98	10%	10%
20	Confirm organization plan and headcount recommendation	Wed 7/1/98	Tue 9/1/98	10%	10%
21	Gain approval and implement dependent on potential	Wed 7/1/98	Tue 9/1/98	10%	10%
22	**Other Areas Nonquantified**	Wed 7/1/98	Thu 12/31/98	50%	50%
23	Medical	Wed 7/1/98	Wed 7/1/98	40%	40%
24	Product Safety	Fri 8/14/98	Thu 12/31/98	50%	50%

- *Week-1*
    1. Complete LP runs, based on common prices/feeds. (All)
    2. Develop Break-even Report format and begin distribution. (All)
    3. Conduct Parametric Review with supply and Product Managers, as appropriate. (All)
    4. Begin process of leveling plant operations on ethylene cost basis. (All)

- *Month-1*
    1. Install T-1 line and provide functionality. (Team D)
    2. Move Corporate personnel from Site A to Newco Site. (Office Services/IS Dept.)
    3. Relocate Plant Engineers to plant sites.
    4. Begin semi-monthly Production Strategy Review Meetings. (All)
    5. Provide economic rationale for start-up decision. (All)

- *First 120 Days*
    1. Lock down synergies. (All)
    2. Develop synergy measurement and reporting format. (Team A)
    3. Develop long-term data base options; establish conversion plan. (IS Dept./All)
    4. Reassess and refocus, as appropriate. (All)
    5. Plan/executive model updates.
    6. Participate in development of 1999 Operating Plan. (All)
    7. Develop business map and begin to mesh with global options. (All)

VI. Issues and Recommendations for Executive Staff Attention

- Purpose: Clarify and prioritize essential issues which are beyond the immediate control of Task Forces; or have resource demands/or other business impact which needs to be sorted at the Executive Staff level
- Remember:
  Brief summary bullets and supporting data as needed by specific issues.
  Remember, this is only a communications and prioritization "backstop" to make sure all obstacles and barriers are effectively dealt with.
  So, don't wait till "report-out" to start working the "showstopper" issues.
  Key issues for officer attention
  - Legacy systems need to be upgraded in time for February, 1998, start-up
  - Must maintain the current legacy systems at Site A until we can operate on upgraded version
  Other important issues
  - Staffing and training of all employees in those functions and critical areas linked directly to the manufacturing process
  - Enough space at Newco Site for all key supply personnel
  - "800" number/continuity and assignment
  - Access to high-quality systems; convert old product spec. process to centralized/integrated approach

RESOURCE C:
EXECUTIVE SUMMARY OF WATSON WYATT WORLDWIDE'S 1998–1999 MERGERS AND ACQUISITIONS SURVEY,
ASSESSING AND MANAGING HUMAN CAPITAL: A KEY TO MAXIMIZING M&A DEAL VALUE

One hundred ninety CEOs, CFOs, and other top executives from companies with M&A experience in the United States, the Asia-Pacific region, and Brazil responded.

A variety of industries are represented, including

- Manufacturing
- Consumer products
- Banking and financial services
- Chemical

Most acquisitions were in the same industry and were embarked on to gain market share and achieve competitive size.

Improving access to markets and reducing costs were more frequently cited objectives for deals in the Asia-Pacific region and Brazil than for deals conducted in the United States.

The Quality of Predeal Assessment Will Affect the Deal Value Realized During and After Integration

WHEN ASKED WHAT HIS COMPANY WOULD DO DIFFERENTLY IN THE NEXT M&A DEAL, ONE PARTICIPANT STATED THAT HE WOULD HAVE HAD A "MORE DEFINED INTEGRATION PLAN IN PLACE IN ORDER TO MOVE MORE QUICKLY IN THE INTEGRATION PHASE."

Survey respondents reported that the predeal stage lasted five to sixteen weeks. Financial information and strategic business developments were consistently rated the most critical areas during due diligence.

The stage at which the HR team becomes involved varies significantly between deals conducted in the United States and those in the Asia-Pacific region and Brazil.

	United States	Asia-Pacific	Brazil
Initial planning	16%	19%	11%
Investigative stage	41%	21%	14%
Negotiation stage	16%	16%	25%
Integration	27%	44%	50%

Our experience shows that conducting an early and thorough assessment of organizational culture can help the acquiring company forecast the deal value more accurately and manage cultural issues before they become bottlenecks and diminish deal value. An early assessment of human capital issues therefore seems to be a weak link in the M&A deal-value chain in the Asia-Pacific region and Brazil.

The information most often sought during the due-diligence process relates to financial data and market share. Information about business competencies is gathered more often for U.S. deals than for others.

Cultural incompatibility was consistently rated as the biggest barrier to successful integration, yet results indicate that this area is least likely to be researched during the due-diligence process.

TYPE OF INFORMATION GATHERED DURING DUE DILIGENCE

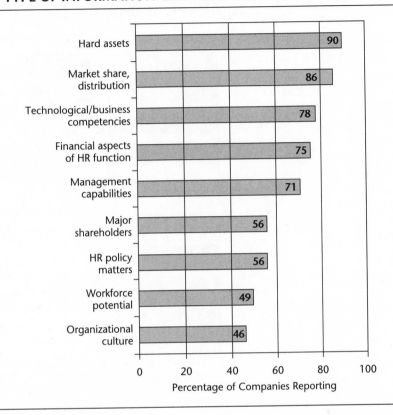

Hard assets — 90
Market share, distribution — 86
Technological/business competencies — 78
Financial aspects of HR function — 75
Management capabilities — 71
Major shareholders — 56
HR policy matters — 56
Workforce potential — 49
Organizational culture — 46

Percentage of Companies Reporting

The Key to Successful Integration Is a Systematic, Thorough, and Expedient Process

Most respondents stated that they spend six months to one year integrating the business operations of the two companies. Employee communication and productivity were noted to be satisfactory during integration, but qualitative answers still indicated that there is room for improvement.

Shareholder value, return on capital employed, and market share were listed as the top three performance measures used to monitor success of the M&A process.

Around the world, retention of key talent, communication, and integration of cultures were most often rated as critical activities in the integration plan, yet only 8 percent of respondents stated that human resources management was a top priority during integration, and just 4 percent of respondents said communication was a priority.

HOW IMPORTANT WERE THE FOLLOWING ACTIVITIES TO THE INTEGRATION PLAN?

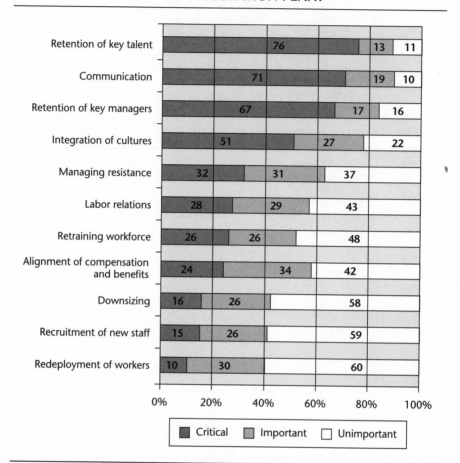

AREAS GIVEN TOP PRIORITY DURING INTEGRATION

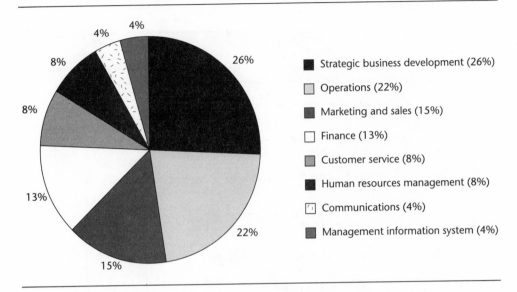

- Strategic business development (26%)
- Operations (22%)
- Marketing and sales (15%)
- Finance (13%)
- Customer service (8%)
- Human resources management (8%)
- Communications (4%)
- Management information system (4%)

M&A Integration Is a Major Change-Management Effort—Having the Right People to Manage It Is Critical

HAVE THE RIGHT LEADERSHIP TEAM APPOINTED EARLY;
APPOINT AND INVOLVE THE HR MANAGER EARLY
IN THE PROCESS—A SURVEY PARTICIPANT ON THE
KEY TO M&A SUCCESS

According to respondents, there are three top risks to a successful integration:

- Employees' resistance to change
- Pressure to address too many issues at the same time
- An unrealistic assessment of business turnaround

Fast-track integration minimizes the period of unrest, keeps the management team fully coordinated and focused, and ensures that anticipated gains are realized as soon as possible.

The success of M&A deals was most often attributed to leadership, well-planned communication, and early management of "me issues."

Indeed, our experience shows that clear and constant communication from senior management provides decisive answers to "me issues" and dispels uncertainty among employees—an essential ingredient of a successful deal.

PERCENTAGE OF COMPANIES CITING ISSUE AS RISK

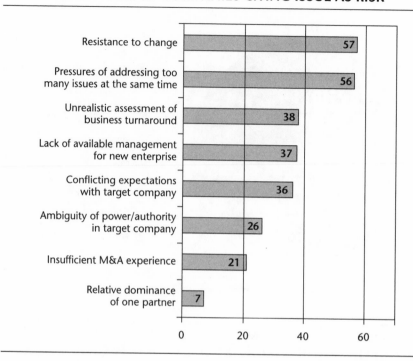

PERCENTAGE CITING REASON FOR SUCCESS

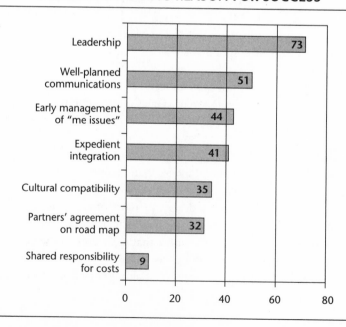

REFERENCES

Arapoff, J. "Mergers and Acquisitions: Making the Deal a Reality—And a Real Value." *Watson Wyatt Strategy @ Work,* Oct.–Dec. 1998, pp. 16–21.

Ashkenas, R. N., De Monaco, L. J., and Francis, S. C. "Making the Deal Real: How GE Capital Integrates Acquisitions." *Harvard Business Review,* Jan.–Feb. 1998, pp. 5–15.

Atkins, R., Carter, B., Nies, C., and Rochelle, D. *Human Capital Integration.* Mergers and Acquisitions Methodology Series. Bethesda, Md.: Watson Wyatt Worldwide, 1998.

Barr, S. "The Morning After: How to Prevent a Post-Acquisition Hangover." *CFO,* 1997, *13*(7).

Bauman, R. P., Jackson, P., and Lawrence, J. T. *From Promise to Performance.* Boston: Harvard Business School Press, 1997.

Carleton, J. R. "Cultural Due Diligence." *Training,* Nov. 1997, pp. 67–75.

Cary, D., and Ogden, D. "A Match Made in Heaven? Find Out Before You Merge." *Wall Street Journal,* Nov. 30, 1998, p. A22.

Clemons, E. K., Thatcher, M. E., and Row, M. C. "Identifying Sources of Reengineering Failure: A Study of the Behavioral Factors Contributing to Reengineering Risks." *Journal of Management Information Systems,* Fall 1995, pp. 9–36.

Collins, J. C., and Porras, J. I. *Built to Last.* New York: HarperCollins, 1994.

Cox, J., "U.S. Companies Buying Up Assets in Troubled Asia." *USA Today,* June 10, 1998, p. 4B.

Galpin, T. J. *The Human Side of Change: A Practical Guide to Organization Redesign.* San Francisco: Jossey-Bass, 1996.

Galpin, T. J. *Making Strategy Work: Building Sustainable Growth Capability.* San Francisco: Jossey-Bass, 1997.

Haslett, S. "Broadbanding: A Strategic Tool for Organizational Change." *Compensation and Benefits Review,* Nov.–Dec. 1995, pp. 40–46.

Hodge, K. "The Art of the Post-Deal." *Management Review,* Feb. 1998, pp. 17–20.

Kim, W. C., and Mauborgne, R. "Fair Process: Managing in the Knowledge Economy." *Harvard Business Review,* July–Aug. 1997, pp. 65–75.

Kotter, J. P., and Heskett, J. L. *Corporate Culture and Performance.* New York: Free Press, 1992.

Longo, S. C. "Has Reengineering Left You Financially Stronger?" *CPA Journal,* Jan. 1996, p. 69.

Lublin, J. S., and O'Brien, B. "When Disparate Firms Merge, Cultures Often Collide." *Wall Street Journal,* Feb. 14, 1997.

Machalaba, D. "Wrong Track: A Big Railroad Merger Goes Terribly Awry in a Very Short Time." *Wall Street Journal,* Oct. 2, 1997, pp. A1, A8.

Marks, M. L., and Mirvis, P. H. *Managing the Merger.* Upper Saddle River, N.J.: Prentice Hall, 1992.

"Mastering Management, Part 11: Summary: Human Resources Management." *Financial Times,* Jan. 19, 1996, p. 3.

May, D., and Kettelhut, M. C. "Managing Human Issues in Reengineering Projects." *Journal of Systems Management,* Jan.–Feb. 1996, pp. 4–11.

Nelson, E., and Lublin, J. S. "Buy the Numbers? How Whistle Blowers Set Off a Fraud Probe That Crushed Cendant." *Wall Street Journal,* Aug. 13, 1998, pp. A1, A8.

O'Donnell, J. "Survey: Americans Slightly Favor Mergers." *USA Today,* June 10, 1998, p. 2B.

Organized Change. "Frequently Asked Questions About Organizational Change: Answers to Questions Often Asked by Heads of Companies." [http://www.electriciti.com/dchaudron/faq.htm]. 1996.

Pandya, M. "Making Mega Mergers Work." *Wharton Alumni Magazine,* Summer 1998, pp. 24–26.

Peck, R. L. "Reengineering: Full Speed Ahead." *Nursing Homes,* Nov.–Dec. 1995, p. 10.

Pritchett, P., Robinson, D., and Clarkson, R. *After the Merger.* New York: McGraw-Hill, 1997.

Reingold, J., and Barrett, A. "M&A Frenzy May Be Scuttling Due Diligence." *Business Week,* Aug. 17, 1998, p. 72.

Sherman, S. "A Master Class in Radical Change." *Fortune,* Dec. 13, 1993, pp. 82–90.

Watson Wyatt Worldwide. *Competing in a Global Economy.* Bethesda, Md.: Watson Wyatt Worldwide, 1997.

Watson Wyatt Worldwide. *Assessing and Managing Human Capital: A Key to Maximizing the M&A Deal Value.* Bethesda, Md.: Watson Wyatt Worldwide, 1998a.

Watson Wyatt Worldwide. *Workforce Management: Demographics and Destiny.* Bethesda, Md.: Watson Wyatt Worldwide, 1998b.

INDEX